CONSUMING THE INEDIBLE

THE ANTHROPOLOGY OF FOOD AND NUTRITION

General Editor: *Helen Macbeth*

CONSUMING THE INEDIBLE
Neglected Dimensions of Food Choice

Edited by

Jeremy MacClancy, Jeya Henry and Helen Macbeth

Berghahn Books
NEW YORK • OXFORD

First published in 2007 by

Berghahn Books
www.berghahnbooks.com

©2007, 2009 Jeremy MacClancy, Jeya Henry and Helen Macbeth
First paperback edition published in 2009

Library of Congress Cataloging-in-Publication Data

Consuming the inedible : neglected dimensions of food choice / edited by Jeremy
MacClancy, Jeya Henry, and Helen Macbeth.
   p. ; cm. -- (Anthropology of food and nutrition ; v. 6)
Includes bibliographical references and index.
ISBN 978-1-84545-353-4 (hbk) -- ISBN 978-1-84545-684-9 (pbk)
1. Food habits. 2. Food preferences. 3. Diet. 4. Nutrition. I. MacClancy, Jeremy. II.
Henry, C. J. K. III. Macbeth, Helen M. IV. Series.
[DNLM: 1. Food Habits--ethnology. 2. Anthropology--methods. 3. Cultural
Characteristics. 4. Diet. 5. Food Preferences--ethnology. 6. Pica--ethnology.]

GT2850 .C65 2007
394.1'2--dc22
                    2007043682

British Library Cataloguing in Publication Data

A catalogue record for this book is available from the British Library

Printed in the United States on acid-free paper.

ISBN 978-1-84545-353-4 (hardback), 978-1-84545-684-9 (paperback)

CONTENTS

LIST OF FIGURES

LIST OF TABLES

Figure 0.1 Epio women, West New Guinea, finding and eating head-lice

PREFACE

Once again, members of the International Commission on the Anthropology of Food (ICAF) have brought together contributors from different subdisciplines within Anthropology and Nutrition to produce this volume in Berghahn's *The Anthropology of Food and Nutrition* series. In June 2005, at Oxford Brookes University, Dr Helen Macbeth, Professor Jeya Henry, Professor Jeremy MacClancy and Dr Paul Collinson, all from the UK section of ICAF, organised a highly successful conference, entitled *Non-Food as Food*. The title caused a considerable amount of email discussion from prospective contributors about what was expected, and it stimulated some interesting perspectives and papers. This volume arises from contributions to that conference.

The idea for the topic arose several years ago during a discussion between Henry and Macbeth about the frequency with which nutritionists neglected, in their intake records, the ingestion of substances which they did not recognise as 'food'. Two of Henry's research students had noticed that the local people they were studying snacked on caterpillars, but caterpillars did not exist in the nutrition composition tables. This led to further consideration of substances, consumed but not tabulated as 'food', and so the idea of including topics, such as geophagia, arose. When the topic was then raised with MacClancy, the basic concept was enriched with the insight from social anthropology on definitions and boundaries, and the conference was planned. However, we owe to the contributors the quality and the diversity of material that this subject stimulated, and we recognise how many other perspectives have been omitted.

The editors are most grateful to the British Academy, to the European section of the International Commission on the Anthropology of Food [ICAF(Europe)] and to the Departments of Anthropology and of Nutrition, Oxford Brookes University, for grants towards the conference; we were also fortunate to be allowed to use the facilities of Headington Hill Hall, Oxford Brookes University. We wish to thank Jackie Wynne and members of the Nutrition Laboratory for their help with the conference, and Sarah Butcher, Chantal Butchinsky and Mandy Archer for their assistance with aspects of the manuscript for this volume.

HMM, CJKH and JVM
March, 2006

LIST OF CONTRIBUTORS

Dr Ricardo Ávila
Departamento de Estudios Mexicanos y Mesoamericanos, Universidad de Guadalajara, Guadalajara, Mexico.

Rachel Black
Universitá degli Studi di Torino, Torino, Italy

Dr Paul Blum
Human Ethology Group, Max Planck Institute, Andechs, Germany

Dr Luis Cantarero
Departamento de Psicología y Sociología, Universidad de Zaragoza, Zaragoza, Spain

Dr Paul Collinson
Anthropology Department, Oxford Brookes University, Oxford, U.K.

Dr Daria Deraga
Social Anthropology Department, National Institute of Anthropology and History, Mexico City, Mexico

Dr Rodolfo Fernández
History Department, National Institute of Anthropology and History, Mexico City, Mexico

Dra. Isabel González Turmo
Departamento de Antropología Social, Universidad de Sevilla, Seville, Spain

Professor Louis E. Grivetti
Department of Nutrition, University of California, Davis, California

Professor Jeya Henry
Department of Nutrition, Oxford Brookes University, Oxford, U.K.

Dr Claude Marcel Hladik
Centre Nationale de la Recherche Scientifique, Musée National d'Histoire Naturelle, Brunoy, France

Dr Peter Hooda	School of Earth Sciences and Geography, Kingston University London, Kingston-upon-Thames, U.K.
Peter Hubbard	Departamento de Lenguas Modernas, CUCSH, Universidad de Guadalajara, Guadalajara, Mexico.
Dr Sabrina Krief	Eco-Anthropologie et Ethnobiologie, Département Hommes, Natures, Sociétés, Museum National d'Histoire Naturelle, Paris, France
Dr Helen Macbeth	Anthropology Department, Oxford Brookes University, Oxford, U.K.
Professor Jeremy MacClancy	Anthropology Department, Oxford Brookes University, Oxford, U.K.
Dr Antonia-Leda Matalas	Harokopio University, Athens, Greece.
Dr F. Xavier Medina	Department of Mediterranean Cultures, European Institute of the Mediterranean, Barcelona, Spain
Dr Ellen Messer	Friedman School of Nutrition Science and Policy, Tufts University, Boston, U.S.A.
Dra. María-Jesús Portalatín	Universidad de Zaragoza, Zaragoza, Spain
Professor Anand Prasad	School of Medicine, Wayne State University, Detroit, Michigan
Dr Professor Wulf Schiefenhövel	Human Ethology Group, Max Planck Institute, Andechs, Germany
Dr Carmen Strungaru	Faculty of Biology, University of Bucharest, Bucharest, Romania
Dr Martín Tena	CUCBA, Universidad de Guadalajara, CUCBA, Zapopan, Mexico
Dr Sera L. Young	Division of Nutritional Sciences, Cornell University, Ithaca, New York, U.S.A.

INTRODUCTION
CONSIDERING THE INEDIBLE,
CONSUMING THE INEFFABLE

Jeremy MacClancy, Helen Macbeth and *Jeya Henry*

Introduction

'I can't find caterpillars in the composition tables', complained the postgraduate nutrition student who had been recording the dietary intake of a rural population sample in Egypt. At much the same time her professor had been carrying out research on geophagia. From this juxtaposition of events arose the idea for this volume and for the conference from which its contributing chapters proceed. The increasing specialisation of disciplines has too frequently meant ignorance of information in other disciplines, and the cases above highlighted the need for interdisciplinary cooperation between anthropologists and nutritionists. Other than in certain special dietary situations, humans do not choose their foods primarily for reasons of nutrition, but for a variety of reasons, e.g. taste and preference (Macbeth 1997), cultural norms (MacClancy 1992; Millán Fuertes *et al.* 2004), status (Wiessner and Schiefenhövel 1996), peer group pressure (González Turmo 1997), belief systems (Portalatín 2004), territorial identity, availability, economics, in response to advertising, etc. Meanwhile, in much of their work, most nutritionists have ignored the work on such topics carried out in other disciplines. The observation that corn provided to victims of the Bengali famine of 1943 was rejected by many of these victims was, however, an early testimony for the view that nutritionists should consider more than the nutrients present in foods.

A recent development in factors affecting food choice has been the increase in advertising based on supposed health promotion, for example there is the concept of a 'Mediterranean Diet' (for a multidisciplinary volume on this, see Cresta and Teti 1998), or the addition of supplements, such as plant sterols and omega 3, into some processed foods. These health promotions and other advertising claims, whether reliably backed by nutritionists or not, have led people to choose foods that were perhaps not traditional in their culture, or to which their tastes had not previously been socialised. It is, therefore, essential for researchers from a wide variety of disciplines, including nutrition and anthropology, to be interested in exchanging cross-disciplinary information on food habits and choices, which this volume achieves. Nutritionists will find many of the chapters rich in new information relevant to their discipline, while the physical results of some consumptions will be drawn to the attention of the social scientists.

Our aim is simple: it is to highlight a neglected topic. It is true that what is considered edible or inedible has been discussed from several angles in quite different disciplines, and that unusual consumptions have been studied critically by medical and psychological researchers. What has been neglected, however, is the importance for anyone considering such consumptions to cross disciplinary boundaries and review all perspectives on the topic. Nutritionists may study nutrition, but they do not always include in their research all that is eaten. Foods consumed may be omitted from their dietary records, for instance, where the foods are not listed in the conventional composition tables, or where subjects do not wish to reveal their consumption of certain items. They should also take into account the differing cultural interpretations of what is 'edible' or 'inedible'. Within nutrition there does exist a debate on whether food taboos may inhibit valuable nutrient intake, but their study of the social aspects of the avoidance behaviour tends to be superficial. Some nutritionists have indeed become interested in unusual consumptions, for example geophagia (see Chapters 5, 6 and 7 below), and considered several theories about its practice, such as the provision of scarce micronutrients, the binding or chelation of toxins, medicinal use, etc., while perhaps ignoring any sociocultural or psychological perspectives on soil consumption.

Meanwhile, social anthropologists have studied a wide range of cultural interpretations of what is inedible. Diversity in such definitions has been central to debates about the boundaries between social groups (Douglas 1966; Feeley-Harnik 1981), but social anthropologists generally have not been concerned with nutritional or other physiological effects, and nutritionists have frequently ignored the flexibility of such definitions. In regard to food intake, biological anthropologists and evolutionary biologists have tended to pursue lines of enquiry more similar to the research methods and science of the nutritionists, and again some substances consumed may have been neglected. Consuming the inedible is a topic ripe for cross-disciplinary attention.

Consideration of the consumption of unusual items does occur in a widely scattered literature (see references in the following chapters). However, what this volume attempts is to bring together different perspectives on the complexity of this topic. That is what has been neglected. The cultural definitions of what is edible or inedible may be relevant to social scientists and nutritionists for quite different reasons, but they are nevertheless relevant in both cases. Yet, the topic is not just one of cultural interpretations of the inedible; the topic includes the consumption of some substances, which are not defined, even in the consumer's own culture, as 'edible'. In some cases the behaviour of eating unusual substances has been in the domain of psychiatrists, in which case the word 'pica' tends to be used. The question arises as to why such substances might be consumed. While psychologists might consider these consumptions to be a behavioural deviance, some substances can be argued to provide nutritional benefits. Other substances provide neither calories nor protein, and the reasons for their consumption should stimulate more cross-disciplinary debate. Some of these items may be consumed because the consumer likes the taste or has come to like the taste. Several practitioners of geophagia claim that the clay or soil that they consume 'tastes' pleasant, although others may not find the taste agreeable. This prompts the question whether the 'taste' for such foods is an indication of nutrient deficiency or whether it is the 'taste' for such substances that causes these unusual consumptions. In some cases the rationale may indeed be the flavour of the substance, but in other cases an altered emotional state or an addiction might be the stimulus. This suggests that humans may develop their 'taste' for such substances because they enjoy their other effects. Reactions to tastes do change in life; coffee tastes bitter, the betel nut has an astringent taste, and children initially dislike the taste of most alcoholic drinks. Taste for such substances is perhaps a topic for another volume.

Multidisciplinary, Interdisciplinary or Cross-disciplinary?

From the very beginning, we did not wish to confine ourselves to a single discipline. That is why we came together: a social anthropologist (MacClancy), a nutritional scientist (Henry) and a biological anthropologist (Macbeth). As an interdisciplinary trio, we fully acknowledged the necessity of studying food choice from several perspectives simultaneously. For food is fuel both for our bodies and our minds. As two of us have put it:

> Food is both 'nature' and 'culture', and bridges many divides: it is both substance and symbol; it is life-sustaining in both biochemical and cognitive modes. Both physically and socially, we consume it and make it part of ourselves (MacClancy and Macbeth 2004: 5–6).

Similarly, what is considered to be either 'food' or not edible is the result of both cultural perceptions and its biochemical nature. The cultivation, distribution, preparation and consumption of foods (after Goody 1982) are always historically contingent cultural acts, as well as biological ones with nutritional consequences. The range of chapters in this volume demonstrates this multidisciplinary approach: besides the chapters by social anthropologists, biological anthropologists and nutritionists, there are contributions from primatologists, evolutionary biologists and a geochemist. This is not to state that one cannot study food practices in a unidisciplinary manner to great benefit: there are too many good examples of this to argue against it (e.g. Lévi-Strauss 1964, 1967, 1969; Douglas 1966; Aylward and Morgan 1975; Berg 1981). Nevertheless, we wish to maintain that in this area of study, given the nature of the subject, combining several different approaches holds the promise of producing otherwise unattainable answers, or at least strong suggestions towards them. Diamond's *Guns, Germs and Steel: A Short History of Everybody for the Last 13,000 Years* (1997) is a well-known, popular example of this.

It is relatively easy to be multidisciplinary, simply stacking together different approaches, as though their contiguity necessarily empowered one's argument. To be rigorously interdisciplinary is another question. Each discipline has its own history, priorities, sets of procedures, objectives, research questions and criteria of evaluation. Very often, their methods necessitate timescales which can differ greatly across disciplines. The resulting admixture can be complementary and clashing by turns. However, just because a productive interdisciplinarity is far harder to achieve than to discuss, that is no reason for not attempting it in a cross-disciplinary project. We would argue that in this multidisciplinary volume, genuine interdisciplinarity has sometimes been achieved, but we acknowledge that in other areas there is juxtaposition, with only limited interrelationship, between some chapters. This is perhaps inevitable given the broad scope of the subject matter.

We follow this introduction with two examples of interdisciplinary chapters, both of which provide surveys of a wide selection of literature on pica as a helpful indication for further reading. Firstly, there is the overview of the evidence for the consumption of the inedible by Sera Young. This chapter progresses from an introduction to pica to a classification of possible aetiologies of such behaviour. Young asks who eats what, when, where, and why. From examining the very varied accounts of these practices, she has isolated eight types of hypotheses: nutrient craving, sensory disturbance, gastrointestinal malaise, detoxification, hunger, stress, mental illness and cultural expectation. It is relevant to the rationale for this volume that she finds that none of these hypotheses alone can explain the majority of the cases quoted in the literature. The implicit corollary is that only a multifactorial approach could account for most cases, presumably with the balance between factors varying from case to case. That conclusion, at the very least, should provide future researchers with a framework within which to work when encountering novel incidents of pica. That framework and the full survey of literature on the subject also provide a valuable start to our volume.

As already mentioned, the reasons for pica are varied and in the next chapter Carmen Strungaru examines the various types of pica from an evolutionary point of view. She describes several types of pica and attempts to classify these in several ways. In a table she creates a classification based on different types of substances ingested. Then, using Tinbergen's ethological approach for understanding biosocial phenomena on four different aetiological levels (causation, ontogeny, phylogeny and evolution, on each of which she provides interesting exemplars) she argues for an adaptive origin for some of these behaviours, finding them explicable in terms of phylogenetically inherited mechanisms. She claims that this is in contrast to the common view, within the medical profession, of these phenomena, which is that people behaving in this way require therapy. She recommends that this pathological typology should be reviewed and balanced with a 'more holistic, evolutionarily inspired approach'.

Scoring Boundaries

Every word has its definitions. What is important is who is defining it when, how, for what reasons, to what end and to what effect.

Anthropologists long ago established very clearly that many foods are culturally defined, and above all that the concept of 'inedible' is wielded as a social strategy to demarcate and highlight the boundaries that groups create between one another. Accusing members of another group of being cannibals is perhaps the most dramatic example of this worldwide tactic (see Macbeth, Schiefenhövel and Collinson, this volume). Derogative stereotyping of the cuisine of another nation is a more common, and less sensationalist, example of the same ploy: the English used to mock the French as 'frogs' because some French ate cooked frogs' legs, while poor 'whites' in the 'Deep South' of the United States used to label African Americans as 'coons' because they occasionally hunted and ate racoons (MacClancy 1992). Similar examples abound.

Since much of our focus tends to be on what Westerners consider to be inappropriate or borderline behaviours in the consumption of food, the topic of definition looms large in our concerns. For that reason, we made the Chapter 3 the one by Isabel González Turmo, in which she outlines various English and Spanish concepts involved in the terminology of 'food' and 'non-food'. In her list of varieties of 'non-food' there are illuminating Andalusian examples of the social definitions of 'food'; these highlight the continuing economic and nutritional contests between the food industry and consumers over what can be classed as 'food' and what not. Leaders of food companies, ever mindful of the bottom line, want to produce items which sell well and can last on the supermarket shelf. They are on the whole quite ready to include non-food ingredients if they increase sales (e.g. colourings), crop yields (e.g. pesticides) or shelf life (e.g. preservatives). To an increasingly suspicious public, whose fears are fed by journalists keen to sell copy, these non-food additives may well be unwanted insertions. The point this chapter highlights is that although many definitions of the edible would specifically exclude these industrial products, the pressure of global food companies to include them continues to grow. In the process, is our everyday definition of food dangerously manipulated, or innocuously extended? Do we trust the advertisers or the journalists?

Ellen Messer, extends the political dimension of González Turmo's analysis by discussing, among others, two cases where industrially produced foods have been publicly questioned: genetically engineered maize in famine-threatened southern Africa and the introduction of Quorn to the USA. To some people, genetically modified (GM) maize has been viewed as a 'frankenfood', the product of a laboratory, not fit for human consumption, while the sale of Quorn has been queried because it is a mould which can trigger allergic responses in sensitive individuals. In accordance with the cross-disciplinary aims of this volume, Messer, after reviewing these cases, concludes that in the reclassification of food into non-food, symbolic, political and economic criteria are paramount. In sharp contrast, the transformation of non-food into food involves concepts and judgments which broaden rather than reduce acceptability. She ends by emphasising the pragmatic value of this work; adding yet another rationale for this volume, she stresses how much biocultural anthropologists studying these topics can and should inform legislators and food trade negotiators about the meaningful construction of food and non-food categories and their transformations.

Eating Earth

From the beginning, the editors knew that geophagia would occupy an important position in our book. For it is both globally widespread and long regarded askance by most Europeans. It is even a subject for literary representation, arising in novels relevant to the United States, South America and Africa, among other places, (see final chapter by MacClancy). The widespread practice of geophagia has also interested nutritionists. Their primary interest was to understand how the practice may have provided any biological advantage to those practising it. Several theories were advanced: first, that soil and clay adhering to some foods, such as potato, cassava, etc., may 'bind' or chelate the toxins present in the food, rendering it edible; secondly, soils may be a valuable source of scarce micronutrients, such as zinc, iron and calcium; finally, soils (e.g. the kaolin-like clays) may help reduce diarrhoea.

Since ethnographers and anthropologists have also observed the practice in non-Western societies and questioned its causes, a review of geophagia and a broad, cross-disciplinary survey of literature on it, produced by the biocultural anthropologist, Sera L. Young, opens this section. In a successful bid to be systematically interdisciplinary, she suggests a useful classification. The editors have included both of her chapters as the first is wide-ranging across all pica, while in Chapter 5 she focuses on the different aspects of geophagia. In this latter chapter she critically reviews the potential biological consequences of earth eating, methodically going through the six mechanisms by which soil substances may act upon the body and the effects, both positive and negative, which have been proposed for them. These relate to: the absorption of minerals; the ability of some soils, especially clays, to bind with substances; the creation of a barrier; the quelling of gastrointestinal upsets; an increase in pH values; and the introduction of organisms. Based on her own biocultural research in Zanzibar, she considers the link of geophagia with anaemia. Highly relevant to the purposes of this volume is her conclusion that instead of some of the general concepts about geophagia and its biological consequences, there should be a much more critical and holistic evaluation of the behaviour, of the soils and of the individuals involved in geophagia. Popularly regarded by Westerners as 'a vile habit', she wants to find out just how 'filthy' eating dirt really is. Such are the questions we hope to stimulate with this volume.

Ananda Prasad, agreed to attend our conference, where he took us through the steps of his investigative career which led him to establish humans' need for zinc and the damaging consequences of its deficiency. What is so significant for this volume is that the initial clue for the significance of zinc came to him through his treatment of stunted clay-eaters, first in Iran, then in Egypt. These were certainly cases where geophagia was gravely maladaptive. The chapter by Peter Hooda, a geochemist, and Jeya Henry, a nutritionist, complements Prasad's chapter. Exploiting an *in vitro* test designed by Hooda, which simulates soil ingestion and its potential impact on human nutrition, they demonstrate that the soils used in several different cases of geophagia, though rich in mineral nutrients (e.g. iron, zinc, calcium, etc.), may in fact reduce the absorption of micronutrients. The fear, therefore, is that eating these soils may exacerbate micronutrient deficiency among geophagics, regardless of their dietary intake of iron and zinc. Another nutritional benefit ascribed to geophagia is the ability to chelate plant toxins. It has been proposed that the alkaloid, solanine, in potatoes and the polyphenols in legumes may be made safe for consumption by the soil ingested, which binds these toxic compounds (Johns 1994).

Sabrina Krief extends these discussions sideways. A primatologist and anthropologist, she examines chimpanzees' consumption of non-foods, including soil, and, thanks to the complementary work of Néomi Klein, is able to demonstrate the degree of overlap between human and chimpanzee selections of soils and plant materials (seemingly for self-medication). To do so, she utilises observational data on the non-human primates, biochemical analyses of apparently 'inedible' substances and ethnographic information on local human medical and geophagic practices. The integration of these perspectives on non-human primate and human behaviour is important and emphasises the value of our cross-disciplinary attempts to understand food-based practices.

Customary Non-food Substances within Diets

For all our concern with the definitions of the edible and the inedible, there are well-established uses of non-food substances in diet, either to enable ingestion or conservation or to enhance nutrition or flavour, or for other hedonistic effects. Thus, Ricardo Ávila, Martín Tena and Peter Hubbard discuss the process, already established in prehistory, whereby maize is made more nutritious through the soaking of raw corn cobs in a lime solution. Millions of Mexicans, in history and today, rely on maize as their major foodstuff and, without its prior treatment with calcium hydroxide, pellagra, among other deficiency diseases, would soon be widespread. Even though this process of *nixtamalization*, as it is known (after the Mexican term *nixtamal*, for maize cooked in water mixed with lime or ash), is by no means a neglected topic of study, we have included it in this volume because it is such a striking example of a popular use of an inedible substance in the processing of a food for daily consumption.

In the following chapter, Marcel Hladik examines to what extent among humans and chimpanzees the perception of taste determines food choice. He suggests that one explanation for geophagia could be that it is a search for sodium chloride. He shows that perception of saltiness is a much more complex sensation than previously thought, and that it shares some of the taste fibres involved in the perception of sweet and bitter substances. He discusses why some peoples consider salty flavours so pleasant (e.g. the Aka and Baka in the African rainforest), while to others it is distasteful (e.g. the Inuit). Since we do not need anything like as much salt as many of us add to food today, Hladik argues that our use of it reaches addictive levels, thus making it as medically contraindicated as some of the toxic items eaten by those exhibiting pica. On these grounds, he contends, salt might today be considered a non-food.

Consumptions in Times of Scarcity

When people's usual access to food is denied, their boundaries of the edible and the inedible shift, sometimes quite dramatically. Some researchers go so far as to speak of 'famine foods' (e.g. Huss-Ashmore and Johnston 1997), i.e. those foods that are recognised as barely eatable but which become acceptable when supplies of usual foods diminish or are absent. However, this idea needs to be very carefully deployed, as work has suggested that many so-called famine foods are in fact consumed for many reasons and in conditions when famine is neither feared nor in evidence (e.g. Sen 1981). There is great variation within and between populations in the times and contexts when substances which some would consider to be 'emergency foods' are consumed (Johns 1994). Moreover, many researchers, because their studies do not occur during exceptional times of shortage (e.g. Lee 1968), under-record the variety and use of emergency foods, which locals often deride in public but still consume outside of times of stress, possibly in private. Rigorous, long-term dietary surveys have shown that even in times of plenty, locals make broad use of a diversity of plants usually labelled as fit only for emergencies (Etkin and Ross 1994; Vickers 1994). As Etkin points out, 'For herbaceous weeds especially, this regular use assures an adequate level of human protection so that species density does not diminish to nonsustainable numbers. Some wild plants are protected as well by the utilization of other, nonemergency, parts of those plants or by their use in other contexts such as medicine or cosmetics' (Etkin 1994: 7).

Food scarcity in less developed countries is, for obvious reasons, a continuing topic of research for academics. What is much less researched is the consumption of what is more generally considered 'inedible' in times of food shortage in recent or modern urban settings in more developed nations. To illustrate this perspective in this volume, Antonia Matalas and Louis Grivetti contribute a chapter describing food practices in Athens during the famine created, first by the Italian invaders, and then by the behaviour of the German occupiers of Greece during the period 1940–44. Their study, based on data obtained by food-intake recall methods among now elderly survivors of this famine, suggests that it was the more adventurous, less hidebound, who were more likely to survive. They were able to surmount the food avoidances upheld in times of abundance while they learned to scavenge wherever and whatever.

Then, in the next chapter, Rachel Black writes about Europeans who have learned to scavenge in contemporary urban settings. This original research is significant in our compilation on the consumption of the inedible, as it reminds us to look at situations close to home. As a basis for her report on this 'urban foraging' she refers to some radicalised youths in Lyons and some impoverished pensioners in Turin. In her innovative study of an under-reported phenomenon, she shows how the main food markets of both cities have become the focus of scavengers, scooping up a small fraction of the enormous waste stallholders produce daily. For the French foragers, their practice is a considered reaction to the conspicuous waste of a capitalist society; for the aging Italians, with diminished pensions, it is a survival strategy reminiscent of their wartime years of hunger.

When Xavier Medina found a recipe for cooking cat in a handwritten, twentieth-century recipe book, he made enquiries about eating cat and found just how hard it can be to ascertain whether denigrated food behaviours were in fact practised. Regularly, in his own recent interviews, consumption of cat was denied and thought disgusting. However, the research he refers to in his chapter deserves a place in this section of the book, because it enables him to state that felines were most likely to have been consumed during the scarcities of the Spanish Civil War of 1936–39 and its immediate aftermath. Again, this exemplifies a form of consumption, which is generally considered unthinkable within a given society, being resorted to within that society in a time of need.

Ineffable, Unexpected or Commonplace?

Discussions of the emotion of disgust are well represented in psychological literature, and Paul Rozin, with a variety of co-authors, has provided a rich collection of articles in regard to disgust and food (e.g. Rozin *et al.* 1997). While the topic of disgust is never far from some of the discussions in this volume, we avoided making it a central issue of any of the chapters. However, in regard to some of the material in the following chapters we were not surprised to encounter evident disgust even in discussions with academic colleagues, as first insects as food, then consuming the product of nose-picking, then cannibalism, then eating disorders including coprophagy, and then the incidental consumption of human faeces, were each discussed.

Today most Westerners regard insects as crop-devouring destroyers, disease carriers or essential agents of biodiversity: they are not generally viewed as flavoursome titbits. It is we, the Westerners, who are out on a limb here, as people in many societies make insects an integral part of their diet. Wulf Schiefenhövel and Paul Blum provide ethnographic and quantitative data about a Melanesian people, where women gather small amounts of essential protein from arthropods, especially insects. Schiefenhövel and Blum go on to discuss the important nutritional and health consequences of this food. Since this particular case exemplifies a global practice shunned by most Europeans and Americans, it is all the more ironic that modern Westerners do in fact eat insects, almost all the time. Given that the industrialised production of food cannot remove all traces of insect carcasses, legislation tends to be less concerned with *which* insects we ingest than with the dosage (MacClancy 1992). Schiefenhövel and Blum identify a final irony in that a small but increasing number of modern-day 'foodies', keen to manifest their gastronomic sophistication, are now prepared to pay fashionable restaurateurs good money for insect-based dishes.

Until María Jesús Portalatín gave her paper, none of the co-editors had ever heard a presentation or read an academic paper which made health claims for people's consumption of their own dried nasal mucus. Portalatín discusses the social prohibitions against and the quotidian reality of people picking their noses and eating the excavated. She includes some psychological dimensions of this behaviour and possible immunological benefits of it. Since we, the co-editors, wished to bring the neglected into greater focus, this chapter has to be our exemplar. This is indeed an under-researched topic, with only extremely rare entries in literature databases and considerable scope for further study.

A volume with this title cannot omit cannibalism, and Helen Macbeth, Wulf Schiefenhövel and Paul Collinson cooperated to review the aspects of cannibalism that have concerned researchers from different disciplines. Initially there would seem to be little overlap between the perspectives of interest to social and biological scientists. However, a cross-disciplinary approach can illuminate some ongoing debates, such as that cannibalism is no 'myth'. The commonality across disciplines, which intrigues these authors and is appropriate for our theme, is the lack of literature on why conspecific flesh is so widely considered unsuitable for consumption. Why does cannibalism stimulate such curiosity and abhorrence in many societies, and yet is verifiably practised under certain circumstances?

Apart from a few references to psychiatric study in the chapter by Portalatín, Luis Cantarero presents the only psychoanalytical approach in this book. Through an examination of parents' socialisation of their children's food

The patent corollary is that any definition of 'marginal' is a cultural reflection on people and their perceptions. What we, the co-editors, have collated here may appear to some as examples of the marginal, but such a view may well say just as much about concepts of what is 'marginal' as it does about the 'marginality' of the food practices examined in the various chapters. A book of this nature produced in the future may well contain different examples of the 'marginal'. In this sense the 'marginal' is a temporally contingent, constructed category, whose content may be easily contested, negotiated, and to those extents remains ever labile. We recognise and accept the consequences of this limiting factor. Nevertheless, our goal was to stimulate further discussion, rather than stand immobile while pondering endlessly what could be meant by the 'inedible'.

Any neglect of a topic has contemporary and political dimensions. What those in any discipline choose to study is, to an important extent, what they think important and worthy of investigation. A food choice that is under-studied may just be evidence of our power, of our ability to choose what is worth studying, according to our own agendas. It is thus all the greater indictment of ourselves if the neglected food choice turns out to be highly significant nutritionally or medically, or at least frequently practised. So, our aim in this volume has been to focus on something we felt was neglected and to approach consumption practices largely regarded until now as marginal with perspectives from different disciplines. We have argued for the value of such research both for food studies and for the people studied themselves. We have put together a broad range of different examples.

Of course the subject is potentially even broader and cannot be contained within the covers of this or any one volume. There are too many examples to list; but one theme, briefly touched upon in some chapters but offering many further avenues of discussion, is that the borderlines between foods and medicines can be obscure and shift; for example, what is inedible (maybe toxic) but considered by some to be curative, or the non-nutritive materials in modern obesity treatments, etc. The list could be lengthened, but our choice was limited by the contributors and the proceedings of a lively conference, and the restrictions of a viable length of book. To these extents, the following chapters are an arbitrary but still indicative collection.

Our other aim was to promote a cross-disciplinary agenda. The study of food lends itself especially well to simultaneous research from multiple perspectives. While each approach has its strengths, it also has its blind spots. Cross-disciplinary research allows us to attempt to answer questions we could not otherwise seriously consider. In particular, the various chapters on geophagia, despite their individual insights, highlight the fact that specific instances of earth-eating have yet to be investigated in a sustained, integrated and interdisciplinary manner. The question remains: what are the nutritional benefits or risks in the different instances of geophagia, and what biological or social factors stimulate their occurrence? Given its global practice, this is an important gap in our research and further investigation is already being planned as an outcome of our conference.

References

Aylward, F. and Morgan, J. (1975) *Protein and Nutrition Policy,* Wiley, New York

Berg, A. (1981) *Malnourished People,* World Bank, Washington, DC

Cresta, M. and Teti, V. (eds) (1998) *The Road of Food Habits in the Mediterranean Area,* Rivista di Antropologia, 76 (supplement)

Diamond, J. (1997) *Guns, Germs and Steel: A Short History of Everybody for the Last 13,000 Years,* Chatto and Windus, London

Douglas, M. (1966) *Purity and Danger,* Routledge and Kegan Paul, London

Etkin, N.L. (2004) The Cull of the Wild. In Etkin, N. (ed.) *Eating on the Wild Side. The Pharmacologic, Ecologic, and Social Implications Of Using Noncultigens,* University of Arizona Press, Tucson, 1–21

Etkin, N.L., and Ross, P.J. (1994) Pharmacologic Implications of 'Wild' Plants in Hausa Diet. In Etkin, N.L. (ed.) *Eating on the Wild Side. The Pharmacologic, Ecologic, and Social Implications of Using Noncultigens,* University of Arizona Press, Tucson, 85–101

Feeley-Harnik, G. (1981) *The Lord's Table: the meaning of food in early Judaism and Chistianity,* Smithsonian Institute Press, Washington, DC

García Marquez, G. (1970) *One Hundred Years of Solitude,* Cape, London

Garine, I. de (2005) Nourritures de Brousse Chez les Muzey et les Masa du Nord Cameroun. In Raimond, C., Garine, E. and Langlois, O. (eds) *Ressources Vivrières et Choix Alimentaires dans le Bassin du Tchad,* IRD Editions/Prodig Editions, Paris, 47–62

González Turmo, I. (1997) The Pathways of Taste: The West Andalucian Case. In Macbeth, H. (ed.) *Food Preferences and Taste: Continuity and Change,* Berghahn Books, Oxford, 115–126

Goody, J. (1982) *Cooking, Cuisine and Class,* Cambridge University Press, Cambridge

Huss-Ashmore, R. and Johnston, S.L. (1997) Wild Plants as Famine Foods: Food Choice Under Conditions of Scarcity. In Macbeth, H. (ed.) *Food Preferences and Taste: Continuity and Change,* Berghahn Books, Oxford, 83–100

James, A. (1979) Confections, concoctions and conceptions, *Journal of the Anthropological Society of Oxford,* X, 83–95

Johns, T. (1994) Ambivalence to the Palatability Factors in Wild Food Plants. In Etkin, N.L. (ed.) *Eating on The Wild Side. The Pharmacologic, Ecologic, and Social Implications of Using Noncultigens,* University of Arizona Press, Tucson, 46–61

Kingsolver, B. (1999) The *Poisonwood Bible,* Faber and Faber, London

Lee, R. (1968) What Hunters do for a Living, or How to Make-Out on Scarce Resources. In Lee, R.B. and De Vore, I. (eds) *Man the Hunter,* Aldine, Chicago, 30–48

Lévi-Strauss, C. (1964) *Mythologiques, Volume 1. Le Cru et le Cuit,* Plon, Paris

—— (1967) *Mythologiques, Vol. 2, Du Miel aux Cendres,* Plon, Paris

—— (1969) *Mythologiques, Vol. 3. L'Origine des Manières de Table,* Plon, Paris

Macbeth, H. (ed.) (1997) *Food Preferences and Taste: Continuity and Change,* Berghahn Books, Oxford

MacClancy, J. (1992) *Consuming Culture. Why You Eat What You Eat,* Chapmans, London

MacClancy, J. and Macbeth, H. (2004) Introduction: How to do Anthropologies of Food. In Macbeth, H. and MacClancy, J. (eds) *Researching Food Habits. Methods and Problems,* Berghahn Books, Oxford

Millán Fuertes, A., Cantarero, L., Medina, F.X., Montejano, M. and Portalatín, M-J. (eds) (2004), *Arbitrario Cultural: Racionalidad e Irracionalidad del Comportamiento Comensal*, University of Zaragoza.

Parker, H. (1909) *Ancient Ceylon*, Luzac, London

Portalatín, M-J (2004) Razón y Sinrazón del Ayuno y la Abstinencia Alimentaria en la Religión Católica. In Millán Fuertes, A., Cantarero, L., Medina, F.X., Montejano, M. and Portalatín, M-J. (eds), *Arbitrario Cultural: Racionalidad e Irracionalidad del Comportamiento Comensal*, University of Zaragoza.

Rozin, P., Haidt, J., McCauley, C. and Imada, S. (1997) Disgust: Preadaptation and the Cultural Evolution of a Food-Based Emotion. In Macbeth, H. (ed.) *Food Preferences and Taste: Continuity and Change*, Berghahn Books, Oxford

Sen, A. (1981) *Poverty and Famine*, Oxford University Press

Steinbeck, J. (1939) The *Grapes of Wrath*, Heinemann, London

Vickers, W.T. (1994) The Health Significance of Wild Plants for the Siona and Secoya. In Etkin, N.L. (ed.) *Eating on the Wild Side. The Pharmacologic, Ecologic, and Social Implications of Using Noncultigens*, University of Arizona Press, Tucson, 143–165

Wiessner, P. and Schiefenhövel, W. (1996) *Food and the Status Quest: An Interdisciplinary Perspective*, Berghahn Books, Oxford

1. EVIDENCE FOR THE CONSUMPTION OF THE INEDIBLE

WHO, WHAT, WHEN, WHERE AND WHY?

Sera L. Young

The causes of pica, the craving and consumption of non-food substances, have remained elusive for more than 2000 years.[1] I became curious about pica during my own research on Pemba Island, Zanzibar, Tanzania. When I asked Pembans why they liked to eat pica substances, typically they smiled and shrugged, 'It's just an addiction.' or, more frequently, 'I don't know.' One elderly woman fired my own question back to me: 'And you, do you know why?' I didn't, but I became committed to answering her.

This chapter is my preliminary response to her. In these pages, I first provide some background on pica: a description of typical pica substances, the regions where and historical periods during which they have been eaten. I conclude by outlining and evaluating the eight most common reasons why pica substances are thought to be consumed.

Which Substances Are Craved?

About the second month of pregnancy, a certain ailment affects the pregnant woman which gets its name (pica) from the noisy bird, the magpie ... To satisfy this depraved humour these women crave various and odd foods, some salty, some acrid; some crave for ordinary sand, oyster shells and ashes (Amida 1542: 758).

Pica pica is the genus and species name with which Linnaeus identified the common magpie. Magpies are birds notorious for what is thought to be an indiscriminate appetite. Ironically, magpies do not have careless appetites; the assorted objects they are observed holding in their beak are materials for nest-building. Similarly, pica eaters, too, do not ingest simply anything. There are particular substances that have been craved throughout history and around the world; they are mostly all dry, powdery substances.

Soil is the oldest and most frequently craved and ingested non-food substance, and, again, not just any soil will do. The smoothest soils, i.e. those high in clay content, are the most sought after (Lacey 1990). For example, Von Humboldt, a German explorer travelling through present-day Venezuela in the early 1800s reported, 'The Otomacs do not eat every kind of clay indifferently; they choose the alluvial beds of strata that contain the most unctuous earth, and the smoothest to the feel' (1889: 197).

Other substances commonly craved for hundreds of years include ash, charcoal, coffee grounds, dried mortar, hair, ice, ground egg- or seashells, shreds of cloth or paper and uncooked rice (Butterworth 1909; Dukes 1884; Edwards et al. 1954; Parry-Jones 1992; Robinson et al. 1990). More recently, pica consumers' tastes have broadened to include manufactured items, such as baby powder, baking soda, baking powder, burnt match-heads, chalkboard chalk, cigarette ashes, cigarette filters, Epsom salts, magnesium carbonate, mothballs, paint chips, (news)paper, paraffin wax, starch, soap and toilet paper (Abu-Hamdan et al. 1985; Chisholm and Martin 1981; De la Burde and Shapiro 1975; DeSilva 1974; Leming et al. 1981; Lopez et al. 2004; Olynyk and Sharpe 1982; Rainville 1998; Simpson 2000).

Although it is possible that cravings for clay are different phenomena from those for other non-food substances, several observations support a commonality. Firstly, those who eat earth are frequently consumers of other non-food substances. Secondly, some who consume the more manufactured substances say they use them as a replacement for earth, either because the desired soil is unavailable or because consumption is socially unacceptable (Cragin 1835; Edwards et al. 1959; Layman et al. 1963). Thirdly, the consistencies of many of the materials are similar: they are mostly dry, powdery substances (ice is an obvious exception).

A final similarity is the intensity with which these substances are craved. 'I feel awful, just about crazy when I can't get clay', one woman from the southern USA explained (Cooksey 1995: 131). Women in Zanzibar use the term 'kileo', the term for drug and alcohol addiction, to describe their feelings for pica substances (Young and Ali 2005). The desire for pica is strong enough that people will go through great difficulty to obtain the substances. For example, Avicenna, writing in the tenth century, suggested that geophagy be cured 'in boys by use of the whip, in older patients by restraints, prison, and medical exhibits' (in Woywodt and Kiss 2002: 144). Thurston wrote, 'I have frequently come across coolie patients with gravel hidden on their persons or actually caught them in the act of eating such dirt, and the craving is so strong that the coolie will cry and beg for the dirt which he so much cherishes' (1906: 543). The most wrenching report of the strength of desire for pica substances is by Cragin, a medical doctor employed by plantation owners, writing in 1835, describing the punishment of slaves who engaged in pica (Cragin 1835: 361):

As curative means, neither promises nor threats (even when put in execution), nor yet the confinement of the legs and hands in stocks and manacles, exert the least influence; and their preventative effect is as temporary as their employment; so great is the depravity of the appetite, and so strongly are the unfortunate sufferers under this complain subjected to its irresistible dominion. A metallic mask or mouthpiece, secured by a lock, is the principal means of security for providing against their indulging in dirt-eating ... nor does this effect a cure or save the life of the patient.

Early Reports of Pica

Pica is not a novel behaviour. The very oldest evidence comes from a prehistoric site at Kalambo Falls, Zambia, where the bones of *Homo habilis*, the immediate predecessor of *Homo sapiens*, have been found alongside special white clay (Clark 1969). Several facts suggest geophagia: the site predates known use of clay for pottery or ornaments by tens of thousands of years, the clay is not found naturally in the area, and it is similar to that which is presently consumed around the world (Root-Bernstein 1997).

Hippocrates (460–380 BC) is responsible for the oldest written record of geophagy. 'If a pregnant woman would like to eat earth or charcoal, and then eats it, the child that enters this world will be marked on its head from these substances' (Hippocrates 1839: 487).

Fewer reports on pica are available from medieval times, partly because gynaecological and obstetric care was mostly given by midwives who did not write texts (Woywodt and Kiss 2002). One surviving document is a textbook written by Trotula of Salerno, a midwife in the eleventh century, who dealt with geophagia as a common but treatable problem for pregnant women. 'If, however, she desires clay or chalk or coals, let beans cooked with sugar be given to her' (Salerno 2001: 96).

Cravings for ice (pagophagia) were first mentioned by the French royal physician Lazarus Riverius (1589–1655), who described women and young girls suffering from 'chlorosis' (an affliction similar to anaemia) desiring 'Earthy, Dry and burnt things, as Cloves, Cinnamon, Nutmegs and other spices, Salt, Ashes, Chalk and the like' and having a compulsion to consume sour things, 'sharp bitter and very cold' leading to 'the continual use of unripe Fruits, Vinegar, Juyce of Lemmons, Pomegranates, and Orenges, cold Water, Snow, Ice and the like' (in Parry-Jones 1992: 564).

Approximately twenty *dissertations* about pica were written by medical doctors in Europe in the seventeenth and eighteenth centuries. Although the aetiologies of pica put forth in these documents (e.g. vapours, humours) and cures suggested (e.g. ash of unicorn horn) are less instructive, they do provide useful descriptive demographics of those who engage in pica (mostly women) and when (during early pregnancy): 'We warn the female sex, as being weaker, of this evil [pica] which is familiar and peculiar to them' (Maler 1692: 6).

The first group who studied pica with techniques that even approximated modern scientific methods were colonial doctors employed by plantation owners in the United States and Latin America to study 'cachexia africana'[2] (Telford 1822). Pallor (indicative of severe anaemia), extreme weakness, and pica were features of this syndrome, and slave owners attributed the very high mortality of their slaves to it. One doctor even reported that mortality due to geophagia had been the cause of the abandonment of two plantations (Imray 1843).

Pica remains a widespread practice today; for example, a 1997 study found that 68 per cent of pregnant women at a Texas clinic engaged in pica (Rainville 1997). Pica clays are even for sale online (http://www.whitedirt.com), and there are Internet chatrooms full of people concerned about their inexplicable cravings for baby powder, chalkboard chalk, cornstarch, facial tissue and broken clay pots (http://health.groups.yahoo.com/group/Cornstarch/).

Where is Pica Done?

Among all the curious perversions of taste existing in various parts of the world, there are few so peculiar or so apparently unaccountable as that of eating earth. Were the habit not very widely extended over the world, it would perhaps hardly be worth any extended investigation; but it is found among the peoples of every continent, and apparently of almost every race (Hooper and Mann 1906: 270).

Pica has been observed as a traditional practice on all inhabited continents, and most frequently in tropical climates. Although I have found more than 1,500 references in which the location of pica is mentioned, these are almost certainly not the only places that pica occurs. Non-food cravings are difficult to study for multiple reasons. Consumers of pica sometimes attempt to conceal their behaviour from researchers because of their fear of judgment or chastisement, because it is an indication of pregnancy status (a private matter) or because they feel it reveals their lack of self-control (e.g. Dickins and Ford 1942; Hooper and Mann 1906; Sayetta 1986). Furthermore, researchers sometimes do not know to inquire specifically about pica and 'discover' it only by accident (e.g. Cooksey 1995; Grigsby et al. 1999; Hooper and Mann 1906; Rainville 1998; Vermeer 1966). An additional difficulty in studying pica is that it does not easily fit into a conceptual category. People may think of pica substances as medicine, a food additive, or 'just a craving', as I encountered in my own research, such that food recall questions do not probe with appropriate prompts (Young 2003). For the purposes of this review, it is sufficient to state that pica has been widely documented in many European countries, the Middle East, Africa, Asia, Australia and throughout the Americas.

Who Engages in Pica?

> When an African female senior government physician in Malawi was asked if village women ate clay in pregnancy, she smiled: 'It would be very surprising if pregnant women in Malawi did not eat clay. That's how you know when you are pregnant!' (Hunter 1993).

Ethnographies and individual case reports in the literature indicate that children, anaemic people, and most frequently of all, pregnant women, are the typical pica consumers (cf. above, Early Reports of Pica). There are only a few accounts of non-anaemic teenagers, adults, and elderly of both genders engaging in pica.

Recently, pica has been documented among people with coeliac disease (e.g. Alvarez Martin *et al.* 1998; Korman 1990) and dialysis patients (e.g. Kensit 1979; Ward 2000).

Why Pica?

Anthropologists, behavioural ecologists, ethologists, geographers, medical doctors, nutritionists, parasitologists, primatologists, psychologists, toxicologists and soil scientists have all posited motivations for pica. I have organised their hypotheses into eight categories: nutrient craving, sensory disturbance, gastrointestinal malaise, detoxification, hunger, stress, mental illness and cultural expectation. This section is an overview of the hypotheses and a sketch of the relevant data, not a systematic evaluation of each argument.

Aetiology 1. A craving for the deficient substance, or '... because I am iron deficient and need more iron':

The most frequent explanation of pica is that individuals are craving a micronutrient that they lack, typically iron (cf. Chapter 6 for more in-depth discussion). In fact, several researchers have stated unequivocally that iron deficiency causes individuals to consume pica substances rich in iron (Castro and Boyd-Orr 1952; Crosby 1976). Initially this hypothesis seems tenable, since pica consumers are frequently iron deficient (Halsted 1968; Kettaneh *et al.* 2005; Lopez *et al.* 2001; Okcuoglu *et al.* 1966). However, this explanation has a number of weaknesses, including the low micronutrient content of the substances craved, an absence of tenable biological mechanisms for craving them, and contradictory clinical evidence.

Most pica substances contain little to no soluble iron, and elemental iron, even when it is soluble has extremely low bioavailability (Hooda *et al.* 2004) (cf. Chapter 6). A second limitation is that the suggested mechanisms by which such a craving might occur are problematic. Hunter states that 'foetal demand' leads to 'strange cravings in Western pregnant women', such as ice cream and pickles, and 'geophagia in peasant societies' (1973: 183). Without the support of an explicit mechanism, such a hypothesis is difficult to test. Furthermore, it is problematic because Western pregnant women do eat earth, and 'foetal demand' would certainly not explain the prevalence of pica among children. Danford posits 'unrecognized nutrient appetites' as the impetus for pica (1982). Johns and Duquette argue that iron deficiency does not cause pica because, although unrecognized nutrient appetites exist, they have not been demonstrated for mineral nutrients (1991: 454).

Finally, experimental evidence offers little support for pica as a means of obtaining increased micronutrients. Although in a single-blind study of 25 iron-deficient patients, one dose of parenteral iron treatment ended pagophagia (pica for ice) (Coltman 1969) and in two studies iron caused the cessation of geophagia in children (Lanzkowsky 1959; McDonald and Marshall 1964), these studies have been criticised for poor follow-up, lack of controls, limited evaluation of iron deficiency and strong verbal messages discouraging pica (Ansell and Wheby 1972). Contradictory clinical evidence is even stronger. In a more carefully controlled double-blind study of geophagia in children, in which no advice was given about pica except when it involved lead poisoning, researchers found that neither iron nor a multivitamin with minerals was significantly more effective than a placebo in 'curing' pica (Halsted 1968). In a randomised, double-blind trial in which Zambian geophagic school children were supplemented with iron, a multivitamin or a placebo, those who received iron actually increased their consumption of soil (Nchito *et al.* 2004).

The discussion of iron deficiency as a motive for pica dwarfs that of calcium deficiency, although calcium deficiency seems more plausible. Although a mechanism to sense calcium deficiency has not been elucidated, pica substances such as chalk, ground shells, and clay are often rich in calcium which is much more readily obtained by the body than is iron. Furthermore, according to a hypothesis-driven literature review, geophagy was more common in non-dairying African cultures, where there was less calcium in the diet than in dairying ones (Wiley and Katz 1998). To date, there is no experimental evidence to test this hypothesis.

Aetiology 2. A functional disturbance caused by an iron or zinc deficiency, or '... because I am iron deficient and lost my sense of taste':

Other researchers propose that a micronutrient deficiency causes pica, but the resultant cravings are not for the substances that will remedy the deficiency, they are simply a product of a malfunctioning brain. Youdim and Iancu attribute abnormal cravings to iron and zinc deficiencies in 'key appetite-regulating brain enzymes' (1977: 298). Von Bonsdorff posits that the iron-rich hypothalamus, responsible for regulating appetite, might not function properly in the absence of sufficient iron, and thus cause pica (1977). Eichner speculates that the 'cells lining the mouth run out of iron and send an alarm signal to the brain,' (in Anderson 2005), but was unable to specify which cells these might be (personal communication, 30th September 2003). More plausible research suggests that taste sensitivity may be altered by zinc deficiency; this in turn could cause non-food substances to have an appealing taste (Chisholm and Martin 1981; Prasad 2001).

This aetiology, however, does not explain the variety of pica substances. Why these dry powdery substances? Why ice? Why not tree bark or sand? Secondly, these researchers all assume that a deficiency precedes pica consumption; this has not been established. If taste perception is altered by zinc deficiency, it should follow that correcting zinc deficiency would cause pica to cease. The cessation of pica has been observed after the correction of zinc deficiency (Prasad 2001), but many factors were altered in addition to zinc concentrations, so that it is not possible to state that the return to normal zinc values was the causal factor.

Aetiology 3. Gastrointestinal malaise, or '… because my stomach is upset':

If pica consumers can give a reason for their pica behaviour (and they rarely can), it is usually related to gastrointestinal malaise, namely heartburn or nausea (Corbett 1995; Frankel 1977). This is physiologically sound. Clays have long been known for their soothing effect on gastrointestinal upset. Although Kaopectate, an over-the-counter medicine to treat diarrhoea, no longer contains the clay kaolin, kaolin is its namesake. Human beings are not the only ones to eat clay when experiencing gastrointestinal distress; rats do it too (McCaffrey 1985; Mitchell *et al.* 1977). Clay, chalk and ground shells also have alkaline properties that can effectively treat heartburn.

The fact that many pica consumers do not attribute their consumption to gastrointestinal upset, nor are experiencing it when they ingest pica substances, indicates that if this is a cause of pica, there are other grounds. Furthermore, an explanation for the consumption of non-alkaline pica substances is still necessary.

Aetiology 4. Exposure to toxins, or '… because I have eaten something harmful':

Johns and colleagues' work on geophagy has shed light on the capacity of clays to neutralise harmful chemicals found in plants (Johns 1996; Johns and Duquette 1991). Profet first proposed the idea that clays could act as detoxifiers of teratogens and thus be beneficial during pregnancy (Profet 1988). Many have found evidence to support her hypothesis (Flaxman and Sherman 2000; Nesse and Williams 1996). Experimental evidence from rats, who are not able to rid themselves of toxins through emesis, support this. Experiments show that they will eat kaolin and successfully reduce poison-related morbidity and mortality (Liu *et al.* 2005; Madden 1999; Mitchell *et al.* 1976).

As for the non-earth pica substances, no research has been done to establish their detoxification potential, although some of these, such as charcoal and starch, are used as detoxifiers in industrial applications (cf. Chapter 6).

Aetiology 5. Hunger '... because I don't have anything else to eat':

Geophagia has been reported during times of hunger (Laufer 1930). In fact, eating dirt for lack of food is where the expression 'dirt-poor' originates (Den Hollander 1935). Although hunger has been a motive for earth consumption during certain periods, the majority of people who have engaged in pica did not do so because they lacked food. For one, it is not an effective solution; although pica substances may fill the belly, few contain significant amounts of calories. Secondly, obesity is common among some populations who engage in pica (Kushner *et al.* 2004; Vermeer and Frate 1979; Ward and Kutner 1999). Thus, hunger seems not to be a major cause of pica.

Aetiology 6. A comforting habit, or '... because I'm upset':

Some scientists propose that pica is a soothing behaviour, associated with childhood memories of one's own mother engaging in pica (Corbett *et al.* 2003). Although children may mimic the pica they see adults engage in, this does not explain why the behaviour disappears in adolescence and why their mothers (and not fathers) ever engaged in pica, and then, only during pregnancy.

Others believe that pica is a response to stress, similar to nail-biting or smoking (Burchfield *et al.* 1977; Singhi *et al.* 1981; Solyom *et al.* 1991). Indeed, there is anecdotal evidence in which pica consumers explain their habit as 'a nervous one' (Hamilton *et al.* 2001). Experimental evidence to support this is minimal. In their study of 553 urban African American women, Edwards and colleagues found that pica was more frequent among those with less social support (Edwards *et al.* 1994). They concluded that during pregnancy 'pica may be a mediator of stress, acting through the immune system' (961s). However, the manifestation of stress in the consumption of starch or ice (as opposed to other stress responses measured in the study) is not adequately explained.

Aetiology 7. Mental illness, or '... because I have a mental disturbance':

Pica is occasionally a feature of several mental problems, including obsessive compulsive disorder, autism, schizophrenia and developmental impairment (Danford *et al.* 1982; McAlpine and Singh 1986; McLoughlin 1988; Roosendaal and Weits-Binnerts 1997). Again, because it is not only mentally impaired people who engage in pica, and not all mentally ill people do, mental health (or a lack thereof) cannot explain the bulk of pica behaviour.

Aetiology 8. Cultural expectation, or '... because that's what we do':

Finally, some scholars argue that it 'makes sense' that women eat earth because their traditional role in some societies as potters and gardeners brings them close to the soil (Hochstein 1968). Others argue the fecundity of the earth makes it appropriate for ingestion, 'The cultural associations of soil-eating with blood, fertility and femininity exist alongside knowledge of its links to illness' (Geissler *et al.* 1999: 1078).

Although it might make sense symbolically in some cultures, there must be additional reasons for pica behaviour. It does not 'make sense' in all cultures, otherwise shame would not be associated with pica. Some people have not learned pica behaviour through acculturation; some women who engage in pica feel 'alone', and had no idea that others shared their tastes (Cooksey 1995). Furthermore, many animals, including primates, turtles, birds, cattle and horses eat clay (Butler 1995; Diamond *et al.* 1999; Krishnamani and Mahaney 2000; Mahaney and Hancock 1990; McGreevy *et al.* 2001; Packard and Packard 2004) and at least one, the Zanzibari red colobus monkey, eats charcoal, (Struhsaker *et al.* 1997). This suggests that culture alone cannot be the impetus for pica.

Conclusion

So how do we answer the Pemban woman who asked why people like to eat pica substances? We cannot, at least not yet. There are many theories but inadequate data to support any one of them. Careful and systematic exploration of each hypothesis is necessary before this 2000-year-old question can be put to rest.

Notes

1. This chapter has been greatly improved by the helpful suggestions made by Julius Lucks, Gretel Pelto, Kathleen Rasmussen and Robin Young, to whom I am grateful.
2. Cachexia africana was also known as 'mal d'estomac' (Dons 1836) 'malacia' (Pancoucke 1818) and 'erdessen' (Wyllie 1909).

References

Abu-Hamdan, D.K., Sondheimer, J.H. and Mahajan, S.K. (1985) Cautopyreiophagia. Cause of life-threatening hyperkalemia in a patient undergoing hemodialysis. *American Journal of Medicine*, 79: 517–519

Alvarez Martin, T., Anso Olivan, S., Prieto Contero, I., Barbadillo Izquierdo, F., Merino Arribas, J.M. and Gonzalez De La Rosa, J.B. (1998) Pica as a form of presentation of celiac disease. *Anales Españoles de Pediatría*, 49: 542–543

Amida, A. (1542) *The Gynaecology and Obstetrics of the Sixth Century*. The Blakiston Company, Philadelphia

Anderson, O. (2005) Self-Diagnosis: Your Workouts Can Reveal What's Wrong With Your Health http://www.pponline.co.uk/encyc/0201.htm

Ansell, J.E. and Wheby, M.S. (1972) Pica: Its relation to iron deficiency. A review of the recent literature. *Virginia Medical Monthly (1918)*, 99: 951–954

Burchfield, S.R., Elich, M.S. and Woods, S.C. (1977) Geophagia in response to stress and arthritis. *Physiology and Behavior*, 19: 265–267

Butler, D.R. (1995) *Zoogeomorphology: Animals as Geomorphic Agents*. Cambridge University Press, Cambridge

Butterworth, M. (1909) Hair ball or hair cast of the stomach and its occurrence in children. *Journal of the American Medical Association*, 53: 617–624

Castro, J.D. and Boyd-Orr, J. (1952) *The Geography of Hunger*. Little Brown and Company, Boston

Chisholm, J.C., Jr. and Martin, H.I. (1981) Hypozincemia, ageusia, dysosmia, and toilet tissue pica. *Journal of the National Medical Association*, 73: 163–164

Clark, J.D. (1969) *Kalambo Falls Prehistoric Site*. Cambridge University Press, London

Coltman, C.A. (1969) Pagophagia and iron lack. *Journal of the American Medical Association*, 207: 513–516

Cooksey, N.R. (1995) Pica and olfactory craving of pregnancy: How deep are the secrets? *Birth*, 22: 129–137

Corbett, R.W. (1995) *The Relationship among Trace Elements, Pica, Social Support, and Infant Birthweight*. Ph.D. Thesis, University of South Carolina

Corbett, R.W., Ryan, C. and Weinrich, S.P. (2003) Pica in pregnancy: Does it affect pregnancy outcomes? *American Journal of Maternal Child Nursing*, 28: 183–190

Cragin, F.W. (1835) Observations on cachexia africana or dirt-eating. *American Journal of the Medical Sciences*, 17: 356–364

Crosby, W.H. (1976) Pica: A compulsion caused by iron deficiency. *British Journal of Haematology*, 34: 341–342

Danford, D.E. (1982) Pica and nutrition. *Annual Review of Nutrition*, 2: 303–322

Danford, D.E., Jr., J.C.S. and Huber, A.M. (1982) Pica and mineral status in the mentally retarded. *American Journal of Clinical Nutrition*, 35: 958–967

De la Burde, B. and Shapiro, I.M. (1975) Dental lead, blood lead, and pica in urban children. *Archives of Environmental Health*, 30: 281–284

Den Hollander, A.N.J. (1935) The Tradition of "Poor Whites". In Couch, W.T. (ed.) *Culture in the South,* University of North Carolina Press, Chapel Hill, pp. 403–431

DeSilva, R. (1974) Letter: Eating cigarette ashes in anaemia. *Annals of Internal Medicine*, 80: 115–116

Diamond, J., Bishop, K.D. and Gilardi, J.D. (1999) Geophagy in New Guinea birds. *Ibis*, 141. 181–193

Dickins, D. and Ford, R.N. (1942) Geophagy (dirt eating) among Mississippi negro school children. *American Sociological Review*, 7: 59–65

Dons, P.L. (1836) Ueber die Sogenannte Africanishe Cachexie, Erdessen (mal d'estomac, dirt eating, Jordaden). *Medizinische Annalen, Heidelberg*, 2: 374–398

Dukes, C. (1884) A remarkable case of a juvenile earth-eater. *Lancet*, 2: 822

Edwards, C.H., Johnson, A.A., Knight, E.M., Oyemade, U.J., Cole, O.J., Westney, O.A., Jones, S., Laryea, H. and Westney, L.S. (1994) Pica in an urban environment. *Journal of Nutrition*, 954s–962s

Edwards, C.H., McDongald, S., Mitchell, J.R., Jones, L., Mason, L., Kemp, A.M., Laing, D. and Trigg, L. (1959) Clay- and cornstarch-eating women. *Journal of the American Dietetic Association*, 35: 810–815

Edwards, C.H., McSwain, H. and Haire, S. (1954) Odd dietary practices of women. *Journal of the American Dietetic Association*, 30: 976–981

Flaxman, S. and Sherman, P.W. (2000) Morning sickness: A mechanism for protecting mother and embryo. *Quarterly Review of Biology*, 75(2): 113–148

Frankel, B. (1977) *Childbirth in the Ghetto: Folk Beliefs of Negro Women in a North Philadelphia Hospital Ward*. R and E Research Associates, San Francisco

Geissler: , Prince, R.J., Levene, M., Poda, C., Beckerleg, S., Mutemi, W. and Shulman, C.E. (1999) Perceptions of soil-eating and anaemia among pregnant women on the Kenyan coast. *Social Science and Medicine*, 48: 1069–1079

Grigsby, R.K., Thyer, B.A., Waller, R.J. and Johnston, G.A. (1999) Chalk eating in middle Georgia: A culture-bound syndrome of pica. *Southern Medical Journal*, 92: 190–192

Halsted, J. (1968) Geophagia in man: Its nature and nutritional effects. *American Journal of Clinical Nutrition*, 21: 1384–1393

Hamilton, S., Rothenberg, S.J., Khan, F.A., Manalo, M. and Norris, K.C. (2001) Neonatal lead poisoning from maternal pica behavior during pregnancy. *Journal of the National Medical Association*, 93: 317–319

Hippocrates. (1839) *Oeuvres Complètes d'Hippocrate*. Hakkert, Amsterdam

Hochstein, G. (1968) Pica: A Study in Medical and Anthropological Explanation. In Weaver, T. (ed.) *Essays on Medical Anthropology, Southern Anthropological Society Proceedings, No. 1,* University of Georgia Press, Athens, USA

Hooda, S., Henry, C.J., Seyoum, T., Armstrong, L.D. and Fowler, M.B. (2004) The potential impact of soil ingestion on human mineral nutrition. *The Science of the Total Environment*, 333: 75–87

Hooper, D. and Mann, H.H. (1906) Earth-eating and the earth-eating habit in India. *Memoirs of the Asiatic Society of Bengal*, 1: 249–273

Hunter, J.M. (1973) Geophagy in Africa and in the United States: A culture-nutrition hypothesis. *Geographical Review*, 63: 170–195

Hunter, J.M. (1993) Macroterme geophagy and pregnancy clays in Southern Africa. *Journal of Cultural Geography*, 14: 69–92

Imray, J. (1843) Observations on the Mal D'estomac or Cachexia Africana, as it takes place among the negroes of Dominica. *Edinburgh Medical and Surgical Journal*, 59: 304–321

Johns, T. (1996) *The Origins of Human Diet and Medicine*. University of Arizona Press, Tucson

Johns, T. and Duquette, M. (1991) Detoxification and mineral supplementation as functions of geophagy. *American Journal of Clinical Nutrition*, 53: 448–456

Kensit, M. (1979) Appetite disturbances in dialysis patients. *Journal of the American Association of Nephrology Nurses*, 6: 194–199

Kettaneh, A., Eclache, V., Fain, O., Sontag, C., Uzan, M., Carbillon, L., Stirnemann, J. and Thomas, M. (2005) Pica and food craving in patients with iron-deficiency anaemia: A case-control study in France. *American Journal of Medicine*, 118: 185–188.

Korman, S. (1990) Pica as a presenting symptom in childhood celiac disease. *American Journal of Clinical Nutrition*, 51: 139–141

Krishnamani, R. and Mahaney, W.C. (2000) Geophagy among primates: Adaptive significance and ecological consequences. *Animal Behaviour*, 59: 899–915

Kushner, R.F., Gleason, B. and Shanta-Retelney, V. (2004) Re-emergence of pica following gastric bypass surgery for obesity: A new presentation of an old problem. *Journal of the American Dietetic Association*, 104: 1393–1397

Lacey, E.P. (1990) Broadening the perspective of pica: Literature review. *Public Health Reports*, 105: 29–35

Lanzkowsky. (1959) Investigation into the aetiology and treatment of pica. *Archives of Diseases in Childhood*, 34: 140–148

Laufer, B. (1930) *Geophagy*, Field Museum of Natural History, Publication 280, Anthropology Series 18, 99–198

Layman, E.M., Mullican, F.K., Lourie, R.S. and Takahashi, L.Y. (1963) Cultural influences and symptom choice: Clay eating customs in relation to the etiology of pica. *The Psychological Record*, 13: 249–257

Leming, P.D., Reed, D. and Martelo, O. (1981) Magnesium Carbonate pica: An unusual case of iron deficiency. *Annals of Internal Medicine*, 94: 660

Liu, Y., Malik, N., Sanger, G., Friedman, M. and Andrews, P.L.R. (2005) Pica-A model of nausea? Species differences in response to cisplatin. *Physiology and Behavior*, 85(3): 271–277

Lopez, L., Langini, S., Fleichman, S., Portela, M. and Ortega Soler, C. (2001) Iron deficiency in pregnant women with pica. *Journal of the American Dietetic Society*, 9: A-104

Lopez, L.B., Ortega Soler, C.R. and De Portela, M.L. (2004) Pica during pregnancy: A frequently underestimated problem. *Archivos Latinoamericanos de Nutrición*, 54: 17–24

Madden, L.J. (1998) *Pica and Peptides: Assessing Gastrointestinal Malaise*. Ph.D. Thesis, University of Washington

Mahaney, W.C. and Hancock, R.G.V. (1990) Geochemical analysis of African buffalo geophagic sites and dung on Mount Kenya, East Africa. *Extrait de Mammalia*, 54: n.p.

Maler, E.C.F. (1692) *Disputatio Medica Inauguralis de Pica*. Typis Joh. Rudolphi Genathii, Basileae

McAlpine, C. and Singh, N.N. (1986) Pica in institutionalized mentally retarded persons. *Journal of Mental Deficiency Research*, 30: 171–178

McCaffrey, R.J. (1979) *Motion Sickness-Induced Pica in the Rat: A Test of the Sensory Rearrangement Theory*. Ph.D. Thesis, University of Georgia

McDonald, R. and Marshall, S.R. (1964) The value of iron therapy in pica. *Pediatrics*, 34: 558–562

McGreevy, Hawson, L., Habermann, T. and Cattle, S. (2001) Geophagia in horses: A short note on 13 cases. *Applied Animal Behaviour Science*, 71: 119–125

McLoughlin, I.J. (1988) Pica as a cause of death in three mentally handicapped men. *British Journal of Psychiatry*, 152: 842–845

Mitchell, D., Laycock, J. and Stephens, W. (1977) Motion sickness-induced pica in the rat. *American Journal of Clinical Nutrition*, 30: 147–150

Mitchell, D., Wells, C., Hoch, N., Lind, K., Woods, S.C. and Mitchell, L.K. (1976) Poison induced pica in rats. *Physiology and Behavior*, 17: 691–697

Nchito, M., Geissler, L., Mubila, L., Friis, H. and Olsen, A. (2004) Effects of iron and multimicronutrient supplementation on geophagy: A two-by-two factorial study among Zambian school children in Lusaka. *Transactions of the Royal Society of Tropical Medicine and Hygiene*, 98: 218–227

Nesse, R.M. and Williams, G.C. (1996) *Why We Get Sick: The New Science of Darwinian Medicine*. Vintage, New York

Okcuoglu, A., Arcasoy, A., Minnich, V., Tarcon, Y., Cin, S., Yorukoglu, O. and Demirag, B. (1966) Pica in Turkey: I. The incidence and association with anaemia. *American Journal of Clinical Nutrition*, 19: 125–131

Olynyk, F. and Sharpe, D. (1982) Mercury poisoning in paper pica. *New England Journal of Medicine*, 306: 1056–1057

Packard, G.C. and Packard, M.J. (2004) To freeze or not to freeze: Adaptations for overwintering by hatchlings of the North American painted turtle. *Journal of Experimental Biology*, 207: 2897–2906

Pancoucke, C.L.F. (ed.) (1818) *Dictionaire des Sciences Medicales* Paris

Parry-Jones, B. (1992) Pagophagia, or compulsive ice consumption: A historical perspective. *Psychological Medicine*, 22: 561–571

Prasad, A.S. (2001) Discovery of human zinc deficiency: Impact on human health. *Nutrition*, 17: 685–687

Profet, M. (1995) *Pregnancy Sickness: Using Your Body's Natural Defenses to Protect Your Baby-To-Be*. Addison-Wesley Publishing Group, Reading, MA

Rainville, A.J. (1997) Pica practices of pregnant women from four WIC clinics in Texas. *Journal of the American Dietetic Association*, 97: A-68

Rainville, A.J. (1998) Pica practices of pregnant women are associated with lower maternal hemoglobin level at delivery. *Journal of the American Dietetic Association*, 98: 293–296

Robinson, B., Tolan, W. and Golding-Beecher, O. (1990) Childhood pica. Some aspects of the clinical profile in Manchester, Jamaica. *West Indian Medical Journal*, 39: 20–26

Roosendaal, J.J. and Weits-Binnerts, J.J. (1997) Aspects of pica in adult psychiatric patients. *Nederlands Tijdschrift voor Geneeskunde*, 141: 306–307

Root-Bernstein, R.S. (1997) *Honey, Mud, Maggots, and Other Medical Marvels : The Science Behind Folk Remedies and Old Wives' Tales*. Houghton Mifflin, Boston

Salerno, T. (2001) *Trotula Major: A Medieval Compendium of Women's Medicine*. University of Pennsylvania Press, Philadelphia

Sayetta, R.B. (1986) Pica: An overview. *American Family Physician*, 33: 181–185

Simpson, E. (2000) Pica during pregnancy in low-income women born in Mexico. *Western Journal of Medicine*, 173: 20–24

Singhi, S., Singhi, P. and Adwani, G. (1981) Psychosocial stress and pica. *Clinical Pediatrics*, 20: 783–785

Solyom, C., Solyom, L. and Freeman, R. (1991) An unusual case of pica. *Canadian Journal of Psychiatry*, 36: 50–53

Struhsaker, T.T., Cooney, D.O. and Siex, K.S. (1997) Charcoal consumption by Zanzibar red colobus monkeys: Its function and its ecological and demographic consequences. *International Journal of Primatology*, 18: 61–72

Telford, W. (1822) On the Mal d'Estomac. *Medical and Physical Journal, London*, xlvii: 450–458

Thurston, E. (1906) Earth-eating. *Ethnographic Notes in Southern India*, Madras: Government Press, 552–554

Vermeer, D.E. (1966) Geophagy among the Tiv of Nigeria. *Annals of the Association of American Geographers*, 56: 197–204

Vermeer, D.E. and Frate, D.A. (1979) Geophagia in rural Mississippi: Environmental and cultural contexts and nutritional implications. *American Journal of Clinical Nutrition*, 32: 2129–2135.

Von Bonsdorff, B. (1977) Pica: A hypothesis. *British Journal of Haematology*, 35(3): 476–477

Von Humboldt, A., Bonpland, A. and Ross, T. (1889) *Personal Narrative of Travels to the Equinoctial Regions of America, During the Year 1799–1804*. (Ed. and Transl. Ross, T.) G. Bell, London

Ward, P.A. (2000) Consequences of pica in dialysis patients. *Seminars in Dialysis*, 13: 57–58

Ward, P. and Kutner, N.G. (1999) Reported pica behavior in a sample of incident dialysis patients. *Journal of Renal Nutrition*, 9: 14–20

Wiley, A.S. and Katz, S.H. (1998) Geophagy in pregnancy: A test of a hypothesis. *Current Anthropology*, 39: 532–545

Woywodt, A. and Kiss, A. (2002) Geophagia: The history of earth-eating. *Journal of the Royal Society of Medicine*, 95: 143–146

Wyllie, L. (1909) Alleged slavery in St. Thomé. *London Times (Weekly Edition)*, 629

Youdim, M.B. and Iancu, T.C. (1977) Pica hypothesis. *British Journal of Haematology*, 36: 298

Young, S. (2003) 'Listen, Without Blood There is No Life': An Ethnography of Anaemia During Pregnancy. *Nutritional Anthropology*, 26: 10–19

Young, S.L. and Ali, S.M. (2005) Conceptual links between traditional treatments of maternal anaemia and iron supplements: A case study from Pemba Island, Zanzibar. *Maternal and Child Nutrition*, 1: 51–58

2. CONSUMING THE INEDIBLE: PICA BEHAVIOUR

Carmen Strungaru

Introduction

'**C**learly, eating is one of the most important things we do – and it can also be one of the most pleasurable' (Carlson, 1994: 396). But often our human conspecifics surprise us by defining as attractive, pleasurable or important the ingestion of materials that we, 'normal humans', consider disgusting, intolerable, noxious and insane to eat. How can such habits be explained?

A topic like 'pica' is unlikely to have a simple explanation because humans, shaped by biological and cultural forces and bridled by constraints rooted in the same domains, are creatures complex enough to deserve an equally complex answer, and because the list of non-food items is made up of a magnitude of diverse substances, which do not seem to form a 'natural' entity. This heterogeneity is also apparent when one looks at the various alternative terms for pica/picatio/picaism: allotriophagia (eating strange things), pseudorexia ('wrong' desire), pellacia (enticement), malacia (decadence), hapsicoria, crissa, citta.

The common European and North American black and white magpie bird *(Pica pica L.)*, well known for collecting, seemingly erratically, all kinds of strange, shiny items, 'lent' its scientific Linnaean name to the strange human habit of compulsive and/or constant eating of unusual, strange, inedible, aversive, disgusting substances. If we take as a reference the Diagnostic and Statistical Manual of Mental Disorders, 4th Edition (DSM IV) of the American Psychiatric Association (1994), 'pica' is defined as behaviour beyond accepted cultural traditions, consisting of constant (i.e. for more than one month) ingestion of inedible substances, which are inappropriate for that developmental stage or age.

Table 2.1 provides a list of substances ingested in pica, derived from a diversity of sources. As can be seen, this list contains a wide variety of natural

Table 2.1 Substances ingested in pica

Animal/human	Vegetal	Mineral/artificial
Insects	Raw potatoes,	Earth, clay (geophagia,
Hair (trichophagia)	potato-skins	geomania)
Faeces (koprophagia)	(geomelophagia)	Charcoal
Genital secretions	Flour (amylophagia)	Ashes (stachtophagia), e.g.
(sexual paraphilia)	Grass, lettuce	of cigarettes
Urine (urolagnia)	(lectophagia)	Dust (koniophagia)
	Wood (xylophagia)	Stones (lithophagia)
	Paper	Burned sulphur of matches
	Rubber	(cautopyreiophagia)
		Colours
		Soap
		Lead containing substances
		(plumbophagia)
		Limestone, chalk, cement
		(and other substances
		containing calcium
		carbonate)
		Snow/ice (pagophagia)
		Textiles, synthetics
		Sharp objects (acuphagia,
		e.g. by prisoners)

substances of mineral, vegetal and animal (including human) origin as well as some artificial, synthetic ones. Several types of pica are described – food-pica, non-food pica, mixed pica, poly-pica, pregnancy pica – in an attempt to classify these and in this way to put order and control upon an apparently disorderly phenomenon. One of the definitions centres on the fact that pica, in contrast to quantitative disturbances of eating (e.g. anorexia, hyperphagia, bulimia), is basically a qualitative disturbance of appetite, a 'pathological' urge or craving.

Fitting the basic principle of pica, but excluded in the medical definition which allows for pica-type ingestions as long as they are culturally accepted, are habits like chewing betel nuts (*Areca catechu*), tobacco *(Nicotiana tabacum),* coca leaves *(Erythroxylum coca),* khat *(Catha edulis),* substances containing eucalyptus or other ether-type products, chewing gum, menthol (peppermint, camphor) lozenges, etc. Ingesting 'products' obtained from autogrooming and social grooming, e.g. pieces of skin, pimples, nasal mucus, (see Portalatín this volume) has so far not been classed as pica.

The Four Tinbergian Questions as a Guideline for Understanding Pica and the Ingestion of Non-food Items

Because of this diversity of pica targets, of 'food' definitions and of behavioural interpretations, I find it useful to dismantle the subject in the classic tradition of ethology by analysing the enigma of 'consuming the inedible' using a similar framework as is laid out in the classic 'Four questions of Tinbergen,' who, building on earlier ideas by Huxley and others, attempted (1963) to explain each meaningful biological, but also biopsychological, biosocial phenomenon on four different levels, here matched for the human species, namely those of:

I.   'causation', i.e. the causal machinery bringing about certain specific, species-typic behaviours, based on evolved cause-effect relationships and involving physiological, biochemical, neurobiological, declaratory, associative and other mechanisms which make us do, in certain rather defined situations, what humans usually do (animals may do very different or very similar things; the latter case is particularly interesting in light of category III below).

II.   'Ontogeny', i.e. the rules involved in bringing about fully developed behaviours, usually based on an interplay between genetic/biological and environmental factors, combining 'nature' and 'nurture'.

III. 'Phylogeny', i.e. when did a specific pattern or behaviour evolve in the line of ancestral precursors and how did it change in the course of time and from one related species to another?

IV.   'Evolution', i.e. the immensely intriguing question, how did it all come about, how were mutation, selection and random genetic drift possibly able to produce the stunning magnitude and variety of life forms, which are so wonderfully adapted to their place on this planet? In modern evolutionary biology, one tries to approach this complex question by asking: how much does a specific trait/behaviour contribute to the spreading of the genome of his/her bearer to his or her descendants, i.e. what is the quantitative impact on 'inclusive fitness'.

(I) and (II) represent 'proximate' causations, which are rooted in the organism and its personal history. (III) and (IV) are usually grouped together as 'ultimate' causations, ones which must be seen and interpreted from a long-term evolutionary perspective, i.e. not in an individual life-history perspective.

In order to answer, within the Tinbergian framework, the question: 'What makes humans consume the inedible?' we must find answers to the following emerging questions:

1.   Why do we ingest different substances and of what kind are they? On what basis do we define what is edible or inedible?

2.   Which factors of our individual development (ontogeny) make us discriminate between edible and inedible?

3. Which factors of our ancient history (phylogeny) make us 'confused' in discriminating between what is edible and what is inedible?
4. What are the evolutionary advantages of 'unnatural' ingestive behaviour?

For a better coverage of the subject, I will mainly use the term 'ingestion' instead of 'eating' and/or 'drinking'. Ingesting a variety of substances is necessary for 'constructing and maintaining the organs, for obtaining energy for muscular activity and for keeping the body warm' (Carlson, 1994: 397). Similarly important are further functions, e.g. maintaining brain activity, fighting disease-producing parasites in our body, keeping our immune system in top form, which, from an evolutionary point of view, are almost as important as personal survival, reproduction, i.e. sexual behaviour, pregnancy, birth as a special kind of 'labour', lactation and other forms of energy and time investment in offspring, 'the currency of life' (as specified by Tinbergen's point IV).

I. What Makes Us, Voluntarily, Ingest Certain Substances and Not Others?

Carlson (1994: 401) wrote: 'It is probably not a coincidence that two of the most successful species on earth, humans and rats, are omnivores. ... The metabolism of omnivores is such that no single food will provide all essential nutrients. Thus, it is advantageous to eat many different kinds of foods.' A problem which omnivorous species have to a much greater extent than other species is that more learning is necessary to distinguish edible, useful and healthy substances from ones which are not edible, harmful or even deadly poisonous. It comes as no surprise, then, that humans, members of doubtlessly the most omnivorous species on the planet, are very much guided in their food ingestion by learning, i.e. culture.

Vast differences in defining what is edible are found. Horse meat is considered as perfectly edible in France and much less so in other parts of Europe; dog meat is eaten by members of some Asian societies. Insects (see Schiefenhövel and Blum, this volume), worms, algae, parasites, are delicacies or common food sources on other meridians. Still, there is possibly some agreement across cultures whether something is basically edible (even though perhaps rejected or disgusting) versus something that is not considered to be food at all, e.g. the substances that are ingested in pica.

The important question arises: how, then, are we humans able to select 'ingestible' items among the huge variety of materials at hand in the environment? I have chosen to introduce external stimuli and internal body states, such as hunger, selective hunger and addictive hunger.

External Natural Stimuli (Releasers)

Smell is important but not essential. We do not ingest flowers despite the fact that they have very attractive odours, but we do often ingest substances that emit neutral and sometimes quite repulsive ones (some cheeses, Durian fruits and many others). Studies on infants suggest that none of the odours are innately repulsive; this repulsion is learned by the imitation of adult reactions and by association of certain odours with bad digestive experiences. This phenomenon is known as conditioned flavour aversion (Engen 1974, 1982).

Another stimulus is taste, which constitutes, together with smell, the flavour of a given substance. This is also very important for the evaluation of food. The problem is that taste and smell alone do not represent a foolproof mechanism protecting us from ingesting nutritionally worthless, harmful, or even lethally poisonous substances. Young children have a tendency for 'tasting' all available objects; this habit is not connected to ingestion (which can accidentally occur) but is part of the exploratory perception of the environment. Carlson states that: '... most mammals come provided with specialized receptors that detect substances that are possibly poisonous. Our tongue contains receptors that detect alkaloids and acids (detectors for bitter and sour) ... Thus we tend to reject bitter and sour tastes.' (1994: 402).

With the exception of some fruits most food items (roots, tubers, etc.) do not have very attractive colours. It is good to keep in mind that in nature intense colour is very often a warning signal, for animals as well as for humans, for example some bright coloured fungi.

Consistency is important but not essential. People do ingest a wide range of substances of various textures, and as for shape there appears to be a certain preference for roundness, e.g. most fruits, some vegetables and some animal products, but it is probably not an essential releaser.

So, it can be concluded that none of the characteristics of food-objects can be considered a foolproof signal for safe ingestion, especially when we refer to natural (unprocessed) food.

Internal Body States Regulating Food Intake

There are two motivational aspects of eating behaviour: a drive-reduction one (we are hungry and want to eat) and a hedonic one (we like eating). 'A reasonable assumption is that liking and wanting are two aspects of a unified process' (Bear et al. 2001 p. 539).

As regards hunger, the glucostatic hypothesis (Mayer 1955) stipulates that a diminished level of blood glucose is the main internal signal driving the organism to become restless and search for food. The lower this level is, the stronger and more indiscriminate is the need and the drive. This mechanism can cause almost any organism to eat any kind of food (an extreme example is the dramatic story of the plane crash in the Andes in 1972 where sheer hunger turned the survivors into cannibals/scavengers). This classic theory of hypothalamic centres regulating hunger and satiety, working on the basis of the glucose level in the blood, has been proven to be a useful schematic way of understanding the mechanisms with which the brain controls nutritive intake, but it is much too simple to explain fully such fundamental, complex, multifaceted behaviour as food ingestion. Recent data show that the lateral and ventromedial hypothalamus participates in the process of food intake by playing both excitatory and inhibitory roles (Campfield and Smith 1990).

However, one must consider other classifications of hunger, such as selective hunger or craving. Sometimes, despite the blood level of glucose being normal, an intense and restless search for particular substances can occur. The urge to consume during pregnancy special foods, e.g. sour substances like lemon, vinegar, pickled cucumbers, etc. or, though it be less socially acceptable, to lick the lime off whitewashed walls or eat clay and other substances which are not part of the ordinary diet and which may, after this episode, be rejected in later life, is a well-known phenomenon in probably all societies, termed 'pregnancy pica', and usually seen as a somewhat normal, albeit slightly odd desire. This craving cannot be explained by the general physiological mechanism of hunger; it is perhaps brought about by very selective mechanisms evaluating specific nutritional needs at specific times. In the case of ingesting substances containing calcium carbonate, there is possibly a need for these compounds. The precise physiological/psychological background of such hunger is not yet fully understood.

Then there is addictive hunger, which can be considered as part of 'selective hunger'. It is present in some persons of both genders and of different ages, who are ingesting certain categories of edible/drinkable substances in excess (chocolate, alcohol) or strange types of substances that do not fit in the traditional or general category of 'food'. In these latter cases one speaks of pica. These substances do not always satisfy nutritive needs in the classic sense of the word and they can develop as an addiction in the consumer.

'Mood and food are connected, one link between the two being the serotonin level in the brain' argue Bear et al. (2001: 539). Depression is often accompanied by increased food intake and weight gain. Chocolate craving does not only bring glucose into the organism, but by its richness in tryptophan, an exogenous serotonin precursor, it reduces depression through facilitating serotonin synthesis. Despite having nutritive qualities, the real reason alcohol is ingested is not hunger (or thirst) but its specific physiological and psychological effects. Tobacco and coca leaves, hallucinogenic mushrooms, menthol and eucalypt, betel nuts, etc. do not have any known nutritive classic qualities. Their usage clearly satisfies biopsychological needs by activating specific receptors in the central nervous system.

II. Some Aspects of the Development of Habits Concerning Food and Non-food during Ontogeny

There are many ways by which organisms are adapting themselves to a species-specific diet. Some animal offspring are able from the very beginning to consume the same type of food as the adults do. Some other altricial birds such as pigeons and doves, and all mammals, start by ingesting special food products provided by the parents through body secretions, and only later in life, when their digestive system is fully developed, will they change to the adult type of diet. The long period of breastfeeding in humans induces a certain psychological resistance to other types of food even if, from an adult perspective, a banana or a piece of meat tastes much better than maternal milk. This refusal of other foods makes weaning difficult, both for child and mother.

The mouth-to-mouth feeding of infants, found in many human societies, has the advantage of softening the food by pre-chewing. It also impregnates it with adult saliva containing some enzymes that facilitate digestion and substances like bacteria, which trigger the immune system of the baby. Perhaps most importantly, this way of feeding signals to the infant that the item is edible. Infants of monkeys and apes do not accept food from their foster human nurses unless they see them chewing or at least pretending to chew it. This learning mechanism, activated mostly by imitation but to a certain degree also by personal trial and error, has the characteristics of imprinting with its fast learning, requiring very few exposures and remaining very stable and not easy to change (Lorenz 1982).

This trait may explain how it comes about that we remain so attached to the food we experienced in our childhood and why we are so resistant most of the time to accept other food items, other ways of preparing the same basic material, or even another order for consuming the same food, than we are used to from early infancy on. The ability to accept unusual foods, exotic tastes, seems to be limited to some adults and to very curious children.

It is an interesting and to my knowledge so far unanswered question, whether it is these highly curious individuals, who are also likely to develop pica, i.e. start to ingest 'strange', culturally non-sanctioned foods. As pica behaviours are often hidden, due to their social unacceptability, it does not seem to be likely that children pick up this habit as an imitation of their parents or other role models. It would seem rather that the onset of pica is very much a personal, individual affair – except in cases where it is seen as a 'normal' phenomenon, as is the case in some African societies where geophagia is widespread (see the chapters by Young and by Hooda and Henry, this volume).

It seems that children and juveniles, as well as adults who develop pica are doing this out of a sudden craving, a kind of physiological or psychomotoric reflex, in situations of stress where such repetitive stereotypic behaviours are known to release the body's own endorphines and, thereby, are part of the endogenous system of regulation and homeostasis (Strungaru 2003).

III. Phylogenetic Aspects of Non-food Ingestion

Carlson (1994: 396) stated: 'Much of what an animal learns to do is
motivated by the constant struggle to obtain food; thus, the need to ingest
undoubtedly shaped the evolutionary development of our own species.' It
is worth keeping in mind that the primate species known to be genetically
most related to us, the four great apes, have very different diets, from one
species to another, and compared to us.

As mentioned above, ingesting is not always equal to eating in the classic
sense. Furthermore, imitative learning phylogenetic insights most likely were
and still are guiding our selective behaviour in finding and using substances,
which are not necessarily 'food', but provide natural remedies and the like. In
the last few years more and more data on self-medicating behaviours in
chimpanzees and other primates, involving plants, clay, charcoal etc. have been
published (Koshimizu *et al.* 1994; Huffman 1997; Struhsaker *et al.*1997; Krief this
volume). These findings show that many of the items normally listed in the non-
food category, are actually fulfilling special curative functions. Interestingly, in
humans as in other primates, once such a remedy is found its usage is usually
transmitted culturally, becoming part of the ethnomedical heritage.

It is more difficult to explain how it can happen that living in a cultural group
which does not use, or even forbids, the ingestion of certain substances,
considering such ingestion to be an abnormal pathological behaviour, some
people still consume them. The most common example is the already
mentioned intake of calcium carbonate, for example in the form of de-coating
the wall beside the bed by infants and young children who are calcium
deficient, despite no one having ever offered them such a 'bite' to eat.

It seems obvious that human pica behaviours must be based on 'building
blocks' which are also present in our contemporary primate relatives and
which existed in our hominid ancestry. From a physiological/biochemical point
of view, craving and pica can be seen as a subconscious and/or conscious set of
perceptions informing the organism about internal changes due to pregnancy,
dietary deficiency, famine, state of health, etc. The ingestion of 'strange'
substances provides:

i.   Supplementation of traditional food with deficit minerals (calcium,
      iron, magnesium, sodium chloride, etc.) by ingesting natural or
      artificial materials containing them (limestone, chalk, cement, clay,
      etc.). Clay eating is probably a form of pica with this adaptive aspect
      (McDonald and Marshall 1964), despite the fact, that there are data
      connecting geophagia with iron deficiency (see the chapters by Young
      and by Hooda and Henry, this volume), while clay therapy is
      presented today as a kind of panacea. Earth is also consumed as a food
      substitute or supplement, or a delicacy (e.g. swallow-nest recipe).
      Among its properties the fact that it binds toxic substances contained

in edible items seems to be an important one (Fessler 2002). Charcoal is used in our modern pharmacopoea as an absorbent of toxic substances, and yet it is given as an example of pica if it is not used in the pharmaceutical way.

ii.   Ethnomedical remedies of vegetal, animal or mineral origin. In this way, substances with very repulsive tastes, as bitter as quinine, absinth wormwood *(Artemisia absinthium)* or *Vernonia amygdalina* (an African medicinal plant used by local people but also by chimpanzees for its antihelminthic properties) (Alawa *et al.* 2003) or as sour as lemons, proved to be very helpful in treating malaria, liver and digestive disturbances, vitamin deficits, endoparasitism, etc.

From the human ethological/psychological perspective, pica can also be seen as an evolved mechanism, which ensures by way of social signalling that family and group respond in an appropriate, supportive manner. For example, in the special case of pregnancy pica it could be argued that the pregnant woman instinctively looks for signs of support, devotion, protection from the people around her, perhaps mainly from her partner. This scenario fits well the general picture of mate selection: the male sends signals indicating his willingness for extended commitment and taking over responsibility for the care of the common offspring. Human culture shaped this biologically based behaviour by enriching it with ritual-food offered specifically to the pregnant wife or young mother and by taboos (Pearn 1983) regulating the ingestion of certain foods during different stages of female reproductive life.

Pica and Social Grooming – Mechanisms for Stress Relief

During social grooming, another archaic part of primate phylogeny, lice and other parasites, scales and other parts of the skin, mucus, etc., all clearly non-food, are commonly eaten, at least in many traditional societies. This is not justified by physiological needs: one grasshopper has more protein than the sum of an entire deloused tribe – and is much easier to obtain. It is most likely that these ingested materials have some hitherto unknown effects on the immune system (see Portalatín, this volume). The active groomers seem to follow in their very intense search and almost automatic movements an innate programme, which is probably also true when they put their finds in the mouth. Natural autogrooming and social grooming are known to have important biopsychological functions by releasing beta-endorphine, building strong emotional bonds, creating a relaxed peaceful atmosphere, etc. (Schiefenhövel 1997).

There is another interesting connection between pica and grooming, especially 'stress grooming'. This may indicate that some forms of pica are motivated by similar neurobiological, psychological mechanisms and might well be some form of extension of excessive autogrooming. The ingestion of nails, hair, finger skin, scales, mucus, etc. is, as mentioned, just the last step of grooming behaviour. Automutilation in captive and domestic animals has also ingestive aspects, e.g. trichophagia. As was said above, these often very stereotyped behaviours have been shown to be part of autoregulation, especially in situations of stress and deprivation.

Yet another aspect is similar in both grooming and pica. For pica purposes, paper, wood, (especially pencil ends, matches, twigs and leaves of trees, etc.), erasers, textiles, etc., are often firstly made into very small pieces, not for ingestive purposes, but, that is my hypothesis, as 'pseudo-grooming activity' and are later eventually eaten. It seems that fingers, hands and mouth have to be in a sort of 'perpetuum mobile' in order to reassure and comfort the stressed brain. Seen from this angle, whatever material is at hand (and mouth) in a stressful situation is likely to enter the list of pica substances. The mouth as part of the stereotyping, receives constant oral stimulation and carries out restless chewing and crushing; it is a phylogenetically ancient motor pattern. A striking example for this is the high success of the chewing gum and cigarette industries. In stressful situations refuge is taken in both these products.

IV. Pica and the Ingestion of the Inedible in Relation to Reproductive Success

Many of the above-mentioned benefits of pica behaviours contribute to the individual's well-being and thus, at least in an indirect way, to the chances of the individual finding a mate and successfully reproducing. From a human ethological evolutionary perspective, I would describe the axis, craving-pica, as the behavioural element in a set of chemically, physiologically and psychologically induced mechanisms. Its most important benefits can be summarised as follows:

- Craving is a form of subconscious or conscious proprioception that informs the organism/the individual about changes in her/his body (e.g. pregnancy, dietary deficiency, famine and others).
- Craving-triggered pica ensures that the body, through initiated changes in nutrition and general behaviour, is receiving substances that are needed for its various subsystems to function well. This is the most unproblematic, medically viable aspect of ingesting inedible items, as it contributes to survival.
- Pica, like other stereotyped behaviours, is part of biopsychological autoregulation (Strungaru 2003) which ensures the maintenance of steady states, contributes to psychological well-being and the like. In this frame, pica has no nutritional, in the widest sense, function but a psychological one.
- By way of social signalling, pica behaviours can inform the family and the surrounding social group about specific or general forms of nutritional or other deprivation, thereby eliciting appropriate social support.

- Individuals, who had in the early days of humanity a tendency towards pica behaviour, were likely to have discovered new useful substances for ethnomedical or other use. This could have given them a high status as healers, group leaders, etc. and thereby raised their reproductive chances.

These factors can, singly or together, contribute to a person's survival, well-being and success in life.

Conclusions

Many possible and nutritionally acceptable or even valuable foods are considered inedible by criteria that are only cultural. Many of the non-food items have metabolic and/or medicinal value. Many of the non-food items are, as in pica, not consumed for ingestive-digestive reasons but just as part of the autoregulatory management of physiology (e.g. in situations of nutritional deprivation) and psychology (e.g. in situations of stress and social deprivation). The latter is likely to occur more frequently in urban than in traditional settings. It would thus be interesting to carry out a comparative study of 'pica' in industrialised versus rural areas and in economically developed versus traditional ways of life.

The evolutionary perspective taken in this contribution presents pica and the ingestion of non-food items as basically adaptive behaviours which can be explained by phylogenetically inherited mechanisms. This view is contrasted by the view held in much of the medical profession where many, if not most, pica cases are seen as requiring therapy. No doubt pica, as other behaviours driven by strong addiction, can become non-adaptive, and a nutritional or social problem or even a psychiatrically relevant disease. So, it seems useful to balance the commonly held view of pica as pathological with a more holistic, evolutionarily inspired approach.

References

Alawa, B., Adamu, A.M., Gefu, J.O., Ajanusi, O.J., Abdu, A., Chiezey, N.P., Alawa, J.N. and Bowman, D.D. (2003) In vitro screening of two Nigerian medicinal plants (*Vernonia amygdalina and Annona senegalensis*) for anthelmintic activity. *Veterinary Parasitology. Apr 2;* 113(1): 73– 81

American Psychiatric Association (1994) *Diagnostic and Statistical Manual of Mental Disorders*, 4th ed. DSM IV, Washington, DC

Bear, M.F., Connors, B.W. and Paradiso, M.A. (2001) *Neuroscience – Exploring the Brain*, Lippincott, Williams and Wilkins, Baltimore

Campfield, L.A. and Smith, F.J. (1990) Systemic factors in the control of food intake: evidence for patterns as signals. In Stricker, E.M. (ed.) *Neurobiology of Food and Fluid Intake. Handbook of Behavioural Neurobiology*, Plenum Press, New York, Vol. 10: 183–206

Carlson, N.R. (1994) *Physiology of Behaviour (5th edition)*, Allyn and Bacon, Boston

Engen, T. (1974) Method and theory in the study of odor preferences. In Turk, A., Johnston, J.W. and Moulton, D.G. (eds) *Human Responses to Environmental Odors*, Academic Press, New York

—— (1982) *The Perception of Odors*. Academic Press, New York

Fessler, D.M.T. (2002) An evolutionary perspective on pregnancy sickness and meat consumption. *Current Anthropology*, 43(1): 19–61

Huffman, M.H. (1997) Current evidence for self-medication in primates: a multidisciplinary perspective. *Yearbook of Physical Anthropology*, 40: 171–200

Koshimizu, K., Ohigashi, H. and Huffman, M. (1994) Use of vernonia amygdalina by wild chimpanzee: possible roles of its bitter and related constituents. *Physiology and Behaviour*, 56: 1209–1216

Lorenz, K. (1982) Vergleichende Verhaltensforschung. *Grundlagen der Ethologie*, DTV Wissenschaft, München

Mayer, J. (1955) Regulation of energy intake and the body weight: the glucostatic theory and the lipostatic hypothesis, *Annals of New York Academy of Science*, 63: 15–43

McDonald, R. and Marshall, S.R. (1964) The value of iron therapy in pica. *Pediatrics,* 34: 558–562

Pearn, J. (1983) Research Studies on Pregnancy Superstitions to Explain Human Congenital Malformations in Two Contemporary Societies. In Schiefenhövel, W. and Sich, D. (eds) (1983) *Die Geburt aus EthnomeDizinischer Sicht*. Beiträge und Nachträge zur IV. Internationalen Fachkonferenz der Arbeitsgemeinschaft Ethnomedizin über Traditionelle Gynäkologie und Geburtshilfe. Vieweg, Braunschweig, Wiesbaden

Schiefenhövel, W. (1997) Universals in Interpersonal Interactions. In Segerstrale, U. and Molnar, P. (eds) *Nonverbal Communication – Where Nature Meets Culture*. Lawrence Erlbaum, Mahwah, New Jersey: 61–79

Struhsaker, T.T., Cooney, D.O. and Siex, K.S. (1997) Charcoal consumption by Zanzibar red colobus monkeys: its function and its ecological and demographic consequences. *International Journal of Primatology* 18: 61–72

Strungaru, C. (2003) Stereotypy vs. Plasticity in Vertebrate Cognition. In Brüne, M., Ribbert, H. and Schiefenhövel, W. (eds) *The Social Brain. Evolution and Pathology*. John Wiley and Sons, Chichester: 7–27

Tinbergen, N. (1963) On aims and methods of ethology. *Zeitschrift für Tierpsychologie,* 20: 410–433

3. THE CONCEPTS OF FOOD AND NON-FOOD
PERSPECTIVES FROM SPAIN

Isabel González Turmo

Introduction

In this paper I shall try to throw light on some questions that arise about the terms which directly or indirectly refer to 'food' and 'non-food' and in general to matter which one cannot or should not eat. The reasons for categorising some materials as not for eating or not 'food' can be economic, nutritional, medicinal, ideological or religious. In fact, in every culture, in every social group and in every different moment in time people can attribute such meaning to different substances. That which is food for some is for others not food. All this can be reduced to one fact, however, that food is that which people eat and non-food is that which people do not or should not eat.

Therefore these are concepts loaded with ethnocentrism and subjectivity (González Turmo 2004). It cannot be forgotten that a person's taste and preferences in food are a most personal matter, as well as being frequently a cultural statement. In Spain, such preferences can be asserted without giving reasons, unlike what happens with regard to preferences and 'taste' in art, cinema or decoration, which must be argued and defended. Each person asserts his/her taste in food with an unquestionable right to do this, and the assertion inevitably contains a categorisation of what is and what is not food.

For this reason, the terms 'not edible' or 'inedible' have served and continue to serve to classify very different food practices and habits. Both actual food intake and ideas about the appropriateness of ingesting certain eatable items can change in time and space. In the same way, completely opposite concepts can coexist in any given time and space in the minds of members of any given social group, whether rich or poor, male or female, young or old, indigenous or immigrant. However, in any case, some classification of what is and what is not food persists, and the interpretation of that distinction is not the same for everyone. It seems evident that what is not food refers to materials which are not recommended for consumption or culturally exotic or even pernicious or prohibited.

A first categorisation of the concepts of 'non-food' could be as follows, although one should always remember that elements of this categorisation are historical and cultural, i.e. the classifications do not always refer to the same items:

- At one extreme is 'non-food' as a commercial category for miscellanea that should not go on to the different 'food' shelves in supermarkets: i.e. toiletries, cosmetics, DIY materials, textile goods, household appliances, toys and so on. These are assumed to have nothing to do with human consumption. Based on this interpretation, publications, websites, conferences, masters and postgraduate courses on 'Non-Food' are already common. This sense of the term, however, has not managed to cross the boundaries into everyday language. People do not talk of 'non-food', but of the edible and the inedible.
- Not recommended substitutes and fake foodstuffs.
- Very close to this interpretation are the 'non-food' substances that are not considered 'food' in any society and scientists do not believe that they provide any known biochemical, nutritional or mineral benefit. There is generally no human consumption of these items in human societies, even in rituals, and the only consumption (if any) is considered abnormal, psychiatric behaviour in any society.
- Then there are the 'non-food' substances that are not considered 'food' in any society, but there are several recorded (perhaps psychiatric) situations of their consumption, and the nutritionists believe that there may be some elements of biochemical, nutritional or mineral benefit, which might explain their consumption, even though these are not recognised by the consumers or doctors or witch doctors. These might range from bodily excreta to clay, etc. (It should be noted here that, for example, clay was used historically as yeast.)
- Not far from this interpretation, but almost the opposite, is the link with local medicines, some of which 'non-foods' may be locally believed to provide some health benefit, but may or may not provide benefit, or may actually cause harm to health.
- Not far from this interpretation are the 'non-foods' consumed in rituals, for presumed ritual benefits, (e.g. for purification, for atonement, for some form of religious belief), whatever their biochemical effects, beneficial or otherwise.
- Then there are the substances considered to be 'non-foods' for religious, ideological and/or political reasons, for example alcohol, cannabis, cocaine, etc.

- Then there are 'non-foods' that in many cultures cause disgust (Rozin *et al.* 1997), perhaps with strong smells, because of their condition (for example rotting, rotten or unclean).
- Among materials, which are not nutritious but are regularly part of foodstuffs and are generally eaten without great concern, are those agents and other additives which add flavour and colour to food.
- Another meaning to consider concerns that which is not very satiating or nutritious or is simply not a basic food.
- Now, we come to items that are perfectly well 'food' in some cultures and yet definitely 'non-foods' in others; this is the level much discussed among social anthropologists (Douglas, 1966).
- Finally, there is the category of 'non-food' as a part of food. This would be defined as a new reality in the context of globalisation, for foods contain substances – both nutrients and non-nutrients – which they used not to contain. These are invisible, sometimes tasteless and above all they are under suspicion.

The Term 'Non-food' When Used for Suspicious Food Materials, in the Context of Globalisation

Both 'food' and 'non-food' can be found in the same food products today. Food has incorporated non-food. The pressure groups lobbying for organic nutrition and ecology campaign to have non-food removed from food. Industrial producers invest in methods that create confidence in the consumer. It could even be that in future that which is today considered non-food will be food and *vice versa*. In fact, non-food has always formed part of food, in the same way that illness is part of health and death is part of life. However, the concepts of purity and the actions of consumers have changed; it is today often not possible to choose between the pure and the impure, as the consumer is not able to differentiate these things and must eat food and non-food at the same time.

For this reason, now more than ever, consumers want to see and touch whatever they eat, and to know its provenance. However, globalisation of the market affects even perishable foods: the bottled water may be French or German, the olive oil Italian or Spanish, the garlics Chinese, the pistachio nuts Iranian, and so on. Consumers are unable to achieve the 'closeness' to the food that they seek. Their only possible recourse is to link themselves symbolically to the food, where the appearance, the wrapping and/or the advertising gives the food-item a natural or 'traditional' image. Here the producer and the advertising agencies together govern the intermediate steps between initial production and eventual sale, and the consumers are led to believe that they can eat their products without concern. Therefore, the producers and advertisers choose messages, slogans and practices, which create a network linking the tastes of infancy with those of adulthood, the familiar with the unfamiliar, the old taste with a new one. Thanks to this, consumers can enjoy what they can believe to be 'their food', even though this food was never in fact their own. Culture is thus the mediating device which allows one to continue eating; it is the tool which allows consumers to recover their capacity as social actors.

Consumers definitely know that what they have to eat might contain something which they do not know about and which they also do not know if they should eat, but they cannot escape the necessity of eating it, nor do they have any means of controlling this. One is dealing here with an almost universal situation, even though the perception of the consumer is not always the same. All these circumstances are new, form no part of previous categorisations, and are not well defined by the terms of ordinary language.

The question is whether the term 'non-food' serves to elucidate this new reality. 'Non-food', as a term, is a product of the global society, of the regular consumption by the masses. It arose to signify domestic, non-alimentary consumption, but almost inevitably it has taken on another meaning: non-food as part of food. These ideas were not really in the term originally, but it has taken on these meanings. Thus one is not here dealing with a meaning which has been incorporated into normal food practices (because culturally there was room for it), but because it forms part of the indissoluble part of food itself.

When one tries to analyse non-food as food from the point of view of different disciplines – in this case, especially from that of social anthropology – the question arises whether this new reality remains sufficiently well expressed by the terms used in ordinary language or whether, in contrast, it would be a good idea to adopt the term coined by industry. The new angle is, above all, that food and non-food form part now of a single 'food', of a single alimentary reality. This situation has been able to exist before, but has now changed into a globalised phenomenon where the consumer has lost control.

About the Terms: 'Food', 'Edible', 'Inedible' and 'Not Edible'

In English, the term 'food' refers to 'any nutritious substance that people or animals eat or drink or that plants absorb in order to maintain life and growth' (*New Oxford English Dictionary* 1998). In Spanish, *comida* (food) is 'what people and animals eat and drink in order to subsist' (*Diccionario de la Lengua Española* 2001). The two definitions are very similar although the British one also includes a reference to plant food.

Yet the Spanish word, *comida,* has a number of other meanings; according to the *Diccionario de la Lengua Española* (2001), *comida* is also the action of eating, as for example in the sentence 'it took me two hours for each *comida*'. Besides this, it can also refer to a gathering for a morning meal or to the lunch people have in the first hours of the afternoon. Finally, it may refer to a meal based on a specific type of food, like the so-called 'meal of fish', a mandatory precept for Catholics, who abstain from meat during a religious fast.

However, there is no direct Spanish translation for the English noun 'non-food'. In Spanish, instead of adding a negative prefix to a noun, speakers use a negative adjective: we talk of *no comestible* (not edible) or *incomestible* (inedible), which are in principle synonymous, although they may convey different shades of meaning. 'Not edible' is what must not be eaten, what might be harmful, whereas 'inedible' may also suggest something with a bad taste. In this case the positive word appears to be richer in meanings than the negative ones. According to the *Diccionario de la Lengua Española* (2001), the adjective *comestible* (edible), which means 'what can be eaten', is only related to biological aspects of food. What is edible may be nutritious, nourishing, wholesome and healthy, but it is not associated with the taste of food or the fact that it may be a source of pleasure.

According to other sources, for example the *Diccionario de Usos del Español*, (Moliner 1998), *comestible* (edible) is anything susceptible to being eaten, and not only that which is recognised as food. *Incomestible* (inedible), however, is synonymous with *incomible* 'uneatable', that is, things which cannot be eaten because they are badly seasoned, cannot be digested or can only be digested with difficulty. Insubstantial food may also fall under this category because it is very quickly and easily digested and is thus considered insufficient.

In this case the negative term for food in Spanish, *incomestible*, rather than being synonymous with the English 'non-food', appears to be the same as 'not-food'. It makes reference to something on a more ambiguous and slippery semantic ground: what may be not tasty, or heavy, or scarce, or such like. In other words, *incomestible* alludes to cultural aspects. These meanings are very different from those that the agrofood industry associates with non-food. In fact, when Hispanic people working in the agrofood sector refer to toiletries, cosmetics, DIY, textile goods, household appliances, toys and so on, they use the English word 'non-food'. It is an Anglicism which seeks to clarify the meaning. So, in Spanish, the use of the English phrase, non-food, has a wider meaning and alludes to all consumption goods that are not food, as in the sentence 'a sample includes 800 food companies and 500 non-food companies'. Likewise, for those publications, websites, conferences, masters and postgraduate courses on 'Non-Food', already common in Spain, the word is used in English, written with capital letters and hyphenated.

On the Uses of the Word 'Food' and Its Opposites

The word, food, and its opposites convey multiple cultural meanings which may even be contradictory. In the case of Spanish, food is related to things that nourish. The *Diccionario Ideológico* (Casares, 1994) boasts nearly one thousand terms connected to food, but none of them can be translated as 'non-food'.

Actually, catering companies use the word 'miscellanea', instead of 'non-food', to refer to packaging and similar materials used, for example for serving food on aircrafts. In Spanish, *misceláneo* means 'mixed, varied, consisting of elements of different kinds'. In other words, something difficult to define, a group of items which should be comprehended in one umbrella-term, nobody knows how.

If, on the contrary, one asks people who are not related to this economic sector what they consider to be non-food, the most frequent answers will refer: (1) to toxic products which people run the risk of ingesting unwillingly; (2) to things that are not nutritious but are part of the food itself and are sometimes ingested; and (3) to things that are not part of the food and yet, are ingested sometimes. In the first case, the list of toxic products is long: heavy metals in fish, pesticides in fruit and vegetables, oils which are not appropriate for human consumption, e.g. canola, which in Spain some decades ago caused the death of many people by intoxication. This meaning of non-food is thus similar to that of water: drinkable versus undrinkable.

Among items which are not nutritious but are part of the foodstuffs and are generally eaten without great concern, are agents and other additives which lend flavour and colour to food. The way people regard these additives is rather different from what they have traditionally thought of spices and, in general, of condiments. The latter, although they are not considered basic forms of alimentation, have always been believed to have nutritious, stimulating and even curative properties. Today, people's conception of flavourings and colourings is closer perhaps to what they think of salami skin, as the casing is not the food itself and it is not advisable to eat it, yet can be eaten. In the case of flavourings, which are an ingredient of the food itself, there is no possible choice though.

The third case includes mucus (see Portalatín this volume), as well as nails, hairs, the blood from one's own wounds, scabs, etc. However, this list should also include mud, which was consumed at the Spanish Court in the seventeenth century, and lime, a traditional means for preserving food in the Mediterranean area. García Marquez made it popular in his novel *Cien Años de Soledad* (1967) where he portrayed a little girl resiliently scratching the walls in order to eat lime. Other items on the list include those items which people take for an altered state of mind, such as cannabis, used in cakes and omelettes or accompanying other culinary preparations; coca leaves and, of course, tobacco and alcohol. The case of tobacco is significant: it is not included in Western food classification systems, but Lévi-Strauss (1972) placed it within one of his food axes. As for alcohol, it is also a clear example of the extent to which culture and ideology influence what people consider to be food or non-food: alcohol is the only consumable item which is regarded as non-food on the FAO's 1,269–strong list of food consumer products, though it has been an essential element in nutrition throughout the history of mankind. Researchers like Shimon Dae (1991), by studying the Talmud, calculated the lowest amount of wine stored by a Palestinian family over a year: between 330 and 375 litres, which were mixed with water in a half to half or one quarter to three quarters ratio. Considering that each litre of wine contains between 600 and 1000 calories, it can be concluded that wine was a basic element of the ancient diet in Palestine. It is similarly known that in Spain during the Middle Ages, the food ration of poor people in hospitals exclusively consisted of bread, wine and meat. The poor could get some 84 centilitres of wine daily; less than a friar, who had four litres a day (Martinez García 1984; Molénat 1984). They were evidently watered wines, yet such watered-down wine or 'wined water', as it was also called, has been a significant nutrient over the centuries.

Comparisons of the Use of the Word '*Comida*' (Food) and Its Opposites

Another matter to consider is what each culture regards as food and non-food. When I started fieldwork in the agricultural areas of Andalusia in Southern Spain nearly twenty years ago, there was one thing that especially caught my attention (González Turmo 1995). I had to keep a weekly record of food and for this reason I asked my informants:

'What did you eat yesterday?'
They answered: 'Food (*comida*)'

At first I was baffled by this answer. I was a green, young anthropologist who lived in the city, where each daily meal and culinary preparation has its own name, and in no way was a meal just called 'food', or even just a 'meal'. Thus, I didn't know if these people were referring to some specific food or simply gave that reply because they were tired of me. Mind you, I had not gone as far as Africa or Oceania to do fieldwork; I was only 30 kilometres away from my home, in the same province, and yet I did not understand what they were saying to me. Since I did not intend to go back without completing the questionnaire which Igor de Garine had recommended my using, I kept asking, each time with greater humbleness:

'Well, but what food?'
'What food should it be?' they answered, 'Why, food!'

Then I had to acknowledge my ignorance, which I should have done from the start; I asked: 'But, what do you call food?'
'What should that be?' they replied, 'A *cuchareo*' (this is a Spanish word with the same root as *cuchara* 'spoon'). Once again I was at a loss. I had never heard that term before. I had to inquire further, and they surely thought that I must have been pretty dumb.

'And what is *cuchareo*?' I asked.
'Why, lentils, stews, potato stews ...'

I hadn't realised before! *Cuchareo* was what people ate with *cucharas* (spoons), especially stews; actually, soups did not fall under that category because they were considered 'weak'.

Some time later, as I noted down people's food intake and discovered that the diet of Andalusian day-labourers was a monotonous one, I understood that what they called food was the single dish they ate at lunchtime. It was the main satiating and nutritional meal of the day and sometimes the only hot one, too. Now it was clear to me what 'food' meant!

Unfortunately, I had not read any Spanish classics before that, like the work of the renowned sixteenth-century orator Fray Luis de Granada, who was beatified in 1997. He did not speak of a type of food (that was not important for him), but of the daily food which allows one, whether a saint, clergyman or ordinary person, to subsist (*Diccionario de Autoridades* 1990). This was exactly the situation of my informants: they had to make do with what they had, i.e. stews based on pulses, bread or potatoes, which they simply termed 'food'. When I eventually understood this, I did not find it odd of them to talk about 'red food' when referring to *cocido* (a stew made of chickpeas, *chorizo*, black pudding and paprika) or 'white food' when referring to *puchero* (the same chickpea stew but with chicken meat and pork fat, and without any colouring). Likewise, I was not surprised to hear that in the evening they did not 'make food', by which they meant that they ate fried fish or omelette. By then, I was already aware that fish and eggs were not regarded as proper 'food'.

Yet, I could not understand why, when I asked about their favourite food, they kept giving me the same answer time and again: 'food'. Were they not tired of always eating the same thing? How could they prefer the same stews they ate on a daily basis? Wouldn't it have been more logical to choose roast chicken, lamb shoulder or sea bream? Well, evidently not. Later on, I realised to what extent each social class asserts its differences through food taste. In the case of my informants, there was nothing they liked more than what they ate every day, even though they were compelled to do so due to poverty.

Food preferences held in common can unite those who share them and serve to distance those who do not. In other words, to use Pierre Bourdieu's words (1979), an opposition is established between the tastes of luxury and the tastes of necessity. In this way, the lower classes, unlike the middle classes, reject those tastes to which they have no access, in a symbolic acceptance of a disadvantaged social position which is difficult to surmount. My informants, and above all the elderly, preferred 'food', that is to say stews, because it was what they had, what they had been eating since they were children, and what marked their identity. At the same time, they rejected those foodstuffs which they could not access, stating that they were 'not food', like caviar, for example, which they thought was disgusting, even though they had never tried it.[1]

The list of meanings related to the word *comida* is not yet complete. This term, in fact, also makes reference to the most important meal of the day. Seventy years ago, when people's lives revolved around solar time, the main meal used to be in the evening and *comida* was the dinner. Nowadays, on the contrary, *comida* is lunch, the meal people usually have in the early afternoon hours. Furthermore, *comida* also refers to various gatherings and celebrations: gala meals, goodbye meals, men's meals, business meals, brotherhood meals, etc. Lastly, *comida* may be one thing for some people or a large list of delicacies for others. It can be either something common or something extraordinary: what people eat sitting down, or what they snack standing in the street. Each social group and culture may interpret food in a different way, but all are sure they know what it is: it is their food.

Conclusion

There is no point in making predictions as to whether the word, non-food, with its objectivising aim, will move from the marketing area into daily life, in order to include new meanings created by a recent reality: spreading information on food production and an increasing distrust in what we ingest. This reality exists and sometimes it is not adequately expressed by the terms that have been in use up to now: *comestible* ('edible'), *no comestible* ('not edible'), *incomestible* ('inedible'). This new reality may require a new term, impressive and malleable, charged with objectivity, and this may be 'non-food'.

Note

1. In Morocco I heard similar remarks to the ones mentioned earlier. When it comes to fish, most of the population can only purchase mackerel (*Decapterus ronchus*) and sardines (*Sardina pilchardus*), which they also use to make fishballs. Sea bream (*Pagellus cantabricus*), sole (*Solea vulgaris*) and prawns (*Parapenaeus longirostris*) are eaten only by a minority of people. A woman of few means told me: 'We hardly ever buy prawns ... besides, they are not nourishing; once you have removed the whiskers there is nothing left'. That prawns are rich in minerals is of little importance; to those who cannot buy them, they are not nutritious.

References

Bourdieu, P. (1979) *La Distinction*. Minuit, Paris

Casares, J. (1994) *Diccionario Ideológico de la Lengua Española*. Gustavo Gili, Barcelona

Dae, S. (1991) Food and Archaeology in Romano-Bizantine Palestine. In Wilkins, J., Harvey, F.D. and Dobson, M., *Food in Antiquity (1996)* University of Exeter Press, Exeter

Douglas, M. (1966) *Purity and Danger.* London: Routledge and Kegan Paul

García Márquez, G. (1967) *Cien Años de Soledad*. Buenos Aires Editorial, Espasa Calpe

González Turmo. I. (1995) *Comida de Rico, Comida de Pobre*. Universidad de Sevilla
—— (2004) Apuntes Para Seguir Trabajando Sobre la Arbitrariedad Alimentaria. In Millán, A., Cantarero, L, Medina, F.X., Montejano, M. and Portalatín, M.J. (eds) *Arbitrario Cultural: Racionalidad e Irracionalidad del Comportamiento Comensal*. La Val de Onsera, Huesca, 489–497

Lévi-Strauss, C. (1972) *Mitológicas*. Fondo de Cultura Económica, Buenos Aires

Moliner, M. (1998) *Diccionario de Uso del Español.* Gredos, Madrid
Real Academia Española (1990) *Diccionario de Autoridades.* Gredos, Madrid
—— (2001) *Diccionario de la Lengua Española.* Espasa-Calpe, Madrid
Rozin, P., Haidt, J., McCauley, C. and Imada, S. (1997) Disgust: The Cultural
    Evolution of a Food-Based Emotion. In Macbeth, H. (ed.), *Food Preferences and
    Taste,* Berghahn Books, Oxford, 65–82

4. FOOD DEFINITIONS AND BOUNDARIES
EATING CONSTRAINTS AND HUMAN IDENTITIES

Ellen Messer

Introduction

The definitions and boundaries of 'real food' are basic subjects of anthropological inquiry, because in all societies, human beings connect eating constraints and human identities. By accepting certain items as 'food' and rejecting others, and also by culturally processing raw items and combining them in structured and patterned ways, human beings define what it means to be a particular kind of human being, one who belongs to a particular community or identifies with a particular social class or way of life.

This chapter builds on previous ICAF explorations of food habits by examining the biological and cultural limits to what human beings will put into their mouths, swallow, and digest, and the ways less or more restrictive nutritional behaviours establish cultural identities. 'Edible food' is defined as all items recognised for their nutritive or additional dietary values, which are ingested via the mouth, swallowed and then digested. 'Inedible, non-foods' are organic or inorganic items that nutritionists or members of particular cultures do not recognise as food because of sensory unattractiveness, anticipated negative physiological effect, predominantly non-nutritive properties, or culturally determined dislike or disgust. Discussions amplify prior studies (Macbeth 1997) that considered the biocultural bases of disgust (Rozin *et al.* 1997), food choice under conditions of scarcity (Huss-Ashmore and Johnston 1997), and changing tastes and acceptance of new foods, such as the potato (Messer 1997) by first reviewing in greater detail the structuring rules by which human beings construct and transform the categories 'edible' versus 'inedible' and then systematically applying these rules to particular animal (e.g. worms), vegetable (e.g. GMO maize), and microbial (e.g. Quorn, from Marlow Foods

Ltd.) 'edible non-food' categories. The concluding section will demonstrate the relevance of this exercise for understanding the acceptance or rejection of new foods, such as GMO maize, in contemporary contexts.

Determinants of Food Intake and Principles of Food Classification

What Are the Classification Rules by Which People Determine Which Items Are Edible and Good to Eat?

Human beings select and rank foods on the basis of sensory, hedonic, and nutritional (anticipated physiological effect) properties. Transformation of 'the inedible' into foods begins with a cultural appreciation of the biological and physical characteristics of particular species and representative specimens, and then their rule-based processing and combination into dietary components and structures. The biocultural criteria for recognising and ranking individual foods and the construction of diet include the biological and physical characteristics of potential food items and also certain symbolic features that make them acceptable or disgusting (Messer 1989; Rozin *et al.* 1997), and more or less preferred, in particular cultural settings. Although any item in the environment might be potential 'food', only some present the sensory criteria that attract gustatory or culinary attention so that they are taken into the mouth, swallowed from mouth to gut, and digested to provide energy and nutrient value, or sense of fullness (to avert hunger pangs). In times of hardship as people start to process and ingest additional 'inedible non-foods' as part of their diets, their criteria for foods shift first from sensory criteria to ones of nourishment and then to criteria of which foods provide a sense of being full (Huss-Ashmore and Johnston 1997).

How Are Classifications of 'Edible' or 'Good to Eat' Achieved or Transformed by 'Cooking', Via Heat or Other Food Processing?

Non-human primates of course consume only raw foods, whereas humans process all but a few whole fruits and vegetables. Potential foods undergo culturally-based food processing, including pounding, grinding, shredding, winnowing, sieving, soaking, drying, fermenting and most importantly, application of heat, all of which affect sensory and biochemical properties that influence presentation, ingestion and digestion. Such physical-chemical-biological processing transforms the edible portion, by removing toughness, so food is easier to chew, and by reducing fibre thereby facilitating digestion. (Toughness and tenderness may or may not be directly connected to fibre content.) In particular, cooking softens tough carbohydrates and makes various classes of starches and proteins more biologically available and utilizable. Processing transforms nutritional value, usually for the better;[1] it also removes toxins, which is important, given that humans have small hind guts, a large small intestine, a fast gut-purge rate, and a reduced ability to detoxify, relative to non-human primates.

Beyond the physical-chemical-biological, cooking also establishes the sociocultural dimensions of human diet: the cultural segregation or combination of 'food' ingredients into dietary components, such as bread or other staple foods, and '*comida*' (in English, 'dishes' or 'meals') renders them 'edible', preferred, and culturally appropriate to eat as part of particular dietary contexts. Cooked food looks 'good to eat', not only because objectionable characteristics like toughness have been removed, but also because it has been transformed into identifiable 'food' items, which define basic diet, in terms such as: (1) 'primary core' cooked grains, starches, gruels, or breads; (2) 'secondary core' dishes, such as soups or stews ('*comida*') (see González Turmo, this volume); or (3) peripheral relishes or condiments that increase the attractiveness of consumption.

During times of duress, less preferred or non-food items may be prepared and disguised as 'food', as in cardboard shredded and boiled into 'pastas' or breads made from flours mixed from grit, tree bark, or other usually 'inedible' substances (see Matalas and Grivetti, this volume). These 'starvation foods' mimic the physical and visual characteristics of ordinary foods and thereby render the emergency product more acceptable, ingestible and (perhaps) digestible. Cues may be not only visual and ideational but also sensory-oral; the mimicking of ordinary foods by processing renders non-food items culturally appropriate and sufficiently palatable that they can be chewed and swallowed and will not stick in the mouth or throat.

As a general principle, in all societies, at all stations of life, non-foods or less preferred items, or items not usually consumed in their raw state, are transformed into 'food' by processing methods that produce a product visually and texturally similar to ordinary food items.

Finally, cooking and the concept of sharing cooked food around a hearth establish the fundamental cognitive categories linking diet and society (see also Lévi-Strauss 1969). Cooking and eating together operationalise the structure, content and combinatorial ideas of 'meals' and their components, which define and set boundaries for what are acceptable and appropriate food items; and when, where and with whom they should be eaten. In sum, food sharing structures cultural identities and social time and space. Consumed commensally, starvation foods also conserve (construct, replicate, mimic) the meal context.

How Are Classifications of 'Edible' Expanded or Restricted by Cultural Context?

Food restrictions are closely linked to social and cultural identities. But categories of 'edible' may be restricted or expanded according to cultural context, including hardship, non-local food-consumption or wilderness settings, where one's group-rules of ordinary civilised food behaviours may be partially or temporarily suspended. Ritual classifications often restrict 'edible' food categories, as in Jewish kosher dietary laws that permit the consumption of ritually 'clean' but forbid ritually 'unclean' animals, and also forbid the consumption of living animals, including their 'life blood'. Alternatively, ritual contexts may allow the consumption of special ritual foods (totemic plants or animals) or 'non-foods', including hallucinogenic mushrooms or plants, which are in ordinary contexts forbidden.

Consumption may also be restricted by cultural location. In the domain of vegetable foods, for example, different Mexican villages follow different culinary customs. Although there may be upwards of a dozen potentially 'edible' wild herb species growing in and around maize fields, each village classifies as edible, cooks and eats, only five or six of these as potherbs. The others are classified as 'fodder' (food for animals) or for other types of people, including those living in nearby or distant towns where villagers do business, and see people eat these other herbs without ill effect. When eating away from home, people may follow the local culinary custom without complaint, but will never collect, prepare or eat species classified as 'not eaten' (a variation on the concept of 'inedible') in the home-hearth context. The reasoning is cultural and contextual, 'they' eat them; 'we' don't. A variation on this non-local identity rule is based on distinctions of social class. Wild-herb consumption of any type may be associated with poverty and hardship. People who have money and are better off eat garden or market vegetables; they don't consume wild herbs. In the interest of projecting higher-class status, economically deprived people may forego the good micronutrient nutrition available in wild greens altogether; a cross-cultural finding that alarms nutritionists (Messer 1984).

Similarly, the preferred stage for consuming such pot herbs is when they are young and tender. But during times of duress, such as the famine years of the Mexican Revolution, elderly people remembered they ate field herbs that were mature, waist-high and dry. They also roasted and ate plant pods and fruits that were ordinarily classified as 'too sweet' or otherwise unpalatable and avoided. Both this knowledge of what was eaten during prior hungry seasons, and the consumption of less preferred greens by non-local (or economically disadvantaged) persons expand the known set of potentially 'edible' items, but do not amend classifications of what is 'not eaten' in ordinary home-village contexts.

As a third example, ordinary rural Mexican adults insist that wild (wilderness context) tubers, succulent stems and leaves, and small spiny fruits of *Opuntia* cactus are 'not edible'. More accurately, they are 'not eaten' by people who have available to them in normal times other, easier-to-eat and more palatable items. Socially and economically marginal members of society, such as shepherd boys out watching their animals in the hills or fields, visibly eat these marginal species without ill effects. Those who reject these potential foods communicate that socially marginalised individuals such as shepherd boys are not quite human, not in an essential sense, but in the context that they are relatively uncivilised, one indicator of which is that 'shepherd boys will eat anything'. However, ordinary adults will occasionally consume these 'not-eaten' items when hiking in the hills, a 'wilderness' context that temporarily sets them apart from the food rules of ordinary civilised contexts.

In sum, 'the inedible' or 'non-foods' are various and variable, defined according to species (or element) and social-cultural context. Principal among these contexts is social-cultural culinary identity (what is food for 'us' versus 'them'), which may be overridden in contexts of hardship, wilderness, or ritual.

Do Food Transformation Rules Change, Depending on Whether the Comestibles in Question Are Animal, Vegetable, or Microbial?

Worms as Edible or Inedible

Worms, taken here to be a generic animal category (earthworms and larvae), inclusive of all manner of squiggling, creeping, swarming, ground-living creatures, illustrate many of these attributes of non-food and/or forbidden animal categories (see Douglas 1966). Worms live in and on the earth, but don't have legs or wings, have a distinctive mode of locomotion, yet are not reptiles. Although most species of larvae and worms are edible, ostensibly nutritious and eaten by peoples across Africa and Asia, if not the Middle East (see Schiefenhövel and Blum, this volume), Biblical sources, along with many who profess modern sensibilities find worms disgusting. This is not only because of their manner of locomotion, origins in the dirt, and anticipated distasteful sensory and health-harmful qualities but also because of their 'wormness', a cognitive construction of their essence, which may also be associated with death (Rozin et al. 1997).

Two American folk songs capture this 'wormness' essence and its associations with social marginality and death. The first depicts worm eating as a suicidal act:

They always always pick on me
They never never let me be
I'm so awful lonely, very sad
It's a long time since I've been glad, but

I know what I'll do by and by
I'll eat some worms, and then I'll die
And when I'm gone, just wait you see
They'll all be sorry that they picked on me.

Via a 'Google' search, I found that the original setting for this song was a popular 1930s film featuring Minnie the Moocher, a cartoon character who represented all unhappy Eastern European immigrant kids of that period. In this particular context, she protests her unhappy life with Papa and her new stepmother, by refusing to eat at the dinner table. The image and idea of 'eating worms', i.e., the consumption of despised, wild 'non-food,' by one who is unhappy and underfed nutritionally and emotionally, contrasts with a happy, well-fed, nutritional and emotional life, and is directly and symbolically associated with death.[2]

The second, with its punch line, 'Think I'll go eat worms', similarly depicts worm eating as a suicidal act by a child who feels socially marginalised:

Nobody loves me
Everybody hates me
Think I'll go eat worms.

It goes on to describe them in disgusting detail, 'Big fat juicy,' 'little skinny hairy,' and other epithets, which are sickening and loathsome. It was often accompanied by another camp song that vividly pictured live worms crawling in and out of (and eating) dead corpses:

The worms crawl in
The worms crawl out
They eat your guts
And they spit them out.

It vividly depicts worms as disgusting not only because they are hairy and crawl about but also because they feed on cadavers and death. In each case eating worms can be construed as a dangerous, rebellious, revolting and suicidal act, which places the rebel either temporarily or forever outside civilised society and its moral definitions and boundaries, symbolised by consumption of civilised, appropriate foods.

Yet worms, the very image of uncivilised fare, also appeal, especially to children. They know that worms are 'inedible', yet will eat worms on a dare or under duress (like when stronger children force worms into the mouths and down the throats of the weaker ones), or, as in the songs, as a symbolic act of desperation. Worms in these 'wild' contexts are a marked category, suggesting titillating and forbidden as well as despised food, which raises emotions straddling the line between fear and exhilaration. Playing on these symbolic and emotional associations, candy makers since the 1980s have marketed stringy, green, gummy 'worms', part of the line 'I like worms', a sweet snack of sugary gum drop and jelly consistency (Brenner 1999).

Such Western symbolism and cultural culinary sensibilities notwithstanding, peoples over much of the world enthusiastically consume worms; they also appreciate the flavours and nourishing qualities of various insect species as common foods and also as delicacies. From a cross-cultural survey of food habits (see Schiefenhövel and Blum, this volume), including the reports presented here, most of these invertebrate items are not harmful to health, generally recognised as safe, and for some peoples, especially appetising. None of these findings, however, convince Westerners that they should eat insects, outside of certain 'wild' ritual ('The Explorers' Society' dinners) or tourism contexts.[3] In sum, Westerners have very different sensory and culturally constructed categories of what are acceptable 'foods', and neither worms nor insects are among them.

Genetically Modified Maize as Famine or Ordinary Food

Genetically modified (GM) foods have been available in the marketplace since the mid 1990s, when genetically modified corn, soya, and canola burst onto the field-crop scene, and soon dominated up to half or more of the US markets for those commodities. Their defining characteristic is their method of development: GM foods involve 'genetic engineering', the interspecies transfer of genes from one to another species by means of an intentional agent of transformation, and have become the flash point for protest against globalisation, the General Agreement on Tariffs and Trade (GATT) and the World Trade Organisation, as well as anti-corporate social activism. This activism involves also anti-hunger, natural food and food safety, environmental and public-health activists, who wrap up their objections into conceptual positions that GM commodities are 'non-foods' and should not be marketed or consumed as food.

Although US government-approved as safe for the environment and for human health, these crops nevertheless failed to meet with approval by many consumers in the US, Europe, Asia and developing countries, who were convinced that they were harmful to the environment, to human health, to the farm economy, and/or to long-term sustainability (biodiversity, local control over the food supply, etc.). Europeans refused to permit genetically-modified maize into their food chain; because African nations market livestock to the EU, their leaders were concerned that they might lose agricultural markets if they, the African nations, permitted production and trade in GM crops. African leaders also expressed concerns about environmental and health risks for their populations. This set the stage for a showdown between the US and its food-aid supply chain, and intended African recipients of US food aid during the Southern African food crisis of 2002–03.[4]

By mid 2002, geographic early warning systems indicated that Southern African nations would need food aid to avert starvation. In simple terms, the governments of Zimbabwe, then Zambia, and intermittently Malawi, the Sudan and Angola, all refused to accept GM maize food-aid as 'food'. Zimbabwe initially would not let the grain into the country. Zambia initially let the grain in, but would not distribute it and then made the World Food Programme (WFP) remove it. The WFP moved the GM maize to Malawi, where officially it was first supposed to be milled, but some was, some wasn't, because Malawi lacked sufficient milling capacity. Later, Zimbabwe and Angola agreed to let in GM maize if it was milled, and very quietly the Sudan did, too. But the Government of Zambia held firm, with the result that the country experienced troubling food-aid shortfalls in November 2002, and some food riots when the government prevented hungry people from accessing the available GM maize that still hadn't been shipped out in January-February 2003. Thereafter, shipments of non-GM millet and bulgur wheat alleviated this crisis.

During this Southern African food crisis, US government officials, like most US scientists, farmers and food-industry leaders, continually asserted that GM maize is 'food' like other maize, and there is no reason to make distinctions or not to eat it (see, e.g., Fedoroff and Brown 2004). Their reasoning drew on:

1. sensory properties, because in their judgment GM maize looked, tasted and performed in cuisine just like conventional maize;
2. nutritional and health qualities, because in their experience GM maize had been tested and observed to be safe for human health, as well as the health of animals and the environment;
3. cognitive construction, because US scientists, farmers and consumers largely shared the concept that GM crops and foods, which had passed government regulations and been approved for environmental release and human consumption, were safe and generally similar to other maize.

As Andrew Natsios, Administrator of USAID, and Colin Powell, US Secretary of State argued, by 2002 Americans had been eating GM maize for seven years with no (apparent) ill effect. They used this 'we eat it, so it must be safe' assertion to argue for African acceptance. Taken together, US promoters of GM maize did not share the anti-GM activists' concept that it was dangerous and disgusting; a 'frankenfood' to be reviled because its pedigree involved genetic engineering. They were willing to meet Zambian and other African governments halfway, however, and try to introduce GM maize as milled flour, rather than whole grains, because they recognised that African agricultural authorities also feared that African farmers, once they acquired the GM seeds for food, might try to plant some, and they knew that Europeans, as well as other GM activists, had instilled a fear of GM crops as environmental contaminants.

Moreover, from the US perspective, GM maize is not only an excellent food, but an example of what GM promoters have been insisting all along is the high value of GM crops as solutions to world hunger (Stone 2002). At the height of the controversy, American officials took African scientists on an American GM tour so that they could see for themselves that all GM-production procedures and outcomes were regulated and safe. All GM products, maize included, must go through stringent testing by the US Department of Agriculture (USDA) before permits allow farmers to plant the seeds in fields, as well as the Food and Drug Administration's regulations to market the products as human food. The promoters also promoted the non-food uses of GM maize as a raw material for biofuels and plastics.

However, the African scientists, to the Americans' surprise, returned unconvinced about GM food safety. Significantly, some GM varieties, such as Starlink corn, had been classified as safe for animals but not for humans, because regulators were not yet certain that they might not raise an allergic reaction. In the year 2000 Starlink corn had accidentally entered the human food chain and anti-GM activists raised an outcry. The uproar over holes in the precautionary procedures was not lost on African scientists and political leaders, who maintained their own precautionary stance. The scientists also questioned whether Americans ate maize, or simply used small quantities of maize products as food ingredients and for non-food industrial products.

African political leaders for their part articulated anger and outrage not only that whole grain maize might contaminate their fields, but also that Americans or transnational corporations might be using starving African populations as guinea pigs to test the health and safety of their GM products. They deplored that under these conditions of duress, American food-aid interests might be forcing Africans to consume food fit and approved only for animals. This added a new dimension to the Zambian food-aid complaints from prior years that Americans had sent low-quality yellow maize fit only for animals. Some experts cautioned that Africans who consume most of their calories from maize should continue to reject GM maize on technical nutritional grounds. Americans, who consume the occasional taco and maize products as components of more complex foods, have not been consuming GM maize as their major source of calories and nutrients. Scientists did not know whether GM maize consumed in large quantities might be harmful to humans.

All the reasons given for this rejection were based on negative health and environmental judgments but they also referred to culture and political identity. From a cultural conceptual standpoint there is no reason why Africans should classify GM foods as good or safe for humans to eat just because Americans eat them. Although US leaders, such as USAID Administrator Andrew Natsios, deplored both the rejection and the timing, and warned that higher mortality would result from not using GM maize, fortunately this appears not to have been the case.[5] Zambian government officials meanwhile reframed the GM maize question entirely, insisting that Zambia needed not food aid, but agricultural investments so Zambian farmers could meet the country's food needs according to agricultural plans and not require foreign food assistance.

Microbial Non-food Transformed into Food: Quorn Mycoprotein

Quorn, manufactured and distributed by Marlow Foods Ltd. provides an instructive counterpoint to the above animal and plant examples. Not exactly a microbial food because biologically it is a mycoprotein (fungal) product rather than a single-cell protein, Quorn's beginnings and the motivations for its development originated in the search for new sources of protein during the 1960s. This was an era of development, dominated by Malthusians, who worried about populations outstripping food supplies and sought solutions for world hunger and malnutrition as lying in the provision of more food, especially protein that could close the alleged 'protein gap', a priority nutrition problem. To meet this demand for more protein, food scientists and nutritionists began searching for promising new sources of protein, most previously considered 'non-foods', including fishmeal and leaf-protein extracts. But mainly they looked for suitable single-celled organisms such as yeasts, bacteria and fungi, which they hoped could be manipulated and multiplied rapidly in industrial processors, on cheap petroleum or organic waste-based hydrocarbon feed stocks, and then feed the world (Garattini *et al.* 1979).

The large UK industrial giant, ICI (Imperial Chemical Industries) hit pay dirt, so to speak, in 1967, when it encountered a soil fungus, *Fusarium venentum,* in Marlow, Buckinghamshire, England (whence the company's name, Marlow Foods). According to the company's product chronology,[6] food scientists identified its promise then worked on flavour and texture characteristics. In 1975, ICI formed a joint venture, a pilot facility, and then scaled up production. Ten years later, in 1985, the product, named Quorn, won UK MAFF (Ministry of Agriculture, Food and Fisheries) approval to be marketed as human food. In that same year, Marlow Foods incorporated, and launched its first product, a vegetable pie.

By then, barely twenty years after the original search for a single-cell protein to solve problems of world hunger, the Green Revolution in grains was well underway. Since the 1970s, nutritionists had been debating whether food energy, protein or micronutrients should be the priority world-hunger problem; by the 1980s, other economic experts and food activists, following Amartya Sen and Frances Moore Lappe, asserted that hunger was a problem of food and nutritional entitlements, i.e. a failure of livelihoods, markets, human rights and social justice, not a problem of food or of particular nutrients. In this transformed context of development, the 'world hunger' rationale for producing mycoprotein disappeared entirely. In its place, Marlow Foods framed and marketed their product to a new target consumer group: First World vegetarians and all those who wanted to limit their intakes of animal foods, whether for ideological, political, environmental, nutritional or health reasons.

These more affluent consumers were located first in the UK, then in the rest of Europe, and later in the US, but not in developing countries. Over the next twenty years (1985–2005), Marlow Foods expanded rapidly into these international markets with increasing numbers of product lines, which now included vegetable pies, quorn pieces, burgers, sausages, fillets, delicatessen 'cold cuts' and an array of ethnic (Indian, Italian and Mexican) dishes.

Curiously, up until 2002, there appeared very little publicity surrounding the health and safety of this novel product. This changed when the product reached the US, with its activist food NGO, the Center for Science in the Public Interest (CSPI), headed by Michael Jacobson. Jacobson (2002), in a letter to the EC Commission for Health and Consumer Protection in Brussels, argued that Quorn was not safe, and furthermore, that it was mislabelled and misrepresented as mushroom-like, when in fact it is a mould, which individuals sensitive to mould eat only at great personal risk. He reported over 500 complaints of food-allergy responses to Quorn, yet the product remained on the market. In 2003 the BBC (British Broadcasting Corporation) followed with its own story about Quorn food allergies and, in 2005, Quorn's food safety was challenged in a lawsuit. Notwithstanding, Quorn sales continued to expand and the company was resold many times. The desirability of eating a 'healthy' low-fat meat-substitute apparently overrode concerns over Quorn's possibly unhealthy fungal and transnational-corporate origins.

The Role of Food Security and Dietary Structure in Processes of Classifying and Ranking Food

The examples above suggest that what is nourishing from a nutritional or nutritionists' perspective may not coincide with social, cultural, psychological and political judgments. The role of diet and nutrition in relation to food security may also enter into this calculation.

GM maize for Africans could be a primary core food; hence the concern over safety, particularly in situations where there appear to be limited alternatives. Quorn, by contrast, is a meat-substitute and secondary core item. There are potentially many alternatives; it meets the desire for variety. Worms are a peripheral food or a relish food, but they may supply critical seasonal protein and nutrients in traditional diets. When analysing the significance of novel or marginal foods, such dietary roles and nutritional contributions are significant. Are the new items snacks or meal foods, dietary staples or herbs and condiments, sources of energy or fillingness, or nutrients essential for health? What are the alternatives?

An additional issue is who renders the judgment on whether a novel food is appropriate or safe to eat? In the case of GM maize, it was African officials and their hungry constituents who judged GM maize to be safe food. In the case of Quorn, food-safety regulators in the UK then EC and US approved it, but individuals reported allergic reactions, and a food activist NGO tried to get the product warning-labelled, if not thrown off the market. Worms tend to be accepted or rejected by individuals who share a local food culture. Yet as worms and insect foods enter the gourmet global food trade, should they be safety regulated? How and by whom?

Do the Same Principles Hold in Both Directions: i.e., Is the Process of Transforming Non-foods into Foods the Same as Deciding Certain Possible Foods Are Inedible Non-foods?

The process of classifying food into non-food suggests that symbolic, social-cultural and political-economic criteria are paramount. In addition to conceptual judgments of what is appropriate, it involves concepts and constraints of status, ranking and judgments of civilised versus non-civilised behaviours.

Transforming non-food into food, by contrast, involves concepts and judgments that expand rather than narrow acceptability; e.g. a return to broad spectrum procurement (Flannery 1968) rather than more constrained dietary specialisation. Non-food also invokes the 'cooking' principle; the novel item should look, taste and feel like known 'food', and meet certain recognised nutritional 'needs', if not for specific nutrients, then for certain types of food (meat-substitute) or for variety, and not be toxic or allergenic.

Conclusions

Globalisation of diet is everywhere in evidence. Yet individuals still search for like-minded, like-nourished reference groups with whom to share food and life. Political activists and politicians understand this and so use food as a key symbol to press their political or health agendas. In the context of globalisation of diet, it is still relevant to consider how eating constraints and preferences continue to be sources of identity, and to influence diet and identity as biocultural forces and outcomes. It is as useful as ever to consider the ways the basic raw versus cooked distinctions apply not only to foods, but also to social identities constructed and manifest in part through food habits.

Biocultural anthropologists studying transformations of non-foods into foods and rejections of foods as non-foods have much to learn and communicate to scientists, legislators and food trade/aid negotiators about the meaningful construction of food and non-food categories and their transformations.

Notes

1. I thank Peter Lucas for discussing with me issues in the evolution of primate diets.
2. I have been fascinated by worm-eating since my maternal grandmother taught me this song on some miserable occasion when I thought that (once again) I had been unjustly punished for fighting with my older sister.
3. Aversion to insect-eating found in their colonies has a recorded European history. Sixteenth and seventeenth century Europeans, who happily ate frogs legs and snails, nevertheless wrote home about the disgusting things that indigenous Americans ate, including pond scum (Spirulina, discussed below), corn smut, larvae and worms. Also, many Europeans reviled African and Asian indigenous food habits that permitted grubs, larvae and other insects. In ordinary eating contexts, Americans and Europeans still do not eat the larvae, ants, beetles and grasshoppers that other peoples eat as common foods or delicacies.

4. The account below is summarised from Hansch *et al.* (2004).
5. Food-aid experts (Hansch *et al.* 2004), who have analysed the significance of GM food in this recent food crisis, on balance concluded that resistance to GM food was not the source of the food crisis or intermediate shortfalls. Instead, they blamed food-aid responders for poor planning and for not having acceptable food-aid available. They also found that for whatever reasons, whether overestimates of the numbers of people at risk of starvation or underestimates of the non-GM food supplies available on commercial terms, no one starved on account of the non-acceptance of GM maize as a starvation food.
6. http://www.quorn.com

References

Brenner, J. (1999) *The Emperors of Chocolate: Inside the Secret World of Hershey and Mars*, Random House, New York

Douglas, M. (1966) *Purity and Danger,* Penguin, Baltimore

Fedoroff, N. and Brown, N.M. (2004) *Mendel in the Kitchen: A Scientist's View of Genetically Modified Foods,* Joseph Henry Press, Washington, DC

Flannery, K.V. (1968) Archaeological systems theory and early Mesoamerica. In Meggers, B. (ed.) *Anthropological archaeology in the Americas*, Washington, DC: Anthropological Society of Washington, 67–87

Garattini, S., Pagialunga, S. and Scrimshaw, N.S. (eds) (1979) *Single-Cell Protein: Safety for Animal and Human Feeding*, Pergamon Press, New York

Hansch, S., Schoenholtz, A., Beyninson, A., Brown, J. and Krumm, D. (2004) *Genetically Modified Food in the Southern African Food Crisis of 2002–2003,* Fritz Institute, Georgetown University

Huss-Ashmore, R. and Johnston, S.L. (1997) Wild plants as famine foods. Food Choice under conditions of scarcity. In Macbeth, H. (ed.) *Food Preferences and Taste. Continuity and Change,* Berghahn Books, Oxford, 83–100

Jacobson, M. (2002) Letter to Mr. David Byrne. Commission for Health and Consumer Protection. European Community, Brussels. March 21, 2002. www.CSPInet.org/quorn/EU_complaint1.pdf Accessed 19 October 2005

Lévi-Strauss, C. (1969) *The Raw and the Cooked.* [Weightman, J. and D., translation], Harper and Row, New York

Macbeth, H. (ed.) (1997) *Food Preferences and Taste, Continuity and Change,* Berghahn Books, Oxford

Messer, E. (1984) Anthropological perspectives on diet. *Annual Review of Anthropology,* 13: 205–249

—— (1989) Sociocultural determinants of food intake. In Pelto, G., Pelto, P. and Messer, E. (eds) *Anthropological Methods for Nutritionists,* United Nations University Press, Tokyo

—— (1997) Three centuries of changing European tastes for the potato. In Macbeth, H. (ed.) *Food Preferences and Taste: Continuity and Change,* Berghahn Books, Oxford, 101–113

Rozin, P., Haidt, J., McCauley, C. and Imada, S. (1997) Disgust: preadaptation and the cultural evolution of a food-based emotion. In Macbeth, H. (ed.) *Food Preferences and Taste: Continuity and Change,* Berghahn Books, Oxford, 65–82

Stone, G. (2002) Both sides now: Fallacies in the genetic modification wars, implications for developing countries, and anthropological perspectives. *Current Anthropology* 43 (4): 611–630

5. A VILE HABIT?

THE POTENTIAL BIOLOGICAL CONSEQUENCES OF GEOPHAGIA, WITH SPECIAL ATTENTION TO IRON

Sera L. Young

Earth-eating, or geophagia, has always incited strongly negative reactions. Even scientists have done little to conceal their 'disgust' for such a 'vile habit' (Cragin 1835) and denounce geophagists 'with the tenacity of ignorance these people cling to their filthy habits' (Anonymous 1897). Positive or even neutral regard for geophagia has only emerged in the last few decades. Yet the grounds for the proclamation of geophagia as 'good' or 'bad' are limited, even today. Most scientists typically evaluate geophagia solely on the basis of their disciplinary concerns, e.g. nutritionists wonder if earth supplies iron, parasitologists evaluate if it spreads helminths. Why? It is difficult to be aware of the ways in which geophagia may affect the body that fall outside of our respective disciplines. None of us has a global perspective of all the possible benefits and all the possible negative consequences of geophagia.

This review of the potential biological consequences of earth-eating is intended to rectify the limited interdisciplinary exchange; in this chapter I synthesise hypothesised consequences from multiple disciplines. Once the hypotheses about geophagia are evaluated systematically, we can judge the 'filthiness' of geophagia on the basis of multidisciplinary scientific data, and not our visceral response.

In this chapter, the six mechanisms by which geophagic substances may act upon the body, and the positive and negative effects that have been proposed for them, are reviewed. These mechanisms are not necessarily mutually exclusive (e.g. clay may add nutrients to the diet as well as quell heartburn). Because of the frequent association of iron deficiency and anaemia with geophagia, I devote the final section to the way that each mechanism can affect iron status.

Mechanism 1: Adds Minerals

Soil consumption may result in the addition of minerals to the diet. Scores of researchers have hypothesised that iron and zinc are acquired through geophagia. Iron and zinc are present in many geophagic soil samples (Caius and Chapgar; 1933, Georgette and Francis 2003; Mahaney et al. 1993; Oates 1978; Voros et al. 2001). However, the only analysis of geophagic soils that considered the elemental bioavailability (the amount that can actually be absorbed by the body) in the presence of food indicated that they do not provide additional 'supplementary' iron or zinc. In fact, they actually bind the iron in foods ingested, thereby reducing the total amount of dietary iron (Hooda et al. 2004; Hooda and Henry, this volume).

It is, however, possible that minerals other than zinc and iron are obtained through earth-eating. The high calcium content of clays and calcium's relatively high bioavailability makes it possible that dietary calcium is provided by geophagic soils (Hooda et al. 2004), but more data are necessary to establish this for certain. Geophagia has been the cause of lead poisoning in several individuals (Fuortes et al. 1996; Shannon 2003; Wedeen et al. 1978). Some clays contain high levels of other harmful elements, such as potassium, mercury, arsenic and aluminum (Campbell et al. 2003; Smith et al. 1998), while others contain harmfully excessive amounts of useful minerals, like potassium and zinc (Garg et al. 2004; González et al. 1982; Hussey 1975; Severance et al. 1988).

Mechanism 2: Binds with Substances

Most geophagic materials contain a high proportion of clay; sandy soils and rich black soils are rarely consumed (cf. Chapter 1). Clay has a high cation exchange capacity, which means that it is very good at holding on to positively charged ions and even microbes.

Some researchers posit that the benefits of geophagia are related to its cation exchange capacity, particularly the capacity of soils to bind with the chemical toxins that plants produce, such as tannins and glycoalkaloids (Dominy et al. 2004; Johns 1996; Johns and Duquette 1991). By adsorbing these plant toxins, pica substances reduce their harmful effect on the body. There are data to support that geophagic materials reduce the effects of these noxious plant chemicals in chickens, elephants, parrots and rats (Gilardi et al. 1999; Houston et al. 2001; Philips et al. 1990; Smith and Carson 1984). This detoxification function provides an alternative explanation for the consumption of soil during famines; the soil was not consumed to fill the belly but to counteract the toxins in the inferior plants and roots that people had resorted to eating.

Other researchers, not interested in pica but in detoxification, have shed light on the effect of clays (attapulgite, bentonite, montmorillonite, Fuller's earth, diatomaceous earth, kieselguhr, kaolin-pectin, termite earth) on microbes. The majority of these materials reduce the harmful effects of certain fungi (Lavie and Stotzky 1986a; 1986b), bacteria (Ditter *et al.* 1983; Gardiner *et al.* 1993; Maigetter and Pfister 1975; Said *et al.* 1980; Vega-Franco *et al.* 1982), and viruses (Dornai *et al.* 1993; Lipson and Stotzky 1983; Rey 1989).

The consequences of binding are not only positive. Because of their high cation exchange capacity, soils may also bind tightly to elemental micronutrients in the diet such as potassium, iron or zinc (Johns and Duquette 1991; Talkington *et al.* 1970). Thus, it seems likely that geophagia can render some micronutrients unavailable and perhaps cause a micronutrient deficiency.

Pica substances have also been shown to reduce the effectiveness of pharmaceuticals including digoxin, chloroquine, aspirin, neomycin and quinidine (Brown *et al.* 1976; McGinity and Hill 1975; Moustafa *et al.* 1987; Tsakala *et al.* 1990; Wai and Banker 1966). The amount of earth that is necessary to inhibit the effectiveness of medicines is unknown.

Mechanism 3: Creates a Barrier

Geophagia may create a barrier in three ways. First, it may help to reinforce the intestinal mucosa that separate recently ingested materials from the rest of the body until they are safely digested enough to be in contact with the blood and other organs. Second, it could also create a blockage in the gut that slows the passage of food; or third, prevent the timely passage of waste.

Smectite is a major component of the soils humans ingest (Mahaney *et al.* 2000). Smectite is also a clay known for its ability to bind to mucus, thereby increasing the effectiveness of the mucus barrier (Leonard *et al.* 1994). It can also repair mucosal integrity and stimulate mucolysis (Mahraoui *et al.* 1997). For these reasons, smectite is used in the treatment of human gastritis and colitis (Moré *et al.* 1987). It seems possible that other clays could work similarly to smectite to protect the body, and even the foetus, from exposure to harmful substances (Profet 1992) or even from invading microbes and helminths that try to latch on to the gut wall.

Oke (1972) has suggested that the consumption of clay could slow gastric motility by creating something of a dam of earth in the gut; he reasons that this would allow more time for nutrients to be absorbed. This seems unlikely as the small quantities of pica substances that are consumed are not enough to slow the passage of food through the gastrointestinal tract. Furthermore, pica substances are not typically eaten before a meal, but afterwards, or as a snack throughout the day.

There are cases of geophagists who have experienced severe constipation (Courbon *et al.* 1987; Robinson *et al.* 1990) and even complete intestinal obstruction (Key *et al.* 1982; Murty *et al.* 1976; Ye *et al.* 2004). Although this is indeed a dangerous consequence of pica, there is no population survey data to indicate how widespread this is.

Mechanism 4: Quelling Gastrointestinal Upset

One of the most easily supported mechanisms of geophagia is the relief of gastrointestinal distress (Wilson 2003). Many of the soils consumed contain the clays kaolin (from which the anti-diarrhoeal medicine Kaopectate® took its name) and smectite. Both clays are known to reduce nausea and gastrointestinal upset. Clinical trials have shown smectite, a type of clay now packaged as the pharmaceutical Smecta® reduces the severity and duration of diarrhoea (De Sola Pool *et al.* 1987; Dupont *et al.* 1992; Guarino *et al.* 2001; Leber 1988; Madkour *et al.* 1993; Narkeviciute *et al.* 2002). The soothing effect of these commonly found clays may be related to the cytoprotective effects discussed above.

Quelling gastrointestinal upset may not be entirely beneficial. Nausea, vomiting and diarrhoea can be useful mechanisms for preventing or minimizing exposure to harmful substances by quickly expelling them from the body. If these functions are muted by the effects of pica substances, the body may be harmed by the unexpelled harmful substances. However, if pica substances work by binding toxins (Mechanism 3) as they quell gastrointestinal upset, expelling the toxic substance may not be necessary.

Mechanism 5: Increases pH

No pica substances are more acidic than the hydrochloric acid in the stomach (pH 2). Thus, another potential benefit is that geophagia, particularly the alkaline clays, could allay heartburn.

Mechanism 6: Introduces Organisms

Geophagia has also been hypothesised to function as a type of inoculation. Callahan has suggested that if a pregnant woman consumes live micro-organisms in soil, she will endow her foetus with immunity to those through the antigens she produces (2003). However, it is unlikely that many micro-organisms will survive the sun drying or baking typically done to prepare geophagic soils. Furthermore, most antigens that a foetus needs will be created through the mother's everyday contact with harmful substances without her needing to purposively ingest large quantities of soil or other non-food substances.

Geophagia has also been hypothesised to be the source of geohelminth infection. In fact, one of the oldest allegations levelled at pica, especially geophagia, is that it is a risk factor for the transmission of parasitic nematodes, namely *Ascaris lumbricoides* (roundworm), *Trichuris trichiura* (whipworm), *Toxocara spp.* and hookworms (Anell and Lagercrantz 1958; Bateson and Lebroy 1978; Glickman *et al.* 1999; Halsted 1968; Hertz 1947; O'Rourke *et al.* 1967; Rogers 1972). There is strong epidemiological and biological evidence that hookworm is not transmitted by geophagia (Geissler *et al.* 1998; Gelfand 1945;

Saathoff *et al.* 2002). However, it remains unclear if pica is an important vector for roundworm and whipworm infection. Several studies have demonstrated a strong association between earth consumption and increased roundworm and whipworm burden in pica consumers (Geissler *et al.* 1998; Glickman *et al.* 1999; Luoba *et al.* 2005; Saathoff *et al.* 2002; Wong *et al.* 1991). However, clay eaten by pregnant women is collected and/or prepared in ways that are not conducive to the spread of worms, e.g. it is baked or sun-dried before consumption (or dug from lower surfaces, where helminths do not reside) (Hunter *et al.* 1989; Vermeer 1966, 1971; Young and Pelto 2006). No helminths were found in soil eaten by adult Zanzibari geophagists (Young *et al.* 2007), but they were present

Table 5.1 Overview of potential benefits and negative consequences of geophagia

Mechanism	Potential Benefits	Potential Negative Consequences
1. Adds elements	• Adds useful micronutrients, e.g. iron, zinc, or calcium	• Adds poisonous elements, e.g. lead, mercury • Adds helpful minerals in excess, e.g. potassium, zinc
2. Binds substances	• Binds with plant toxins • Binds with pathogens: bacteria, viruses, fungi, protozoa • Binds with dietary iron (causing nutritional immunity)	• Binds with dietary iron (causing iron deficiency) • Reduces the effectiveness of pharmaceuticals
3. Creates a barrier	• Protective coating of intestine • Slows gastric motility	• Damages intestinal mucosa • Gastric/intestinal obstruction, constipation
4. Quells gastrointestinal upset	• Reduces upper and lower gastrointestinal upset	• Inhibits useful mechanisms for detoxification (e.g. diarrhoea)
5. Increases pH	• Soothes heartburn	• Makes iron less available • More hospitable environment for enterotoxins and/or helminthes
6. Introduces organisms	• Live micro-organisms	• Geohelminths

in soil eaten by children in Jamaica and Kenya (Geissler *et al.* 1998; Wong *et al.* 1991). To date, there is not sufficient evidence to prove or disprove a causal relationship between pica and other geohelminth infections.

Anaemia, the Disease of Earth-eating?

Geophagia is often found concurrently with anaemia. This observed association between geophagia and anaemia was first documented around 30AD by Cornelius Celsus, a Roman textbook author who observed, 'People whose colour is bad when they are not jaundiced are either sufferers from pains in the head or earth eaters' (cited in Woywodt and Kiss 2002). A second of many examples of the conflation of anaemia and geophagia was recorded on 29th November, 1870, by David Livingstone. While visiting Zanzibar, he wrote about 'safura' in his journals, calling it 'the local name of the disease of clay or earth eating' (Livingstone 1874). Safura, however, is translated from Swahili to English as 'anaemia' not 'geophagia'. Because the geophagia and anaemia continue to be found in association, in this section I explore how geophagia can affect iron status.

Earth as a Supplement

If iron is present in biologically relevant quantities and is bioavailable, it will increase iron status, thereby reducing anaemia. On the other hand, the presence of high amounts of zinc or lead in pica substances would compete with iron uptake, which could cause anaemia. Furthermore, the presence of other elements such as aluminum and mercury can interfere with the production of red blood cells, thus negatively impacting indicators of iron status.

The Binding Capacity of Earth

The high cation exchange capacity (binding capacity) of soils may mean that they will bind with elemental nutrients in the diet, making them impossible for the body to absorb. Minnich demonstrated (1968) and Cavdar, Arcasoy and colleagues replicated (Arcasoy *et al.* 1978; Cavdar *et al.* 1980, 1983) the impairment of iron absorption by clays. While Talkington and colleagues found no appreciable impairment of iron absorption by two popular Texan clays or laundry starch, they did see impairment with Turkish clays (1970). To date, there is sufficient evidence to support the concept that some, but not all, clays interfere with elemental iron absorption[1] and, in turn, contribute to iron deficiency (Reid 1992).

Typically, iron deficiency has been thought to be detrimental to health. However, the chelation of iron may help to prevent the proliferation of

Figure 5.1 Zanzibar woman collecting rocks

pathogens that are dependent on the hosts' iron stores (Nesse and Williams 1996; Ratledge and Dover 2000). Geophagia may be one way to keep iron away from parasites.

Alternatively, if pica substances can inhibit the proliferation of microbes, or bind with bacterial enterotoxins, gut inflammation may be reduced. This would increase the intestine's ability to absorb iron, and in turn increase the geophagist's iron status.

Earth as a Barrier

If the surface of the intestinal mucosa is covered with a layer of clay (or starch or charcoal) or is damaged by pica substances, fewer nutrients may be absorbed, including iron. Because the intestine is the site of iron uptake, this could quickly decrease iron status. However, there has been no research to substantiate the plausibility of this effect.

Earth as an Anti-nausea Treatment

Quelling nausea may increase iron intake by enabling a person to consume (more) food that contains iron. Furthermore, the nutrients that are consumed are able to stay in the digestive tract long enough to absorb minerals such as iron if a person does not have diarrhoea or emesis. Geophagia may permit more food ingestion, which could increase iron status. However, if the earth that is consumed contains clay, it will likely have a high cation exchange capacity and be able to bind dietary iron, thus decreasing overall iron status.

Earth as an Antacid

Increasing the pH of the gastrointestinal tract has two potentially negative consequences. The first is that an increased gastrointestinal pH may make elemental iron less available by inhibiting the oxidisation of ferric iron (Fe^{3+}) to ferrous iron (Fe^{2+}), which is more readily absorbed. Second, if the gut environment is less acidic, it may create a more hospitable environment for microbes and intestinal helminths already present that prefer a more neutral pH. The blood loss that many geohelminths cause would result in a decreased iron status.

Parasites and Earth Consumption

If geophagic soils are a vector for geohelminth infection, the bleeding they cause could explain the association of anaemia and geophagia. If soils inhibit helminths from latching onto the gut wall, this may shield geophagists from a loss of iron.

Conclusion

Before sweeping statements can be made about the biological consequences of geophagia, each of these mechanisms needs to be critically, and deliberately, evaluated using many samples of geophagic soils from around the world. Furthermore, the biological status of the person both before and after earth consumption must be established. Then, and only then, can we make judgments about just how 'filthy' eating dirt really is.

Note

1. Because haeme iron is not converted to a free ionized form before it is absorbed, geophagia probably does not affect absorption of haeme iron (Prasad *et al.* 1983).

References

Anell, B. and Lagercrantz, S. (1958) *Geophagical Customs*. Almquist and Wiksells Boktryckeri, Uppsala

Anonymous (1897) The clay eaters. *Scientific American*, 76: 150

Arcasoy, A., Cavdar, A.O. and Babacan, E. (1978) Decreased iron and zinc absorption in Turkish children with iron deficiency and geophagia. *Acta Haematologica*, 60: 76–84

Bateson, E.M. and Lebroy, T. (1978) Clay eating by Aboriginals of the Northern Territory. *The Medical Journal of Australia*, 1, Supplement 1: 1–3

Brown, D.D., Juhl, R.P., Lewis, K., Schrott, M. and Bartels, B. (1976) Decreased bioavailability of digoxin due to antacids and kaolin-pectin. *New England Journal of Medicine*, 295: 1034–1037

Caius, J.F. and Chapgar, S.K. (1933) Earth-eating and salt-licking in India. *Journal of the Bombay Natural History Society*, 37: 455–459

Callahan, G. (2003) Eating dirt. *Emerging Infectious Diseases*, 9: 1016–1021

Campbell, L., Dixon, D.G. and Hecky, R.E. (2003) A review of mercury in Lake Victoria, East Africa: implications for human and ecosystem health. *Journal of Toxicology and Environmental Health. Part B, Critical Reviews*, 6: 325–356

Cavdar, A.O., Arcasoy, A., Cin, S. and Gumus, H. (1980) Zinc deficiency in geophagia in Turkish children and response to treatment with zinc sulphate. *Haematologica*, 65: 403–408

Cavdar, A.O., Arcasoy, A., Cin, S., Babacan, E. and Gozdasoglu, S. (1983) Geophagia in Turkey: iron and zinc absorption studies and response to treatment with zinc in geophagia cases. In Prasad, A., Cavdar, A.O., Brewer, G. and Aggett, P. (eds) *Zinc Deficiency in Human Subjects: Proceedings of an International Symposium held in Ankara, Turkey, April 29–30, 1982,* Alan R. Liss, Inc, New York, 71–97

Courbon, B., Boulloche, J. and Mallet, E. (1987) Plaster geophagia in an immigrant Maugrabin child. *Archives Françaises de Pédiatrie*, 44: 145

Cragin, F.W. (1835) Observations on cachexia africana or dirt-eating. *The American Journal of the Medical Sciences*, 17: 356–364

De Sola Pool, N., Loehle, K., Radzik, A.J. and Kinsley, J. (1987) A comparison of nonsytemic and systemic antidiarrheal agents in the treatment of acute nonspecific diarrhea in adults. *Today's Therapeutic Trends*, 5: 31–38

Ditter, B., Urbaschek, R. and Urbaschek, B. (1983) Ability of various adsorbents to bind endotoxins in vitro and to prevent orally induced endotoxemia in mice. *Gastroenterology*, 84: 1547–1552

Dominy, N.J., Davoust, E. and Minekus, M. (2004) Adaptive function of soil consumption: an *in vitro* study modelling the human stomach and small intestine. *Journal of Experimental Biology*, 207: 319–324

Dornai, D., Mingelgrin, U., Frenkel, H. and Bar-Jospeh, M. (1993) Direct quantification of unadsorbed viruses in suspensions of adsorbing colloids with the enzyme-linked immunosorbent assay. *Applied and Environmental Microbiology*, 59: 3123–3125

Dupont, C., Moreno, J.L., Barau, E., Bargaoui, K., Thiane, E. and Plique, O. (1992) Effect of diosmectite on intestinal permeability changes in acute diarrhea: a double-blind placebo-controlled trial. *Journal of Pediatric Gastroenterology and Nutrition*, 14: 413–419

Fuortes, L., Weisman, D., Niebyl, J., Gergely, R. and Reynolds, S. (1996) Pregnancy, pica, pottery and Pb (lead). *Journal of the American College of Toxicology*, 15: 445–450

Gardiner, K.R., Anderson, N.H., McCaigue, M.D., Erwin, P.J., Halliday, M.I. and Rowlands, B.J. (1993) Adsorbents as antiendotoxin agents in experimental colitis. *Gut*, 34: 51–55

Garg, M., Shaver, M.J. and Easom, A. (2004) Pica. An underappreciated cause of electrolyte abnormalities. *Nephrology News Issues*, 18: 28–9, 33

Geissler, P., Mwaniki, D., Thiong, F. and Friis, H. (1998) Geophagy as a risk factor for geohelminth infections: a longitudinal study of Kenyan primary school children. *Transactions of the Royal Society of Tropical Medicine and Hygiene*, 92: 7–11

Gelfand, M. (1945) Geophagy and its relation to hookworm disease. *East African Medical Journal*, 22: 98–103

Georgette, K. and Francis, T. (2003) *A Study of the Hydrochloric acid (HCL) Extractable Mineral Components of a Clay Substance Eaten in Ghana* (unpublished manuscript) Department of Nutrition and Food Sciences, University of Ghana

Gilardi, J.D., Duffey, S.S., Munn, C.A. and Tell, L.A. (1999) Biochemical functions of geophagy in parrots: detoxification of dietary toxins and cytoprotective effects. *Journal of Chemical Ecology*, 25: 897–922

Glickman, L.T., Camara, A.O., Glickman, N.W. and McCabe, G.P. (1999) Nematode intestinal parasites of children in rural Guinea, Africa: Prevalence and relationship to geophagia. *International Journal of Epidemiology*, 28: 169–174

Gonzalez, J.J., Owens, W., Ungaro, P.C., Werk, E.E. and Wentz, P.W. (1982) Clay ingestion: a rare cause of hypokalemia. *Annals of Internal Medicine*, 97: 65–66

Guarino, A., Bisceglia, M., Castellucci, G., Iacono, G., Casali, L.G., Bruzzese, E., Musetta, A. and Greco, L. (2001) Smectite in the treatment of acute diarrhea: A nationwide randomized controlled study of the Italian Society of Pediatric Gastroenterology and Hepatology (SIGEP) in collaboration with primary care pediatricians. SIGEP study group for smectite in acute diarrhea. *Journal of Pediatric Gastroenterology and Nutrition*, 32: 71–75

Halsted, J.A. (1968) Geophagia in man: Its nature and nutritional effects. *American Journal of Clinical Nutrition*, 21: 1384–1393

Hertz, H. (1947) Notes on clay and starch eating among negroes in a southern urban community. *Social Forces*, 25: 343–344

Hooda, P.S., Henry, C.J., Seyoum, T.A., Armstrong, L.D. and Fowler, M.B. (2004) The potential impact of soil ingestion on human mineral nutrition. *The Science of the Total Environment*, 333: 75–87

Houston, D., Gilardi, J. and Hall, J. (2001) Soil consumption by elephants might help to minimize the toxic effects of plant secondary compounds in forest browse. *Mammal Review*, 31: 249–254

Hunter, J.M., Horst, O.H. and Thomas, R.N. (1989) Religious geophagy as a cottage industry: The Holy Clay Tablet of Esquipulas, Guatemala. *National Geographic Research*, 5: 281–295

Hussey, H.H. (1975) Geophagia-induced hyperkalemia. *Journal of the American Medical Association*, 234: 746

Johns, T. (1996) *The Origins of Human Diet and Medicine*. University of Arizona Press, Tucson

—— and Duquette, M. (1991) Detoxification and mineral supplementation as functions of geophagy. *American Journal of Clinical Nutrition*, 53: 448–456

Key, T.J., Horger, E.R. and Miller, J.J. (1982) Geophagia as a cause of maternal death. *Obstetrics and Gynecology*, 60: 525–526

Lavie, S. and Stotzky, G. (1986b) Adhesion of the clay minerals montmorillonite, kaolinite, and attapulgite reduces respiration of histoplama capsulatum. *Applied and Environmental Microbiology*, 51: 65–73

—— and —— (1986a) Interactions between clay minerals and siderophores affect the respiration of histoplasma capsulatum. *Applied and Environmental Microbiology*, 51: 74–79

Leber, W. (1988) A new suspension form of smectite (liquid 'diasorb') for the treatment of acute diarrhoea: A randomized comparative study. *Pharmatherapeutica*, 5: 256–260

Leonard, A., Droy-Lefaix, M.T. and Allen, A. (1994) Pepsin hydrolysis of the adherent mucus barrier and subsequent gastric mucosal damage in the rat: Effect of diosmectite and 16,16 dimethyl prostaglandin E2. *Gastroentérologie Clinique et Biologique*, 18: 609–616

Lipson, S.M. and Stotzky, G. (1983) Adsorption of reovirus to clay minerals: Effects of cation-exchange capacity, cation saturation, and surface area. *Applied and Environmental Microbiology*, 46: 673–682

Livingstone, D. (1874) *The Last Journals of David Livingstone in Central Africa from 1865 to his Death*. London

Luoba, A., Geissler, P.W., Estambale, B., Ouma, J., Alusala, D., Ayah, R., Mwaniki, D., Magnussen, P. and Friis, H. (2005) Earth-eating and reinfection with intestinal helminths among pregnant and lactating women in Western Kenya. *Tropical Medicine and International Health*, 10: 220–227

Madkour, A.A., Madina, E.M., El-Azzouni, O.E., Amer, M.A., El-Walili, T.M. and Abbass, T. (1993) Smectite in acute diarrhea in children: a double-blind placebo-controlled clinical trial. *Journal of Pediatric Gastroenterology and Nutrition*, 17: 176–181

Mahaney, W.C., Hancock, R.G.V. and Inque, M. (1993) Geochemistry and clay mineralogy of soils eaten by Japanese macaques. *Primates*, 34: 85–91

Mahaney, W.C., Milner, M.W., Hs, M., Hancock, R.G.V., Aufreiter, S., Reich, M. and Wink, M. (2000) Mineral and chemical analyses of soils eaten by humans in Indonesia. *International Journal of Environmental Health Research*, 10: 93–109

Mahraoui, L., Heyman, M., Plique, O., Droy-Lefaix, M.T. and Desjeux, J.F. (1997) Apical effect of diosmectite on damage to the intestinal barrier induced by basal tumour necrosis factor-alpha. *Gut*, 40: 339–343

Maigetter, R.Z. and Pfister, R.M. (1975) A mixed bacterial population in a continuous culture with and without kaolinite. *Canadian Journal of Microbiology*, 21: 173–180

Mcginity, J. and Hill, J. (1975) Influence of monovalent and divalent electrolytes on sorption of neomycin sulfate to attapulgite and montmorillonite clays. *Journal of Pharmaceutical Sciences*, 64: 1566–1568

Minnich, V., Okcuoglu, A., Tarcon, Y., Arcasoy, A., Cin, S., Yorukoglu, O., Renda, F. and Demirag, B. (1968) Pica in Turkey II: effect of clay upon iron absorption. *American Journal of Clinical Nutrition*, 21: 78–86

Moré, J., Benazet, F., Fioramonti, J. and Droy-Lefaix, M.T. (1987) Effects of treatment with smectite on gastric and intestinal glycoproteins in the rat: a histochemical study. *Histochemical Journal*, 19: 665–670

Moustafa, M.A., Al-Shora, H.I., Gaber, M. and Gouda, M.W. (1987) Decreased bioavailability of quinidine sulphate due to interactions with adsorbent antacids and antidiarrhoeal mixtures. *International Journal of Pharmaceutics*, 34: 207–211

Murty, T.V., Rao, N.N. and Bopardikar, K.V. (1976) Geophagia with mechanical obstructive symptoms. *Indian Pediatrics*, 13: 575–576

Narkeviciute, I., Rudzeviciene, O., Leviniene, G., Mociskiene, K. and Eidukevicius, R. (2002) Management of Lithuanian children's acute diarrhoea with gastrolit solution and dioctahedral smectite. *European Journal of Gastroenterology and Hepatology*, 14: 419–424

Nesse, R.M. and Williams, G.C. (1996) *Why We Get Sick: The New Science of Darwinian Medicine*. Vintage, New York

O'Rourke, D.E., Quinn, J.G., Nicholson, J.O. and Gibson, H.H. (1967) Geophagia during pregnancy. *Obstetrics and Gynecology*, 29: 581–584

Oates, J.F. (1978) Water-plant and soil consumption by Guereza monkeys (*Colobus guereza*) A relationship with minerals and toxins in the diet? *Biotropica*, 10: 241–253

Oke, O.L. (1972) Rickets in developing countries. *World Review of Nutrition and Dietetics*, 15: 86–103

Philips, T.D., Clement, B.A., Kubena, L.F. and Harvey, R.B. (1990) Detection and detoxification of aflatoxins: prevention of aflatoxicosis and aflatoxin residues with hydrated sodium calcium aluminosilicate. *Veterinary and Human Toxicology*, 32S: 15–19

Prasad, A., Halsted, J.A. and Nadimi, M. (1983) Nutrition classics. syndrome of iron deficiency anaemia, hepatosplenomegaly, hypogonadism, dwarfism, and geophagia. *Nutrition Reviews*, 41: 220–223

Profet, M. (1992) Pregnancy Sickness as Adaptation: A Deterrent to Maternal Ingestion of Teratogens. In Barkow, J.H., Cosmides, L. and Tooby, J. (eds) *The Adapted Mind: Evolutionary Psychology and the Generation of Culture*, Oxford University Press, New York, Oxford, 327–366

Ratledge, C. and Dover, L.G. (2000) Iron metabolism in pathogenic bacteria. *Annual Review of Microbiology*, 54: 881–941

Reid, R.M. (1992) Cultural and medical perspectives on geophagia. *Medical Anthropology*, 13: 337–351

Rey, C. (1989) Rotavirus viral diarrhoea: The advantages of smectite. *International Review of Pediatrics*, 196: 1–4

Robinson, B.A., Tolan, W. and Golding-Beecher, O. (1990) Childhood pica. Some aspects of the clinical profile in Manchester, Jamaica. *West Indian Medical Journal*, 39: 20–26

Rogers, M.E. (1972) *Practice of Pica among Iron Deficient Pregnant Women*. Ph.D. Thesis, Auburn University

Saathoff, E., Olsen, A., Kvalsvig, J.D. and Geissler, P.W. (2002) Geophagy and its association with Geohelminth infection in rural schoolchildren from Northern Kwa

Zulu-Natal, South Africa. *Transactions of the Royal Society of Tropical Medicine and Hygiene*, 96: 485–490

Said, S.A., Shibl, A.M. and Abdullah, M.E. (1980) Influence of various agents on adsorption capacity of kaolin for *Pseudomonas Aeruginosa* toxin. *Journal of Pharmaceutical Sciences*, 69: 1238–1239

Severance, H.W., Holt, T., Patrone, N.A. and Chapman, L. (1988) Profound muscle weakness and hypokalemia due to clay ingestion. *Southern Medical Journal*, 81: 272–274

Shannon, M. (2003) Severe lead poisoning in pregnancy. *Ambulatory Pediatrics*, 3: 37–39

Smith, B., Chenery, S.R.N., Cook, J.M., Styles, M.T., Tiberindwa, J.V., Hampton, C., Freers, J., Rutakinggirwa, M., Sserunjogi, L., Tokins, A. and Brown, C.J. (1998) Geochemical and environmental factors controlling exposure to cerium and magnesium in Uganda. *Journal of Geochmical Exploration*, 65: 1–15

Smith, T. and Carson, M. (1984) Effect of diet on T-2 toxicosis. *Advances in Experimental Medicine and Biology*, 177: 153–167

Talkington, K.M., Gant, N.F., Scott, D.E. and Pritchard, J.A. (1970) Effect of ingestion of starch and some clays on iron absorption. *American Journal of Obstetrics and Gynecology*, 108: 262–267

Tsakala, M., Tona, L., Tamba, V., Mawanda, B., Vielvoye, L., Dufey, J. and Gillard, J. (1990) In vitro study of the adsorption of chloroquine by an antidiarrheal remedy traditionally used in Africa. *Journal de Pharmacie de Belgique*, 45: 268–273

Vega-Franco, L., Velasco-Sanchez, F. and Perez, J.E. (1982) Effect of the administration of adsorbents on the bacterial flora of the rat intestine. *Boletín Médico del Hospital Infantil de México*, 39: 259–263

Vermeer, D.E. (1966) Geophagy among the Tiv of Nigeria. *Annals of the Association of American Geographers*, 56: 197–204

—— (1971) Geophagy among the Ewe of Ghana. *Ethnology*, 10: 56–72

Voros, J., Mahaney, W.C., Milner, M.W., Krishnamani, R., Aufreiter, S. and Hancock, R.G.V. (2001) Geophagy by the bonnet macaques (*Macaca radiata*) of Southern India: a preliminary analysis. *Primates*, 42: 327–344

Wai, K.N. and Banker, G.S. (1966) Some physicochemical properties of the montmorillonites. *Journal of Pharmaceutical Sciences*, 55: 1215–1220

Wedeen, R.P., Mallik, D.K., Batuman, V. and Bogden, J.D. (1978) Geophagic lead nephropathy: case report. *Environmental Research*, 17: 409–415

Wilson, M.J. (2003) Clay mineralogical and related characteristics of geophagic materials. *Journal of Chemical Ecology*, 29: 1525–1547

Wong, M.S., Bundy, D.A. and Golden, M.H. (1991) The rate of ingestion of ascaris lumbricoides and trichuris trichiura eggs in soil and its relationship to infection in two children's homes in Jamaica. *Transactions of the Royal Society of Tropical Medicine and Hygiene*, 85: 89–91

Woywodt, A. and Kiss, A. (2002) Geophagia: the history of earth-eating. *Journal of the Royal Society of Medicine*, 95: 143–146

Ye, D., Kam, K., Sanou, F., Traore, S.S., Kambou, S., Yonaba, C., Dao, F. and Sawadogo, A. (2004) Intestinal obstruction and geophagia in a 14–year-old child. *Archives de Pédiatrie*, 11: 461–462

Young, S.L. and Pelto, G.H. (2006) Core Concepts in Nutritional Anthropology. In Temple, N.J., Wilson, T. and Jacobs, D.R. (eds) *Nutritional Health: Strategies for Disease Prevention.* Humana Press, Totowa, NJ, 425–437

6. THE DISCOVERY OF HUMAN ZINC DEFICIENCY

A REFLECTIVE JOURNEY BACK IN TIME[1]

Ananda S. Prasad

Introduction by the Editors

No discussion of geophagia would be complete without alluding to the pioneering work of Professor Ananda S. Prasad. Professor Prasad is the 'Godfather' in the scientific study of geophagia. His classic paper published in 1961 firmly established the role of geophagia in human zinc and iron deficiency. It was, therefore, an honour that he attended our conference and a privilege to include his unabridged talk in this book to capture the history and spirit of his work.

History Leading to the Evidence of Zinc Deficiency in Humans

In 1869 Raulin discovered that zinc was essential for growth factors in micro-organisms. This was followed by the connection to higher plant life in 1926 by Sommer and Lipman. In 1934 Todd *et al.* showed that zinc was essential for growth in rats and in 1958 O'Dell *et al.* showed this in poultry. There was enough evidence around that zinc was a growth factor, but it was not known if it had any role in humans. When reading textbooks on biochemistry, medicine or nutrition before 1963 it would state that it is very unlikely that zinc will be found to be deficient in humans as it can be found everywhere, including air, soil and plants. Therefore it was not imagined that zinc would ever be a problem. However, in 1963, I and my colleagues discovered zinc deficiency in humans (Prasad *et al.* 1963).

The Chief of Paediatric Haematology at Harvard, who was a very good friend of the Shah of Iran, and Hobart Reimann, the former Chief of

Table 6.1 Zinc deficiency in micro-organisms, plants and animals

Paulin in 1869	– Aspergillus niger
Sommer and Lipman in 1926	– Higher Plant Life
Todd, Elvehjem and Hart in 1934	– Rats
O'Dell and Savage in 1958	– Poultry
Prasad *et al.* in 1963	– Man

Medicine in Minnesota, were looking for someone to set up the medical curriculum in Iran to train students and residents. A proposal of an academic position at the Nemazee Hospital in Shiraz was put to me, which I accepted after initial reservations due to not being familiar with the country or the language. The Nemazee Hospital mainly cared for rich Iranians. However, I also had access to the Saadi Hospital, caring for the poor Iranians with complicated clinical problems.

During my first week in Iran I was invited by Dr James A. Halsted to visit and discuss the case of a twenty-year-old patient who was very anaemic. The boy was found to have severe growth retardation, hypogonadism, anaemia, no pubic or facial hair, hepatosplenomegaly, slightly protruding stomach, very rough and dry skin, as well as indulging in geophagia (clay eating) and being mentally lethargic.

A question that puzzled me was why a boy was anaemic with haemoglobin level of 5g/dl without any blood loss, who also showed stunted growth. I was convinced that iron deficiency could not account for the growth retardation. Therefore, iron deficiency was discarded as a possibility.

The dietary history of the boy showed a diet of mainly bread, some vegetables and no protein. He also had a history of prolonged geophagia, consuming approximately half a kilo each day. This was found to be a common occurrence in and around Shiraz.

I had never had a case like this, a clay eater with iron deficiency who did not bleed. In order to investigate the cause behind the deficiency, twelve anaemic patients were admitted into the hospital and studied in great detail. We then looked at the Periodic Table for transitional metals. If iron is unavailable for absorption due to clay eating and bread (it was not known what was in the bread), it is possible that another trace mineral would be affected similarly. Zinc was selected because of its growth factor history with plants and animals.

I had a difficult time convincing my colleagues of my beliefs and tried to have a zinc analysis done. There was only one laboratory in the world at that time capable of measuring zinc in plasma, and it was in Boston, Massachusetts, USA. The samples were sent for analysis, but unfortunately they went bad and had to be thrown away. I decided to publish my data anyway, speculating about zinc deficiency and hoping it would create some interest and invitation for further funding and research. When submitting the paper, I wrote a note to the editor about the lack of data and asked for the paper to be published anyway even if the speculating part had to be removed. Nothing was changed, as they found the paper to be very interesting and thought it might be found to be of great importance at a later date.

The paper, 'Syndrome of Iron Deficiency Anaemia, Hepatosplenomegaly, Hypogonadism, Dwarfism and Geophagia' was published in the *American Journal of Medicine* 1961 and republished in 1983 as a nutrition classic in *Nutrition Review*. (In Figure 6.1 the cover of this edition in *Nutrition Classics* is shown.)

I left Iran in 1961. I had been invited by the Chief of Biochemistry at Vanderbilt University to carry on with my research into zinc deficiency at the Medical Research Unit in Cairo after I had shared my belief of its widespread prevalence in the Middle East. The Research Unit was to provide me with all the resources necessary for the research as they were so fascinated by my work about zinc deficiency. It was of concern to me that there might not be any dwarfs in Cairo, so before accepting the post we traveled around the local villages to find out if there were any dwarfs. We found ten to twelve dwarfs in just one day from four villages. The Chief of Biochemistry had seen these people before and had assumed they were children around eight to ten years old, not adults in their twenties. These people had very similar dietary habits to the people in Iran.

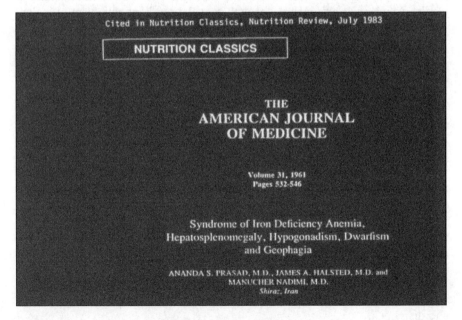

Cited in Nutrition Classics, Nutrition Review, July 1983

NUTRITION CLASSICS

THE
AMERICAN JOURNAL
OF MEDICINE

Volume 31, 1961
Pages 532-546

Syndrome of Iron Deficiency Anemia,
Hepatosplenomegaly, Hypogonadism, Dwarfism
and Geophagia

ANANDA S. PRASAD, M.D., JAMES A. HALSTED, M.D. and
MANUCHER NADIMI, M.D.
Shiraz, Iran

Figure 6.1   Cover of the 1961 article republished in 1983

Zinc analysis in plasma, red cells, hair and urine and Zn^{65} turnover rate and 24–hour exchangeable zinc pool were consistent with the diagnosis of zinc deficiency in the dwarf.

The next step was to give the dwarfs zinc supplements to see if they would grow. No changes were expected, but during the first year of giving zinc the subjects grew five to six inches in height. Also, their secondary sexual characteristics were corrected within three months, and they grew pubic and facial hair. The condition was reversible and it is very hard to find other such examples in textbooks.

There Were Three Subject Groups

The first group was given a placebo, the second group a zinc supplement, and the third group was given an iron supplement. The zinc group had their gonad dysfunction and growth corrected but no change to their haemoglobin levels; the anaemia was corrected in the iron supplement group, but there were no changes in the gonads or growth dysfunction. This was the first demonstration of tissue effects of zinc and iron in human subjects. Zinc was shown to be a growth factor, *not* iron.

In 1990, a landmark article of mine was published in the *Journal of Laboratory and Clinical Medicine*: 'clinical and experimental zinc metabolism in patients with the syndrome of iron deficiency anaemia', Zinc deficiency was shown here for the first time to occur in humans. The clinical manifestations of zinc-deficient dwarfs include: growth retardation, hypogonadism in males, rough skin, poor appetite, mental lethargy and recurrent infections.

Aetiological Factors in Human Zinc Deficiency

The poor availability of zinc from the village diet prevalent in wheat was known to contain high amounts of phytate and fibre, which is believed to limit zinc availability. Hookworm infestation causes blood loss and excessive sweating causes loss of zinc from the body.

I never saw any dwarfs older than twenty-five as they all died from infections and I was sure that zinc had a major role to play, and that zinc is critical for T helper cell 1 function when the function shifts from T helper cells 1 to 2.

Acrodermatitis Enteropathica: A Genetic Disorder

The manifestation of acrodermatitis enteropathica includes growth retardation, weight loss, skin changes, immunity disorders, gastrointestinal (GI) problems and diarrhoea.

Professor Moynahan from the London School of Medicine was treating children with acrodermatitis enteropathica, a genetic disorder where they die by the age of thirteen from infection. In 1973, Professor Moynahan and his colleague, Dr Barnes, were studying a two-year-old girl suffering from a severe case of acrodermatitis enteropathica. They were not having a good response from her treatment and did further investigation. She was not growing and her serum zinc concentration was found to be low. Because of my work on zinc she was given zinc supplementation and her skin lesions and GI problems cleared up. The symptoms returned when the supplementation was stopped. They found that the zinc was fundamental in the treatment for this rare genetic disorder since giving zinc to these children cured them. Therefore, for this disease zinc must be given. Professor Moynahan published his results in *The Lancet*, which helped put a stop to any previous doubt and controversy surrounding my work regarding zinc.

The National Academy of Sciences (NAS) in the US decided to include zinc as an essential trace element for humans. The NAS took this to Congress and it was made law in 1974. Zinc is now included in the Recommended Daily Allowance. There was no more controversy or further need for me to defend my thesis after that.

Zinc and Immunity

I have spent the last fifteen years working on zinc and the immune function. I went to Michigan where I received funding to carry out some work to produce a human model of zinc deficiency. The biochemical, clinical and diagnostic aspects of severe and moderate levels of zinc deficiency in humans were now well recognised, but it was important to carry out some study into mild or marginal zinc deficiency as it is easily corrected if detected early.

In 1960 there were only three known enzymes requiring zinc; there are now over 300. Zinc is also required for gene expression in Interleukin 2 (IL2). An experimental human model showed that in mild cases of zinc deficiency the activity of thymulin, a hormone with immunoregulatory properties, was reduced, but increased after giving zinc supplementation.

Therapeutic Uses of Zinc

Therapeutic uses of zinc include the treatment of infants and children in developing countries with acute diarrhoea and respiratory tract infections, Wilson's disease, when there is an excess of copper in the body, sickle-cell disease, the common cold and the prevention of blindness due to age-related macular degeneration (AMD). Eight to ten years ago the National Eye Institute invited me to see if anything could be done. Zinc supplementation alone has succeeded in reducing blindness by 25 per cent in patients.

Zinc deficiency is very common, with 2 billion people in the world having zinc deficiency. Zinc supplementation is important in the prevention and treatment of Wilson's disease, as the zinc lowers the copper levels in the body. Zinc acetate lozenges can halt a cold if taken correctly at the onset (within 24 hours) every three hours. It disappears within 3.5 days. Subjects with AMD who received zinc supplements live longer than placebo groups. Why? Does it play a beneficial role in major diseases such as cancer, cardiovascular disease, heart attacks and infections?

At present I am continuing to work hard at finding out what is affected by zinc and what is happening in the elderly population. There has been considerable progress made in the field of zinc metabolism in humans since 1963 when I first discovered the connection between zinc deficiency and human disease.

Note

1. This paper is presented as an *ad verbum* text of the presentation made by Professor Prasad at the conference. It has been deliberately kept in the first person to reflect the excitement and context of his work.

References

O'Dell, B.L., Newberne, P.M. and Savage, J.E. (1958) Significance of dietary zinc for the growing chicken. *The Journal of Nutrition.* 65: 503–518

Prasad, A.S., Halstead, J.A. and Nadimi, M. (1961) Syndrome of iron deficiency anaemia, hepatosplenomegaly, hypognadism, dwarfism and geophagia. *American Journal of Medicine,* 31: 532–546

Prasad, A.S., Miale, A. Jr., Farid, Z., Sanstead, H.H. and Darby, W.J. (1963) Biochemical studies on dwarfism, hypogonadism and anaemia. *Archives of Internal Medicine* 111: 407–428

Raulin, J. (1869) Chemical studies on vegetation. *Annales de la Societe Royal des Sciences Medicales et Naturelles de Bruxelles* XI: 93–99 (in French)

Sommer, A.L. and Lipman, C.B. (1926) Evidence of indispensable nature of zinc and boron of higher green plants. *Plant Physiology* 1: 231–249

Todd, W.R., Elvehjem, C.A. and Hart, E.B. (1934) Zinc in the nutrition of the rat. *American Journal of Physiology* 107: 146–156

Tucker, H.F. and Salmon, W.D. (1955) Parakeratosisor zinc deficiency disease in pigs. *Proceedings of the Society for Experimental Biology and Medicine* 88: 613–616

The Editors Wish to Add the Following:
Honours and Awards Received by Professor Ananda S. Prasad

2005:   Appointed to the Advisory Council for Asian and Pacific Affairs, Council for Asian and Pacific Affairs

2003:   Outstanding and Inspiring Leadership Award, Consul General of India, Dr. Prasad's landmark discovery of the essentiality of zinc for human nutrition and that nutritional deficiency of zinc with serious health consequences was widely prevalent

2003:   Inducted into the Heritage Hall of Fame, International Institute Foundation

2003:   Director of Research, Division of Hematology-Oncology, Wayne State University School of Medicine, Detroit, Michigan

2002–3:   NIH Council for the National Heart, Lung, and Blood Institute, NIH

2002:   Honourable Member of Russian Society of Trace Elements in Medicine, Russian Federation, Moscow

2001:   Klaus Schwarz Medal, International Association of Bioinorganic Scientists, Salt Lake City

2000:   Elected as Corresponding Member of the European Academy of Sciences, Arts and Humanities

2000:   Turkish Academy of Sciences Award, Ankara

2000:   Distinguished Professor of Medicine, Division of Hematology-Oncology, Wayne State University School of Medicine, Detroit, Michigan

2000:   Mastership of the American College of Physicians

1999:   Doctor Honoris Causat, Claude Bernard University, Lyons

1997:   Pioneer Award in Sickle Cell Research, National Heart, Lung and Blood Institute, NIH

1993:   Michigan Laureate Award, American College of Physicians

1992:   Elected to Academy of Scholars, Wayne State University, Detroit, Michigan

1989:   Raulin Award, International Society for Trace Elements Research in Humans (ISTERH)

1989:   Medal of Honour, Lyons, France

1988:   Gopalan Oration Gold Medal, Nutrition Society of India

1986:   Distinguished Faculty Fellowship Award, Wayne State University, Detroit, Michigan

1984:   Robert H. Herman Award, American Society of Clinical Nutrition

1983–4:   Hoffman-La Roche Lecture, Canadian Society of Nutritional Sciences

1976:   American College of Nutrition Award, Montreal

1975:   Goldberger Award American Medical Association

1964:   Research Recognition Award, Wayne State University

1960:   Honorary Professor of Medicine, University of Shiraz, Shiraz

7. GEOPHAGIA AND HUMAN NUTRITION

Peter Hooda and *Jeya Henry*

Introduction

Geophagia is the practice of intentional and repeated ingestion of soil or other geological materials and has been found to occur among both animals and humans (Abrahams 1997). Geophagia occurs all over the world, and among all age groups of all populations (Halsted 1968; Reid 1992). Historically, the practice can be traced back to 1000AD with most evidence originating from Africa, and the earliest indication being from a site near Kalambo Falls on the border of Tanzania and Zambia (Clark 2001). From its origin in Africa, the practice of geophagia spread across the world. However, there are regions (e.g. Japan, Madagascar, South America) with only little evidence of it (Laufer 1930).

In human society, geophagia is considered as a form of pica, (the eating of non-food items), and is a complex eating behaviour which may be found across a range of socio-economic settings, and is frequently culturally instilled in indigenous communities (Hunter 1973). There are many reasons that have been put forward to explain geophagia in humans. The dominant theories include soil ingestion for medicinal purposes (Reid 1992), cultural practices and religious purposes (Vermeer and Ferrell 1985), as well as for physiological needs, and as a result of psychiatric disorders (Hunter 1973).

Soils have been found to possess numerous pharmaceutical properties and have been used in a medicinal context for centuries (Simon 1998). Geophagic soils are sold in markets across those parts of Africa and Asia where geophagia is particularly common (Vermeer and Ferrell 1985; Simon 1998), and are consumed mainly by childbearing women for their various 'remedial' properties or because of cultural beliefs. Geophagia is also a widespread occurrence among people with psychological difficulties. Mentally retarded and developmentally impaired persons are particularly prolific consumers of soils (Halsted 1968; Simon 1998), as are children who exhibit 'hand to mouth' behaviour, which frequently continues into adulthood. Childbearing women have also been found to deliberately ingest soil for the perceived purposes of stress mediation (Edwards *et al.* 1994), enhanced digestion and to prevent frequent vomiting in early pregnancy (Simon 1998).

Geophagia and Human Health

In addition to cultural, religious and psychological reasons, a number of health benefits have been put forward as possible explanations for the practice of geophagia. In Africa, for example, childbearing women eat clays probably as a mineral nutrient supplement (Hunter 1973), though there is no conclusive evidence to support the perceived benefit or the belief. Soil ingestion has also been used as a remedy for diarrhoea and intestinal parasites (Hunter 1973; Vermeer and Ferrell 1985). Vermeer and Ferrell (1985) showed that clay sold in West African markets is similar in mineral composition to the clays used in the pharmaceutical Kaopectate™ for general gastrointestinal problems. Ingestion of at least certain soils may therefore provide medicinal benefits similar to commercially produced pharmaceuticals for general gastrointestinal ailments.

Geophagia has also been associated with a range of health/medical problems. It can bind potassium in the intestine, resulting in severe hypokalaemia. Potassium replacement in patients who are otherwise healthy is often enough to treat this condition. However, it can be life-threatening in patients with chronic renal failure (Gelfand *et al.* 1975). In extreme cases, persistent soil ingestion has been identified as a cause of mechanical bowel disorder and perforation, and of maternal death (Key *et al.* 1982). Intestinal parasitic infections are commonly related to aberrations, such as pica, including geophagia (Danford 1982; Giacometti *et al.* 1997).

Association between geophagia and iron-deficiency anaemia or low iron status has been widely reported (e.g. Danford 1982; Geissler *et al.* 1997), and studies have shown that iron supplementation enables patients to improve their iron nutrition as well as help them give up geophagia (Arbiter and Black 1991). The common occurrence of nutrient deficiency, particularly that of iron in geophagic individuals, has led to suggestions that iron deficiency causes geophagia (Lanzkowsky 1959), although this view has never been substantiated in control studies. It is however not clear whether iron-deficiency triggers geophagia or the persistent soil ingestion causes the deficiency because of the interference of the soil in iron absorption. It appears that geophagia may be common in certain population groups, which are at greatest risk of iron deficiency (e.g., poorly nourished, pregnant women). The occurrence of iron or another mineral nutrient deficiency in geophagic individuals therefore seems to be an association rather than a causal relationship (Danford 1982; Simon 1998). A syndrome occurring in males, characterised by severe iron-deficiency anaemia, Zn-deficiency, hypognadism, hepatosplenomegaly and dwarfism, was first reported by Prasad *et al.* (1961). This syndrome was observed in villages in Iran, with patients suffering from general malnutrition. The relationship of this syndrome with geophagia is not clear; however, geophagia is recognised as at least a contributory factor, as it was a common factor among the patients (Prasad 2001; see also Prasad, this volume).

Geophagia and Human Mineral Nutrition

Many researchers have concluded that geophagia is caused by a physiological requirement for basic nutrient elements that are deficient or completely lacking in the diet (Lankowsky 1959; Vermeer and Ferrell 1985; Abrahams 1997), and that it is triggered by the human body as a mechanism to obtain specific nutrients. Geophagia has also been perceived as a means of supplementing essential mineral nutrients, particularly in subsistence communities. This view, however, stems largely either from total elemental contents of the soils or from their partial extractions (Aufreiter *et al.* 1997; Abrahams 1997; Smith *et al.* 2000). Based on total elemental contents and their partial extractions, Aufreiter *et al.* (1997) predicted dietary/nutritional benefits of geophagia soils collected from the US, China and Zimbabwe. However, strong acid-soluble (total) nutrients are unlikely to be available for absorption into the body, as a large fraction of the total nutrient content will not be soluble in environments like the gastrointestinal tract, and adsorption on to ingested soil can remove food-borne potentially bioavailable nutrients from the intestine. Mineral nutrients released in the stomach (pH 2) may be readsorbed through cation exchange and adsorption as the soil enters the intestine (pH 7–10), since the retention of nutrient-ions by these processes tends to increase with pH.

Geophagia may be successful in preventing body-fluid losses, and alleviating physical stresses associated with the early stages of starvation (when used as famine food). Recent findings, however, have discounted the theory that soil ingestion may be a method of nutrient supplementation (Hooda *et al.* 2002). A major factor supporting this hypothesis is that geophagia often produces an iron or zinc deficiency as opposed to being a curative, and this phenomenon is particularly prevalent where specific highly adsorptive clays are ingested (Simon 1998). The type of soil selected by geophagia-practising individuals is extremely influential in determining the probability of nutrient-release in the gastrointestinal tract (Aufreiter *et al.* 1997). Studies analysing the mineralogical composition of geophagic soils have discovered the presence of clay minerals that are very effective at retaining nutrients. Therefore, consumption of soils predominantly of clay mineralogy may result in nutrient adsorption from the gastrointestinal tract, thereby further exacerbating the problem of nutrient deficiency.

Assessing the Impact of Geophagia on Nutrient – an *in vitro* Case Study

In vivo studies of assessing the impact of geophagia on human nutrition are difficult to conduct and raise ethical issues. Recently, Hooda *et al.* (2002) developed an *in vitro* test, which simulates soil ingestion and its potential impact on human nutrition. The *in vitro* soil ingestion method simulates conditions which are broadly similar to those expected, when the soil is digested in the gastrointestinal tract (GI), where release of soil-borne nutrients, as well as soil-retention of already available nutrients, can occur following soil ingestion. Although the test does not model the entire physiological process controlling the absorption of nutrients in the gastrointestinal tract or their dissolution from the soil, it is considered useful in assessing broad potential impacts of soil ingestion on human nutrition (Hooda *et al.* 2002).

The *in vitro* test involves simulating soil ingestion with nutrient solutions to represent nutrients that are already available for absorption in the gastrointestinal tract. It is important to recognise that nutrients were included in the solutions so that an *in vivo* type environment could be simulated for nutrient sorption-desorption reactions. The nutrient solutions used in this study were prepared on the basis of recommended daily allowances (RDA) of mineral nutrients that are required for optimum growth and functioning of the human body (Hooda *et al.* 2002). Three nutrient solutions, i.e. RDA-50, RDA-80 and RDA-100, corresponding to 50, 80 and 100 per cent, respectively, of the recommended daily intake of the nutrients were prepared to represent a cross section of their dietary intake, as geophagia may occur in people from low as well as high socio-economic backgrounds, with potential major differences in nutrient intake. The test also included a control nutrient solution, containing no Fe, Ca or Zn, but other nutrients as in RDA-50 (Hooda *et al.* 2002), in order to assess the impact of geophagia on someone with an extremely poor diet. The simulations were carried out at two pH values, 2 and 10, representing the stomach (Phase 1) and the intestine (Phase 2), respectively. The potential impact of geophagia in terms of nutrient gain or loss was determined by the difference in nutrient concentrations/contents before and after *in vitro* simulations for both phases (1 and 2).

Geophagic Soils

The case study is based on five soils collected from geophagia-prevalent communities in Uganda, Tanzania, Turkey and India (Table 7.1). These were: herb-mixed dark brown soil from Uganda (S-1); brown earth from Tanzania (S-2); chalky clay from Turkey (S-3); clay-oven lining (S-4) and pond alluvium clay (S-5) from India. Samples S-1, S-2 and S-3 represent traditional 'remedies' sold in local markets, and are eaten by pregnant women in Uganda, Tanzania

Table 7.1 Soil descriptions

Soil no.	Description	Country
S-1	Herbs mixed bar	Uganda
S-2	Brown earth	Tanzania
S-3	Calcareous pellets	Turkey
S-4	Clay-oven lining	India
S-5	Pond alluvium clay	India

and Turkey, respectively. In Northwest India, pond alluvium clay is excavated when village ponds dry up in summer months. This clay-rich material is used for making clay-ovens as well as for coating huts.

Table 7.2 presents the total contents of calcium, iron and zinc in milligrams per kilogram (mg/kg-1) in the soils. The results of total nutrient analysis show that, if available for absorption in the gastrointestinal tract, the soils could be a significant source of nutrient supplementation. Notable examples are the two Indian clays (S-4 and S-5) for Fe, Zn and Ca; the Tanzanian brown earth (S-2) for Fe; and the herbal-mixed clay from Uganda (S-1) for Ca. Whether or not ingestion of these relatively nutrient-rich soils becomes a source of nutrient supplementation will be determined largely by two factors. Firstly, the solubility of soil minerals in the gastrointestinal tract, and secondly, the nutrient-binding capacity of the soils. Large proportions of the soil nutrients (Table 7.2) are expected to become soluble in conditions (pH 2) like the stomach. However, a combination of large binding capacity of the soils and neutral to alkaline conditions (pH 7–10) in the intestine may lead to their readsorption and precipitation, rendering them unavailable for absorption in the GI tract.

Table 7.2 Total concentration (mg kg^{-1} air-dried soil mass) of calcium, iron and zinc in the geophagic soils (after Hooda *et al.* 2002)

	Geophagic Soil				
Nutrient	S-1	S-2	S-3	S-4	S-5
Calcium	4077	139	4456	37756	30295
Iron	14825	94007	17253	43856	37176
Zinc	24	33	27	88	81

Iron

Figure 7.1 summarises an example result of geophagia for potential impact on iron nutrition, using the brown earth soil from Tanzania. It should be stressed here that this geophagic soil (S-2) had the largest amount of iron among the five soils (Table 7.2). The geophagia simulation test clearly shows significant losses of Fe from the solutions after phase-1 simulation (Figure 7.1). The loss of iron differed between the soils and nutrient solutions, ranging from 26 to 79 per cent of iron present in the original nutrient solutions. It is not surprising to note that the greatest iron loss occurred when the Turkish soil (S-3) was tested, which had the lowest amount of iron among the soils (Table 7.2). The results clearly demonstrate that soils can retain iron even under acidic conditions like those of the stomach (pH 2).

The phase-2 stage of the experiments representing the passage of the soils through the intestine had a more spectacular impact on the availability of iron for potential absorption in the GI tract. The soils retained 85–95 per cent of the iron that was present in the solutions, as seen for the soil from Tanzania, S-2 (Figure 7.1). It should be stressed here that nutrient absorption occurs in the intestine. The data show that eating soils can potentially remove significant amounts of iron from the GI tract and there was no major effect of dietary iron intake, which means eating soils may have similar impacts regardless of dietary

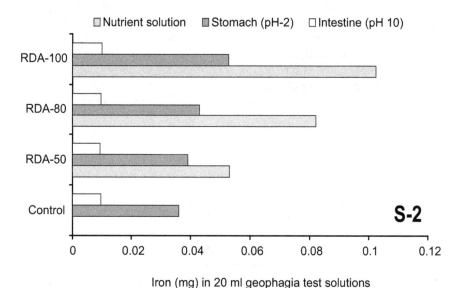

Iron (mg) in 20 ml geophagia test solutions

Figure 7.1 The potential impact of geophagia on iron availability for absorption in the gastrointestinal tract. Solution labelled as control contained no iron. Any decrease in iron content in the nutrient solutions following geophagic simulation represents a potential loss in the bioavailability

iron intake. However, cases of extremely low dietary Fe intake may benefit from the small iron release observed (Figure 7.1).

Zinc

Figure 7.2 shows an example of the geophagia test for zinc, using alluvium clay soil from India (G-5), which had a reasonable amount of zinc. The phase-1 simulation stage shows that zinc was retained by all five soils, as for G-5, resulting in the loss of zinc from the nutrient solutions (Figure 7.2). The impact, however, varied widely between the soils and the three nutrient solutions. The Tanzanian brown earth (S-2) removed the minimum zinc (about 10 per cent); this was closely followed by the Ugandan herbal-mixed sample (S-1), whilst the highly calcareous Turkish soil (S-3) did not leave any zinc in any of the solutions, i.e. 100 per cent removal (Hooda *et al.* 2002). The data provides clear evidence of zinc removal by the soils even when subjected to highly acidic conditions (pH 2). As with iron, a small amount of zinc was released from the soils when the test was performed in the presence of nutrient solutions containing no zinc (Figure 7.2).

The phase-2 part of the test analogous to the reaction in the intestine showed that no detectable zinc was left in any of the solutions across all five soils, as

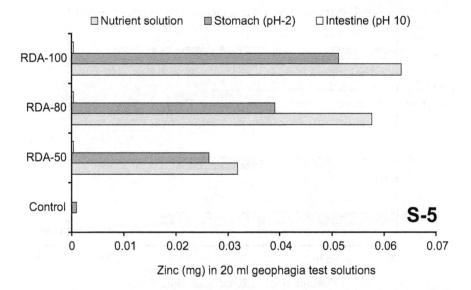

Figure 7.2 The potential impact of geophagia on zinc availability for absorption in the gastrointestinal tract. Solution labelled as control contained no zinc. Any decrease in zinc content in the nutrient solutions following geophagic simulation represents a potential loss in the bioavailability.

seen for S-5 (Figure 7.2). The findings have an important bearing on zinc nutrition of geophagic subjects. That is, eating soil can potentially remove a large amount of dietary-zinc and could lead to zinc-deficiency associated medical/health problems (e.g., dwarfism, as reported by Prasad *et al.* 1961). Another important finding is that the zinc content of soils being eaten may not have any positive or negative impact on the availability of zinc for absorption in the body (see Table 7.2 and Figure 7.2).

Calcium

For calcium, in contrast to iron and zinc, the geophagia simulation test significantly increased the calcium contents in the solution as seen for the clay-oven material (S-4) from India (Figure 7.3). The Tanzanian Brown earth (S-2), however, showed little or no change in the solution calcium concentrations (Hooda *et al.* 2002), primarily because this soil had a relatively small amount of calcium (Table 7.2). For a given soil, the amount of calcium released during the phase-1 stomach simulation was often similar, regardless of the initial calcium concentration in the solution. The maximum calcium release occurred from the pond alluvium clay from India (S-5), followed by the clay-oven lining sample (S-4); the amount of calcium released from the Ugandan herbal mixed

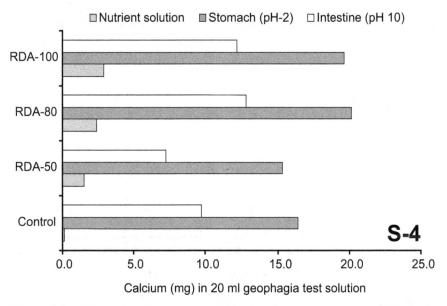

Figure 7.3 The potential impact of geophagia on calcium availability for absorption in the gastrointestinal tract. Solution labelled as control contained no calcium. Any decrease in calcium content in the nutrient solutions following geophagic simulation represents a potential loss in the bioavailability.

(S-1) and the Turkish (S-3) geophagic samples was similar, but much less compared to the Indian samples.

Calcium contents in the nutrient solutions decreased in phase 2 compared to phase 1 in all five soils, as seen for the clay-oven material, S-4 (Figure 7.3). The retention by S-1, S-2 and S-3 during the intestinal phase reduced solution calcium contents below the initial concentration. However, for the two Indian soils there was still a relatively large positive balance in terms of calcium in the solutions that might be available for absorption in the intestine. All five soils when tested with nutrient solutions containing no calcium showed varying degrees of calcim release. This implies that eating soil may become a potential source of calcium supplementation for individuals with little or no dietary calcium supply.

Conclusion

The case study clearly demonstrates that the mineral nutrient composition of geophagic soils, if used for assessing nutrient bioavailability to geophagic subjects, can lead to completely misleading conclusions. Geophagic soils can retain nutrients, such as iron and zinc even in the acidic environment of the stomach (Hooda et al. 2002). The extent of nutrient retention was found to be variable among the study samples, demonstrating the importance of different soil properties in controlling nutrient availability in the gastrointestinal tract.

In conclusion, it appears that despite being rich in mineral nutrients, geophagic soils can potentially reduce the absorption of micronutrients such as iron and zinc, which may exacerbate their deficiency in geophagic individuals regardless of their dietary iron and zinc intake. This is consistent with numerous clinical nutrition studies on geophagic subjects (cited in Halsted 1968; Danford 1982) which reported iron-deficiency, and in some cases zinc-deficiency related growth and developmental problems in children such as dwarfism (Prasad et al. 1961). The practice of deliberate soil ingestion, however, could be a means of calcium supplementation if the material is calcareous.

References

Abrahams, P.W. (1997) Geophagy (soil consumption) and iron supplementation in Uganda, *Tropical Medicine and International Health*, 2: 617–623

Arbiter, E.A. and Black, D. (1991) Pica and iron deficiency anaemia, *Child Care Health and Development*, 17: 31–34

Aufreiter, S., Hancock, R.G., Mahaney, W.C., Stamolic-Robb, A. and Sanmugadas, K. (1997) Geochemistry and mineralogy of soils eaten by humans, *International Journal of Food Sciences and Nutrition*, 48: 293–305

Clark, J.D. (2001) Geophagy and Kalambo Falls clays. In Clark, J.D. (ed.), *Kalambo Falls Prehistoric Site*, vol. 3, *The Earlier Cultures: Middle and Earlier Stone Age*, Cambridge University Press, Cambridge

Danford, D.E. (1982) Pica and nutrition, *Annual Review of Nutrition*, 2: 303–322

Edwards, C.H., Johnson, A.A., Knight, E.M., Oyemade, U.J., Cole, O.J., Westney, O.E., Jones, S., Laryea, H. and Westney, L.S. (1994) Pica in an urban-environment, *Journal of Nutrition*, 124: 954–962

Geissler, P.W., Mwaniki, D.L., Thiong'O, F. and Friis, F. (1997) Geophagy, iron status and anaemia among primary school children in Western Kenya, *Tropical Medicine and International Health*, 3: 529–534

Gelfand, M.C., Zarate, A. and Knepshield, J.H. (1975) Geohagia – Cause of life-threatening hyperkalemia in patients with chronic renal failure, *JAMA-Journal of American Medical Association*, 234: 738–740

Giacometti, A., Cirioni, O., Balducci, M., Drenaggi, D., Quarta, M., DeFedericis, M., Ruggeri, P., Colapinto, D., Ripani, G. and Scalise, G. (1997) Epidemiologic features of intestinal parasitic infections in Italian mental institutions, *European Journal of Epidemiology*, 13: 825–830

Halsted, J.A. (1968) Geophagia in man: its nature and nutritional effects, *American Journal of Clinical Nutrition*, 21: 1384–1393

Hooda P.S., Henry, C.J.K., Seyoum, T.A., Armstrong, L.D.M. and Fowler, M.B. (2002) The potential impact of geophagia on the bioavailability of iron, zinc and calcium in human nutrition, *Environmental Geochemistry and Health*, 24: 305–319

Hunter, J.M. (1973) Geophagy in Africa and in the United States: a culture-nutrition hypothesis, *Geography Reviews*, 63: 170–195

Key, T.C. Jr., Horger, E.O. III and Miller, J.M. (1982) Geophagia as a cause of maternal death, *Obstetrics and Gynaecology*, 60: 525–526

Lanzkowsky, P. (1959) Investigation into the aetiology and treatment of pica, *Archives of Disease in Childhood*, 34: 140–148

Laufer, B. (1930) Geophagy, *Field Museum of Natural History, Anthropology Service*, 18: 99–198

Prasad, A.S., Halsted, J.A. and Nadimi, M. (1961) Syndrome of iron deficiency anemia, hepatosplenomegaly, hypogonadism, dwarfism and geophagia, *American Journal of Medicine*, 31: 532–546

Prasad, A.S. (2001) Recognition of zinc-deficiency syndrome, *Nutrition*, 17: 67–69

Reid, R.M. (1992) Cultural and medical perspective on geophagia, *Medical Anthropology*, 13: 337–351

Simon, S.L. (1998) Soil Ingestion by humans: a review of history, data and aetiology with application to risk assessment of radioactively contaminated soil, *Health Physics*, 74: 647–672

Smith, B., Rawlins, B.G., Cordeiro, M.J.A.R., Hutchins, M.G., Tiberindwa, J.V., Sserunjogi, L. and Tomkins, A.M. (2000) The bioaccessibility of essential and potentially toxic trace elements in tropical soils from Mukono District, Uganda, *Journal of the Geological Society London*, 57: 885–891

Vermeer, D.E., Ferrell, R.E., Jr., (1985) Nigerian geophagical clay: a traditional anti-diarrheal pharmaceutical, *Science*, 227: 634–636

8. CONSUMPTION OF MATERIALS WITH LOW NUTRITIONAL VALUE AND BIOACTIVE PROPERTIES

NON-HUMAN PRIMATES VS HUMANS

Sabrina Krief

Introduction

Non-human animals are of considerable significance in terms of the topic of this volume because, while many are considered edible, others are not. Also, some of the edible ones may be considered inedible under certain circumstances; for example, when animal matter consumption is linked to pica, deviant behaviour, or taboos. Also, as discussed at the conference from which this volume arises, such a subject is relevant when one considers different types of autophagy, such as nail, hair or nasal mucus ingestion (see Portalatín, this volume), placenta consumption (as Maria Menges discussed at the conference), or cat consumption (see Medina, this volume). In this paper, I shall consider the concept of food and non-food as part of our study into chimpanzee behaviour and examine if animals may also be viewed as consumers of non-food items. Ruth Kutalek at the conference emphasised the overlapping boundaries between food, non-food and medicine. Chimpanzees are great apes, our closest relatives, and their organisms and bodies were considered, for a while, to be a convenient model for human physiology and medicinal experiments. Today, for ethical reasons, chimpanzees can no longer be considered as a pharmacological model. However, it might be useful to observe apes in their natural habitat and their consumption of non-food items from the forest in order to gain a greater understanding of plant selection for phytochemical study. This perceived boundary between food and non-food was the basis for our study of self-medicative practices in non-human primates. In addition, we observed that, depending on the method of consumption and the health status of the consumer, the same items might be considered both as food and as non-food. During our study, we also noticed an overlap between items that we considered to be non-food items consumed by chimpanzees and non-foods used in traditional medicine by villagers of the same area.

Non-food Consumption in Animals: Reasons, Consequences and Relevance of Such a Study

The effects of non-food consumption in humans lead us to consider the possible reasons for an animal's ingestion of non-food items and the consequences, both positive and negative, on its health. The production of secondary metabolites is considered to be an evolutionary adaptation to help plants fight off predation from insects and herbivores. Eaten frequently or in large amounts they could be noxious. Animals have to cope with such compounds present in their diet. Janzen (1978) first suggested that incidental ingestion of plants with secondary products may be toxic, but may also help to cure or combat parasite infection. If animals can avoid eating toxic food, they can also ingest plants that appear both to make them feel better and control pathogens. Similarly, ingesting soil may be a way to alleviate digestive upsets or to provide supplementary minerals, even if some negative effects such as parasite infection may occur.

The most convincing evidence of self-medicative behaviour comes from research on chimpanzees. Chimpanzees are susceptible to a wide range of pathogens that also infect humans. Investigations into the feeding behaviour of wild apes reported two particular types of behaviour, namely bitter-pith chewing and leaf swallowing, which have both been described as self-medicative behaviours. The ingestion of whole leaves was first observed by Richard Wrangham in 1971, as reported by Wrangham and Nishida (1983). They noted that the rough-surfaced *Aspilia* leaves are selected one at a time and are not chewed, but instead swallowed whole. At least thirty-four other species of plants have now been observed to be eaten in the same way in other study sites across Africa and by other subspecies of chimpanzees, by bonobos and by eastern lowland gorillas (Wrangham and Goodall 1989; Huffman 1997). This behaviour is now thought to be used by chimpanzees to control parasite infection and alleviate symptoms caused by worms (Wrangham 1995). Observations showed that some worms were firmly stuck to the leaf surface by short flexible hairs called trichomes. Moreover, because of their irritative physical properties, whole leaves may act by repeated flushing of the gastrointestinal tract, leading to the expulsion of parasites (Huffman and Caton 2001).

In contrast to the mechanical effect of the rough leaves, the bitter pith of *Vernonia amygdalina* is thought by Huffman and Seifu to be eaten for its pharmacological properties. In 1989, they published a detailed study of a sick chimpanzee recovering after having ingested a medicinal plant. The chimpanzee removed the leaves and the outer bark of the pith and chewed and sucked the bitter juice. Within 24 hours, it had recovered from its lack of appetite and malaise. *Vernonia amygdalina* is prescribed by African healers to treat stomach aches and parasite infections. Chemical analyses revealed the presence of sesquiterpene lactones, a group of compounds previously known for their bioactivities (Jisaka *et al.* 1992, 1993). Eleven new compounds from steroid glucosides were isolated and identified.

- Vernonioside B1 and vernoniol B1 are effective against *Schistosoma japonicum*
- Vernodalin is active against *Schistosoma japonicum*, *P. falciparum* and *Leishmania*, but it is also highly toxic. Recent studies have shown this product is found only in the leaves of the plant.

The 'feeding' behaviour of wild chimpanzees sometimes appears unusual to observers in several respects. Chimpanzees have a digestive tract very similar to that of humans (Milton 1999). Taste perception is also thought to be close to that of humans, because of their phylogenetic similarities (The Chimpanzee Sequencing and Analysis Consortium 2005), evidence from neurophysiological studies (Hellekant and Ninomiya 1994) and experimental tasting of chimpanzee plant foods by humans (Nishida *et al.* 2000). Most of the chimpanzee foods tested by human observers (Nishida *et al.* 2000, personal observations) were found to be palatable, even if the Nishida *et al.* (2000) study confirmed that of Hladik and Simmen (1996) by suggesting a higher tolerance for bitter substances in apes than in humans. However, the duration of the consumption of bitter plants was low: they conclude that either a high nutritional value or medicinal properties may explain the ingestion despite bitterness. On this basis, we define what might be considered as non-food consumption for chimpanzees:

1. items of unusual texture sometimes eaten in an unusual way (e.g. rough leaves ingested whole without chewing);
2. items of unpalatable taste (bitter, astringent items);
3. items obtained with a high expenditure of energy (removing bark from trees) or with unpleasant side-effects (urticant or thorny plants) without any clear caloric benefit (the tiny fruits of an *Urticaceae*, etc.);
4. items without any apparent nutritional value (soil, sawdust, rotten wood, etc.);
5. items usually ignored or avoided (seed-picking in dung);
6. items eaten regularly, but only over a short period of time, despite abundance.

Behavioural observations usually supported the fact that such items are not eaten for nutritional purposes. Such a study may be a way of providing new arguments for the study of non-food consumption in human beings: some behaviours, considered as pica or deviant in humans, are widespread in chimpanzees, thus psychological reasons put forward as explanations for human behaviour might be re-examined from this perspective.

In chimpanzees, several hypotheses could be suggested to explain puzzling behaviour related to non-food ingestion: this consumption could happen by chance or by error. Nevertheless, primates have coexisted and co-evolved with the plants of the tropical rainforests for millions of years and such behaviours, even if rare, are not anecdotic. Such behaviours could be considered as perverted or induced by psychological reasons. However, these behaviours are observed in wild chimpanzees living in natural conditions and are not practised only by one given individual or by only those that have suffered a period of stress. Chimpanzees might be driven to ingest non-nutritional food in periods when food is scarce. The consumption of non-nutritional parts of plants or soil happens regularly and, generally, we have not observed a seasonal pattern. As an alternative hypothesis, these non-nutritional items may contain bioactive compounds that could have therapeutic benefits. They may reduce the effects of pathogens on their health.

Our hypothesis is that a study of wild chimpanzees might be an original and alternative method to screen useful natural products: phytochemists faced with the rapid disappearance of tropical forests and, by consequence, the disappearance of sources of natural products, could investigate primates' and other animals' behaviour as a new method to screen bioactivities. We could use the results to bring awareness of the importance of conserving vegetal resources as a major heritage for human and wildlife species. Moreover, the use of chimpanzees for our study provides a convenient model for investigating the mechanisms that lead to the selection of such compounds. The phylogenetic proximity of the model chosen may provide interesting information on the origin of medicine among humans. In addition, this might be a way to better understand some of the prominent behaviours related to non-food consumption in humans.

Methods

The study was mainly focussed on a phytochemical study of plants ingested by chimpanzees. In the course of this study, some other behaviours, related to various items which appeared to be of no nutritious value, were observed. The basis and the control methods of our hypothesis are through monitoring health. Three methods of faeces analysis were performed in order to gain the most comprehensive view of the animals' parasite burden.

The chimpanzee community of Kanyawara, in the Kibale National Park in Western Uganda, is free-ranging and used to being followed by humans. We based our selection of plants on those chosen because of unusual feeding habits. Another way of selecting plants was by observing the diet of sick chimpanzees. In order to monitor the health of the chimpanzees without disturbing their behaviour, we followed the individuals throughout the day and paid attention to any abnormal activities. We monitored faecal and urine samples from specific individuals. We also checked which plants were used in traditional African medicine, through bibliographic studies and interviews with the traditional healer of the village near the field station.

Plant specimens were collected and dried, and extracts were taken with ethyl acetate and methanol. Each extract was tested for its biological properties on different protozoan parasites such as *Leishmania donovani, Trypanosoma brucei brucei* and *Plasmodium falciparum*. We also carried out anthelminthic assays against *Rhabditis pseudoelongata*. Extracts were also tested against bacteria, fungi and viruses. Cytotoxicity assays used KB cell lines. In addition, we looked for their immuno-stimulating properties. This screening has led us to work on a small number of plants and to isolate natural products.

I. Consumption of Non-food by Kanyawara Chimpanzees, as Defined by Observers

I shall, therefore, describe the consumption of a few items that might be considered as non-food ingestion for the following reasons:

- consumption of low amounts of plant that contained a bioactive product: leaves of *Trichilia rubescens* and bark of *Albizia grandibracteata*
- non-chewed items: *Aneilema aequinoctiale*
- non-caloric items: soil
- toxic items: *phytolacca dodecandra*

The results of monitoring health could be summarized as follows: the parasitic load was low, but most of the samples and all the chimpanzees were infected. In a group with such close contacts, and according to these results, we suggest there may be a regulation factor responsible for low parasitic levels. Moreover, the analysis of urine samples from the chimpanzees confirmed that health problems are rare, even though urinary infections seem to be quite common. The major problem observed came from poaching: many of the chimpanzees suffer from injuries caused by traps. Some other health problems, such as bronchitis or wounds, have been observed (Krief *et al.* 2005c).

1. Swallowing Whole Leaves

The first evidence of non-food being used was the consumption of rough leaves, which are not chewed and are expelled whole, so are unlikely to have been eaten for a nutritional purpose.

Several species of plants are consumed as part of this unusual behaviour at Kanyawara (as described by Wrangham in relation to *Aspilia* leaves), such as *Rubia cordifolia, Aneilemea aequinoctiale* and species of *Ficus* with rough leaves (*Ficus asperifolia, Ficus exasperata*). Leaves of *Aneilema* are chosen slowly and carefully, the chimpanzee testing the texture by clipping its lips onto the plant's limb and folding the leaf while it is still attached to the stem. The leaf is then rolled inside the mouth and the ingested leaves appeared whole a few hours later in stools, where worms and tapeworms are often found, too. Mature leaves of *Ficus exasperata* are very rough and are used as sandpaper by local people. Small undigested pieces of leaves from this species are sometimes found in dung.

2. Occasional Ingestion of Low Amounts of Different Species Containing Bioactive Compounds

Trichilia rubescens Oliv. (*Meliaceae*) leaves are one of the 170 items recorded as being consumed by the Kanyawara chimpanzees (Wrangham, personal communication). The chimpanzee diet is dominated by fruit (during 700 hours of observation, 81 per cent of feeding time was spent eating fruit) and although the diet varied from month to month, in the nineteen species on which chimpanzees spent 0.5 per cent or more of feeding time during this study, *Trichilia rubescens* leaves were not present. Usually, in each bout of observation, only one individual from the party ingested a few leaves of *T. rubescens* for a short time, leaving the shrub before all the leaves had been eaten. Different individuals in the community were observed consuming *T. rubescens* leaves. Others present in the party did not even try to feed on the shrub after the consumer had left it. Moreover, this plant generally grows in a cluster, meaning leaves would be available to several chimpanzees. These observations suggest that chimpanzees eating *T. rubescens* leaves may be individuals with a temporarily different criterion for food choice from other individuals in their party, even if symptoms observed in the consumer were not always related. Fractionation of the leaves' crude extract results in pure compounds, limonoids named trichirubine A and B, with significant antimalarial properties ($IC_{50} = 0.3$ µg/ml) (Krief *et al.* 2004).

It has been previously reported that young *Albizia grandibracteata* leaves, consumed by red colobus monkeys (*Procolobus badius*) in the Kibale National Park, have the highest level of saponins in the diet of the two groups of monkeys observed (Chapman and Chapman 2002). Nevertheless, regardless of its availability, this item was one of the six most preferred foods for these folivorous monkeys, which possess a ruminant-like digestive system. This consumption might be explained by the high protein content of this leaf compared to other species.

I have twice observed the consumption of bark of this species by chimpanzees that do not share the digestive system of the colobus, but that are monogastric, like humans: firstly, by a young, female chimpanzee suffering from an intestinal disorder; secondly, by an adult male also with parasites. A decrease in the problem was observed in the dung samples of the young female collected a few days later and observations of her general health status were normal. Some data about their potential activity are already known, as a patent was deposited forty years ago about the activity of this species. *Cercopithecus* species monkeys dosed with aqueous or alcoholic extracts of *Albizia grandibracteata* leaf or bark developed a steady increase in spontaneous uterine activity (Lipton 1964). Abortion occurred in gravid rats, rabbits and cats at any stage of gestation when dosed intravenously, intraperitonally or orally, with appropriate amounts of the extracts.

Nevertheless, the products responsible for such occurrences were not isolated. The bark of this species is also used in traditional medicine to treat digestive problems, such as bloat in Uganda and parasitism and lumbago in the Democratic Republic of Congo (Balagizi and Ntumba 1998; Defour 1994; Heine and König 1988). Bioassays that we conducted confirmed this antihelmintic activity, but also confirmed high cytotoxic activity against tumoral KB cells and led to isolation of saponins with significant *in vitro* antitumoral activities (Krief *et al.* 2005b).

3. Soil Consumption

Another such case, where the boundaries between food and non-food are very small, is soil consumption. Geophagy is widespread among animals, for example, in primates, horses, parrots, elephants or koalas (Laufer 1930; Hladik and Gueguen 1974; Davies and Baillie 1988; Mahaney *et al.* 1990, 1995, 1996; Gilardi *et al.* 1999; Houston *et al.* 2001), as well as in traditional human societies (Laufer 1930; Johns 1996). In Kanyawara, both humans and chimpanzees consume soil. The traditional healer uses red soil as an antidiarrhoeal in humans and to fight oedema in cows. Chimpanzees ingested red soils quite often. They selected earth from two types of sites: either from between the roots of fallen trees or from a natural hole below the humus layer. Noémie Klein has conducted her Master's study on this comparison between two soil samples, one corresponding to the soil used by the traditional healer, the second collected after observing soil consumption by a chimpanzee in February 2005 (poster in the conference from which this volume arises). According to simple observation, both soils have similar colour, aspect and texture. Initial results confirm that both soils have similar clay texture. The clay mineralogy is dominated by kaolinite and the rest of the sample is made up of quartz. No difference was discernable between the soils. Organic matter was very low in both samples and mineral nutrients released through digestion were not significant in comparison with the *Trichilia* nutrient released and the intake corresponding to a daily intake by vegetal matter.

Many studies have considered the benefits of geophagy in adsorbing organic compounds. I have observed, in the field, that geophagy sometimes occurs for a short period before or after consumption of toxic or active plants. We wonder if, in the chimpanzees' case, such associations are coincidental or intentional. In the village, the traditional healer also combined several items: some usually considered as food, others as non-food; some inorganic, others organic. From the point of view of our Western medicine, such additives may be viewed as 'formulation', a delivery vehicle for bioactive compounds. Other associations can also be observed in chimps. Meat is never eaten without chewing vegetal items such as leaves or bark. Caterpillars are reported to be eaten with leaves.

We used a simple model that mimics digestion to test the hypothesis of a possible interaction between soil and plants (Klein *et al.* in preparation). Accordingly, it appears that there is no nutritional reason for chimpanzees to eat soils. This material more likely serves to coat the intestinal tract, to adsorb toxins and enhance bioactivities, therefore having a pharmaceutical rather than a nutritional benefit.

4. Ingestion of Potentially Toxic Food

Chimpanzees ingest the fruits of *Phytolacca dodecandra*, a plant used for abortion in traditional medicine and which is known for its use in suicides in Africa (Esser *et al.* 2003). Poisoning by *P. dodecandra* has also been reported in sheep and reproduced experimentally, leading to death following general neurological symptoms, diarrhoea, and digestive hyperaemia and necrosis (Peixoto *et al.* 1997). In rats, LD_{50} (the dose killing 50 per cent of the subjects of the experiment) was 1g/kg for males and 0.92 g/kg for females. In gross anatomy, stomach irritations were observed, and histological examinations of organs showed mucosal haemorrhages in the two highest-dose groups in both sexes (Hietanen 1996). The chemistry of berries has been investigated, as they were used as soap by African women and their use in washing streams was associated with a reduction in snails, vectors of a severe parasitic disease named shistosomiasis. Saponins with significant molluscidal properties were isolated and identified. The information suggests that such berries should be considered as non-food, likely to have some benefits that are greater than their toxicity.

II. Is There a Concept of Non-food in Chimpanzees?

A Food Taboo?

Observations show that chimpanzees may have assimilated the notion of death (Boesch and Boesch-Achermann 2000). Whereas male chimpanzees may kill and eat the infants of females from another community, usually, when infants died, their bodies were kept by the mothers, but not eaten and no cannibalism was observed in such cases (Boesch and Boesch-Achermann 2000). So we may wonder if there is evidence to show that some items are considered as non-food for reasons other than toxicity, inedible taste or unpleasant texture.

A Juvenile Palm Civet Is Such Easy Prey: Why Not Eat It?

Why did some chimpanzees not eat one young mammal, which was not risky and was easy and very quick to catch?

On 18 June 2005, a party of eight chimpanzees were feeding on a *Ficus natalensis*. Observers (A. Houle and S. Krief) had climbed 26 metres into this fruiting tree before the chimpanzees arrived. Since dawn, when they had arrived in the tree (6.30 a.m.), the observers could hear a young palm civet (*Nandinia binotata*, Order Carnivora, Family Viverridae, tail 15 cm, body and head 15 cm) almost continuously mewing. No other palm civet was observed in the tree during this four-hour spell of observation. At least four chimpanzees were feeding close to the young animal (up to 20cm away) and were looking at it. One of them approached the young individual at two metres and vigorously shook the branch the palm civet was on three times. The observers and chimpanzees came back to the same tree in the following days. The next day, photos were taken by J.M. Krief that enabled species identification, and mewing was still heard for a few days, confirming that the chimpanzees did not prey on the young animal. The chimpanzees at Kanyawara usually like the meat of young monkeys and eat the entire bodies of very young ones, whereas they usually eat only the viscera of adults. The reason for the non-predation and non-consumption of this young palm civet has not been explained.

Non-food as Food

We have already described the consumption of mature leaves of *F. exasperata* that are rough and brittle, and are ingested as non-food. Conversely, the young leaves are soft and nutritious, but also contain bioactive compounds with antibiotic properties – six times higher than those in mature leaves (Rodriguez and Wrangham 1995). Young leaves are sometimes consumed early in the morning and not chewed; sometimes later in the day, in which case they are eaten quickly and chewed as regular food. Such an example highlights the diversity of food processes related to one species which it seems can be either food or non-food and which enables the chimpanzees to take advantage of different properties (caloric intake or medicinal value) of a same species.

III. Do Human and Non-human Primates Share Non-food Items?

Some non-food species consumed by chimpanzees are used by the local traditional healer for what appears to be the same reasons. In addition, the traditional healer included medicinal plants or items in preparations, mixing them with food. For example, seeds of *Ficus natalensis* are mixed with fatty meat to treat cancer and the seeds of *P. dodecandra* mixed in butter are used to cure skin diseases. The bark of *Celtis africana* mixed with chicken soup is used for people who have collapsed. As well as underlining the narrow borderline between food and non-food in human practices, these examples also show the similarities in plant selection between the two species. From a conservational point of view, it emphasises the necessity of preserving natural resources for the well-being of both humans and animals.

IV. Non-food Consumption in Chimpanzees: A Conditioned or an Intentional Choice?

In general, chimpanzees are very conservative in their feeding habits. Experience and knowledge may pass between individuals: young chimpanzees have been observed processing the techniques of bitter-pith chewing and leaf swallowing performed by their sick mothers. Even if their daily diet includes a wide range of secondary metabolites in small amounts, non-palatability of certain items acts as a signal of danger: a new food, bitter or astringent in taste, will be consumed in only small amounts, preventing poisoning. We might suggest that taste perception changes for sick chimpanzees, or they temporarily have a higher tolerance to usually unpalatable items or a specific taste, such as bitterness, is looked for by sick individuals. This hypothesis may explain how a newly immigrating female may acquire empirical knowledge in a new area. Some behaviours, such as soil consumption or the swallowing of rough leaves, may occur regularly, helping self-maintenance and preventing pathogenic effects; others may be practised only rarely or in cases of illness. In addition to the question of the chimpanzee's awareness of its own malaise, relieved by unusual food consumption, for an individual's empirical acquisition, a socially learned self-medicative practice would mean, firstly, an awareness of a shared disease or of the disease of another individual (which might be possible, as empathy has been described in chimpanzees) and, secondly, the acknowledgement of unusual consumption linked to the state of being ill. Observations related to mother-juvenile behaviours and those of immigrating females will be a way to understand better the acquisition and transmission of such behaviours.

Conclusion

In conclusion, we can underline the good health, the low parasitic load, the longevity and the quick and apparently spontaneous recovery of the wild chimpanzees. Their feeding behaviour, the common use of plants by chimpanzees and humans for the same illnesses and the bioactivities are all consistent with the hypothesis that the chimpanzees' diet contains a set of products with medicinal properties. As well as providing information about chimpanzee behaviour, this study could help to provide evidence for the evolution of medicine and, lastly, it offers a new strategy in the search for natural compounds. An increasing number of plant and animal species are threatened by the destruction of their habitat. This study emphasises the necessity both for humans and for wild fauna to protect (and to correct any negative impact on) the environment.

References

Balagizi Karhagomba, I. and Ntumba Kayembe, F. (1998) Plantes utilisées dans le traitement des helminthoses gastro-intestinales des petits ruminants dans le groupement d'irhambi-katana (Région du Bushi, Province du Sud-Kivu, RDC), *Recherches Africaines* 1: 90–99

Boesch, C. and Boesch-Achermann, H. (2000) *The Chimpanzee of the Tai Forest: Behavioral Ecology and Evolution*, Oxford University Press, Oxford

Chapman, C.A. and Chapman, L.J. (2002) Foraging challenges of red colobus monkeys: influence of nutrients and secondary compounds. *Comparative Biochemistry and Physiology* 133: 861–875

Davies, A.G. and Baillie, I.C. (1988) Soil-eating by red leaf monkeys (*Presbytis rubicunda*) in Sabah, Northern Borneo, *Biotropica* 20: 252–258

Defour, G. (1994) *Plantes Médicinales Traditionnelles au Kivu (République du Zaïre)*, Documentation du Sous-Réseau Prélude [Prelude medicinal plants database, available at: http://www.metafro.be/prelude]

Esser, K.B., Semagn, K. and Wolde-Yohannes, L. (2003) Medicinal use and social status of the soap berry endod (*Phytolacca dodecandra*) in Ethiopia. *Journal of Ethnopharmacology*, 85: 269–277

Gilardi J.D., Duffey, S.S., Munn, C.A. and Tell, L.A. (1999) Biochemical functions of geophagy in parrots: detoxification of dietary toxins and cytoprotective effects, *Journal of Chemical Ecology* 25(4): 897–922

Heine, B. and König, C. (1988) *Plant Concepts and Plant Use. An Ethnobotanical Survey of the Semi-Arid and Arid Lands of East Africa. Part 2: Plants of the So (Uganda)*, Band Kolner Beiträge zur Entwicklungsländerforschung/Cologne Development Studies, Verlag Breitenbach Publishers, Saarbrücken, Fort Lauderdale

Hellekant, G. and Ninomiya, Y. (1994) Bitter taste in single corda tympani taste fibers from chimpanzee. *Physiology and Behavior,* 56: 1185–1188

Hietanen, E. (1996) Toxicity testing of endod, a natural plant extract, as a prerequisite for its safe use as a molluscicide. In D'itri, F. (ed.) *Zebra Mussels and Other Aquatic Nuisance Species,* Ann Arbor Press

Hladik, C.M. and Gueguen, L. (1974) Géophagie et nutrition minérale chez les primates sauvages, *Compte Rendu de l'Académie des Sciences* 279: 1393–1396

—— and Simmen, B. (1996) Taste perception and feeding behavior in nonhuman primates and human populations. *Evolutionary Anthropology*, 5: 58–71

Houston D.C., Gilardi, J.D. and Hall, A.J. (2001) Soil consumption by elephants might help to minimize the toxic effects of plant secondary compounds in forest browse, *Mammal Review* 31(3): 249–254

Huffman, M.A. and Seifu, K.M. (1989) Observations of illness and consumption of a possibly medicinal plant *Vernonia Amygdalina* (Del.), by a wild chimpanzee in the Mahale Mountains National Park, Tanzania, *Primates* 30(1): 51–63

——— and Caton, J.M. (2001) Self-induced increase of gut motility and the control of parasitic infections in wild chimpanzees, *International Journal of Primatology*, 22: 329–346

——— (1997) Current evidence for self-medication in primates: a multidisciplinary perspective, *Yearbook of Physical Anthropology*, 40: 171–200

Janzen, D.H. (1978) Complications in interpreting the chemical defenses of trees against tropical arboreal plant-eating vertebrates. In Montgomery, G.G. (ed.) *The Ecology of Arboreal Folivores*, Smithsonian Institute Press, Washington, D.C., 73–84

Jisaka, M., Ohigashi, H., Takagaki, T., Nozaki, H., Tada, T., Hirota, M., Irie, R., Huffman M.A., Nishida, T. Kajie, M. and Koshimizu, K. (1992) Bitter steroid glucosides, vernoniosides A1, A2 and A3, and related B1 from a possible medicinal plant, *Vernonia amygdalina*, used by wild chimpanzees, *Tetrahedron* 48: 625–632

Jisaka, M., Ohigashi, H., Takegawa, K., Hirota, M., Irie, R., Huffman, M.A. and Koshimizu, K. (1993) Steroid glucosides from *Vernonia amygdalina*, a possible chimpanzee medicinal plant, *Phytochemistry* 34(2): 409–413

Johns, T. (1996) *The Origins of Human Diet and Medicine*. University of Arizona Press, Tucson

Krief, S., Hladik, C.M. and Haxaire, C. (2005a) Ethnomedicinal and bioactive properties of the plants ingested by wild chimpanzees in Uganda, *Journal of Ethnopharmacology* 101: 1–15

Krief, S., Huffman, M., Sévenet, T., Guillot, J., Bories, C., Hladik, C.M., Wrangham, R.W. Krief, S., Thoison, O., Sévenet, T., Wrangham, R.W. and Lavaud, C. (2005b) Novel triterpenoid saponins isolated from the leaves of A*lbizia grandibracteata* ingested by primates in Uganda, *Journal of Natural Products* 68: 897–903

Krief, S., Huffman, M.A., Sévenet, T., Guillot, J., Bories, C., Hladik, C.M., and Wrangham, R.W. (2005c). Non-invasive monitoring of the health condition of wild chimpanzees (*Pan troglodytes schweinfurthi*) in the Kibale National Park, Uganda. *International Journal of Primatology*, 26: 467–490

Krief, S., Martin, M.-T., Grellier, P., Kasenene, J. and Sévenet, T. (2004) Novel antimalarial compounds isolated after the survey of self-medicative behavior of wild chimpanzees in Uganda, *Antimicrobial Agents and Chemotherapy* 48(8): 3196–3199

Laufer, B. (1930) Geophagy, *Publication 280, Anthropological Series*, Field Museum of Natural History, Chicago, 18(2): 99–198

Lipton, A. (1964) *A Material Having Uterine Contractant Activity and a Process for Its Extraction from the Plants of the Genus Albizia*, Patent 952 588

Mahaney, W.C., Aufreiter, S., and Hancock, R.G.V. (1995) Mountain gorilla geophagy: possible strategy for dealing with effects of dietary changes, *International Journal of Primatology* 16: 475–488

Mahaney, W.C., Milner, M., Aufreiter, S., Hancock, R.G.V., Wrangham, R. and Campbell, S. (in press) Notes on geophagy soils eaten by chimpanzees of the Kanyawara Community in the Kibale Forest, Uganda, *International Journal of Primatology*

Mahaney, W.C., Milner, M.W., Sanmugadas, K., Hancock, R.G.V., Aufreiter, S., Wrangham, R. and Pier, H.W. (1997) Analysis of geophagy soils in Kibale Forest, Uganda, *Primates* 38(2): 159–176

Milton, K. (1999) A hypothesis to explain the role of meat-eating in human evolution, *Evolutionary Anthropology* 8(1): 11–21

Nishida, T. Ohigashi, H., Koshimizu, K. (2000) Tastes of chimpanzee foods. *Current Anthropology,* 41 (3): 431–438

Peixoto, P.V., Wouters, F., Lemos, R.A. and Loretti, A.P. (1997) Phytolacca decandra poisoning in sheep in Southern Brazil, *Veterinary and Human Toxicology* 39(5): 302–303

Rodriguez, E. and Wrangham, R.W. (1993) Zoopharmacognosy: The Use of Medicinal Plants by Animals, In K.R. Downum, J.T. Romeo and H. Stafford (eds), *Recent Advances in Phytochemistry, 27: Phytochemical Potential of Tropic Plants,* Plenum Press, New York, 89–105

The Chimpanzee Sequencing and Analysis Consortium (2005) Initial sequence of the chimpanzee genome and comparison with the human genome, *Science* 437: 69–87

Wrangham, R.W. (1995) Leaf-swallowing by chimpanzees and its relationship to tapeworm infection, *American Journal of Primatology* 37: 297–304

Wrangham, R.W. and Goodall, J. (1989) Chimpanzee use of medicinal leaves, In Heltne, P.G. and Marquardt, L.A. (eds), *Understanding Chimpanzees,* Harvard University Press, Cambridge, Massachusetts, 22–37

Wrangham, R.W. and Nishida, T. (1983) *Aspilia* spp. Leaves: a puzzle in the feeding behavior of wild chimpanzees. *Primates* 24(2): 276–82

9. LIME AS THE KEY ELEMENT
A 'NON-FOOD' IN FOOD FOR SUBSISTENCE

Ricardo Ávila, Martín Tena and *Peter Hubbard*

Food and *'Non-food'*

People in general seldom concern themselves with the boundaries between what is edible and what is not. The distinction lies deep within what might be called their cultural universe, where children learn, almost without realising it, what is food and what is not food. That is to say, for humans, cultural patterns are the means by which they distinguish what is eatable. However, there are other fundamental aspects which influence this: for example, the physical/ chemical composition of substances. These establish edibility at a quite different level.

In our view, there are two clear major factors that establish the boundaries between the edible and the inedible. The first of these is the physical/chemical composition. There are a number of products in our environment that cannot be eaten because they do not yield nourishment or permit digestion, or may even be toxic. We cannot consume metallic objects, granite rocks or wooden logs, unless these are reduced to miniscule particles (Vasquéz 1997). The second factor is the cultural one, which is arbitrarily determined, and separates the eatable from the uneatable (Millán *et al.* 2004). What is more, cultures differ in relation to these concepts, and such differences are well exemplified in this volume.

This chapter concerns lime (calcium hydroxide), which is generally not considered to be 'food', though the vast majority of Mexicans, almost unaware of the fact, daily consume it. This is because it is mixed with maize grains in order to produce *nixtamal*, which once washed and ground is transformed into the dough used to prepare *tortillas*, a food which is the physiological and cultural basis of subsistence for Mexican people, together with *tamales, atole* and a great variety of other products and dishes.[1]

Introducing *Nixtamal*

The term *nixtamal*[2] refers to the process of treating maize so as to transform it into a basic food. *Nixtamal* is both the process of treating maize (*Zea mays*) and the product of this process. The nixtamal process incorporates two fundamental actions: the gradual soaking of the grain, and the insertion of the calcium ion into it. Firstly, the penetration of water into the grain is extremely important, since it enables the gelatinisation of the starch, which is a fundamental condition for the development of the physical and transformative properties of the final product: the tortilla and other foods derived from the dough. Secondly, the integration of lime into maize provides the following advantages to maize. It makes it easier to remove the pericarp; it controls the development of undesirable micro-organisms; it facilitates the soaking of the grains; it increases the calcium content; it strongly modifies the physical/chemical and structural properties of the grain by integrating chemically the chains of starch and oils; it increases the yellow colour of the grain; it increases its alkalinity; it causes greater gelatinisation of the starch granules, producing changes in texture; and it improves its nutritive qualities, releasing niacin (vitamin B3), which is to be found in the grain, but needs to be processed so as to become available for human consumption. Finally, it increases the quantity of an important amino-acid, tryptophan, which in turn enables niacin to form and makes it available for digestion (Cámara Nacional del Maíz Industrializado 2004; Bell n.d.; Mejía 2004; Sánchez and Durán 2004).

Moreover, it has been demonstrated that the nixtamal process reduces the total quantity of fumocins in tortillas by up to 80 per cent compared to the raw grains (Durham and McGraw 2001). These are micro-toxins that occur naturally in the grains and are dangerous because of their ability to cause leuco-encephalitis in horses and lung oedema in pigs, and have been associated with cases of cancer of the oesophagus in humans (Food and Agriculture Organisation 2003; Palencia *et al.* 2003). The penetration of calcium into the grain (or at least its contact with it) is interesting from a nutritional point of view, because the naturally occurring quantity of calcium in maize is very low and the nixtamal process provides a higher amount. In fact, the level of calcium in maize dough depends on the quantity of lime used in the process, the time the grain is soaked in alkaline water and the number of times it is rinsed after treatment (Dickerson 2003; Pless *et al.* 2004; Fernández *et al.* 2004).

Teosinte possibly first appeared in the River Balsas basin in south-central Mexico. It is assumed that the first interactions between this plant and humans occurred five or six thousand years ago (Salvador 2001; Benz 2001), although there are writers that speculate whether this was the result of an isolated event or a lengthy process (Salvador 2001). Despite this, other researchers suggest that there is evidence of deliberate manipulation of grains by humans from the earliest stages of Meso-American societies, as indicated by ancient sites in Tehuacán, in the Mexican state of Puebla, and Guila Naquiz and Coxcatlán in the neighbouring state of Oaxaca (Benz 2001). In these sites, there is evidence

Figure 9.1 Mexican woman with pot of boiling maize

of manipulation of a type of popcorn, perhaps the ancestor of our modern popcorn, which had between six and nine grains on each cob (Salvador 2001). This evidence is derived from studies on bird and human digestive tracts (Doebley 2003). It is also thought that this proto-maize was ground, and its flour made into some kind of flat bread (Salvador 2001).

The Importance of Lime for this 'Non-food'

From the sixteenth century onwards, maize was taken to the four corners of the earth by navigators, travellers and merchants; and was quickly installed in each place, as demonstrated by a Chinese engraving dating from 1597 (Salvador 2001). In general, in those societies where subsistence from other cereals had already been established, the consumption of maize was not immediately accepted for human consumption, primarily for cultural reasons, but the grain was used for the feeding of livestock. (One exceptional case was that of southern Italy.) It seems, however, that the plant had been exported, but not appropriately processed for its preparation and consumption, and failure to use the nixtamal process can cause, among other problems, pellagra. Owing to its natural, relatively low content of proteins and vitamins, maize outside Mexico was unable to guarantee its consumers adequate nutrition. Untreated maize, for example, is deficient in lysine and tryptophan (Salvador 2001).

Nevertheless, the point of this paper is that in ancient Mexico this defect had already been overcome thousands of years before the arrival of Europeans. Maize had long been prepared and cooked in water containing lime, in other words through the nixtamal process. Use then of this chemical non-food provided a significant increase in the quantity of essential amino acids available. The niacin present in nixtamal-processed maize increases the nutritional level of those who consume it, especially when eaten in combination with legumes; in the Mexican case, this is the bean (*Phaseolus vulgaris*).

A Food Today

In poorer regions of Mexico and Central America, for the majority of people today, the calcium absorbed nutritionally is almost entirely derived from maize which has been processed in this way. This has occurred to such an extent that this food product has become an indispensable element in human nutrition in the region. It is of basic importance for osseous growth and maintenance, as well as for heart movement, muscular movements and coagulation of the blood, among other functions (Gutiérrez *et al.* 2004).

To give an idea of the quantity of maize in the form of tortillas consumed in Mexico, it is calculated that the *per capita* consumption is 185 kilograms a year, which comes to half a kilogram daily. However, it is estimated that in rural areas, especially the poorer ones, consumption of the tortilla constitutes 70 per cent of calorific daily input, which is to say a substantial part of the nutritional needs in these areas. In fact whole maize kernels contain a calorific value equivalent to 3,578 calories per kilogram. Apart from this, people from the lower socio-economic classes, being about 50 per cent of the population (50 million people, at least), obtain 84 per cent of the protein they consume from maize and beans. This explains to a large extent why millions of Mexican peasants retain the ancestral custom of sowing maize and beans for their own consumption, rather than to sell to others. As a result, it has been calculated that 60 per cent of arable land in Mexico is used for cultivating maize (Salvador 2001).

Although nowadays the nixtamal process continues to play a part even in the industrial production of tortillas, which is the principal source of nourishment in urban areas today, people who have tried food products made from maize that have been processed in traditional ways 'know' that the proper nixtamal processing of maize and the good grinding of it is what makes it possible to produce really tasty tortillas, as well as other food products made with this type of dough (Souza 2004). However, while many ecologists and defenders of traditional food habits strive to retain organic maize, traditional processing and responsible consumption, economic and cultural development tends to indicate that there is no escaping the mass production of tortillas and other maize products. What is more, the increase in maize production through increasingly complex agricultural methods and its integration into a sophisticated production process is ensuring mass consumption of the industrial version, that in turn sustains an enormous industry, which is growing and powerful in the United States and which maintains the industrial production of this cereal worldwide. Although maize products developed by sophisticated industrial procedures still involve a form of the nixtamal process, it is unlikely that they will achieve, in popular Mexican imagination, the level of acceptance of the time-honoured methods of production.

Conclusion

For the inhabitants of ancient Mexico two food-related achievements were thus of great importance. One was the provision of sustenance, and the other was the development of the miraculous and complex process of becoming civilised. The first achievement in this was the transformation of a wild plant with hard seeds, *teosintle*, into another organism, modern maize, which depended and depends completely upon man's care in order to survive. The second was the idea of using a toxic 'non-food' alkali to convert maize into a food that was completely digestible, with greater nutritional capacity.

It is probable that there are a large number of materials in the natural environment, which in the cultural environment are not considered to be food, but which are consumed. They may or may not remain undetected, but may greatly benefit nutrition in indirect ways. Such is the case with the lime added to maize for the nixtamal process. This is a *non-food*, in the strict sense, but one that helped to initiate one of the three or four great agricultural revolutions on this planet. Still, its role in this process was not a chance one: it was the result of human intervention. The cultural influence, which both emerged from the natural and acted upon nature, is a clear historical paradigm in which a cultural perspective – essentially arbitrary – has managed to prevail over natural conditions.

If there were greater awareness among those who consume nixtamal-processed maize around the world, of the fact that they are taking in calcium hydroxide, albeit indirectly, there might be psychological reactions and perhaps many individuals would refuse to consume many of these maize products. Still, the majority continue to consume this non-food, which while it remains toxic in its isolated state, manages to make the final food products with which it combines more nutritious and productive. In the final instance, it provides the nutrition that people need and it sustains life.

Notes

1. Because of its malleable consistency, dough obtained from the *nixtamal* process is not only used to prepare tortillas, which we might call the Mexican bread, but also *tamales*, which are a thicker more elaborate preparation, as well as a wide variety of products that give rise to the dishes of regional cookery in Mexico. At the same time, by adding water and other ingredients, the same dough can be made into a number of different drinks, of which *atole* is the most notable.
2. This is a Nahuatl word from the roots *nixtli* (ash) and *tamalli* (the food referred to in the previous footnote). Strictly speaking, *nixtamal* is maize cooked in water with lime or ash, that is later ground to prepare the dough from which tortillas and tamales are made (EdeM, 1993: 5813).

References

Bell, A. (n.d.) *Nixtamalization and its Effects on the Physiochemical and Functional Properties of Maize*. (Key research skills in Bioscience F13 664), School of Food and Biosciences, The University of Reading, Reading

Benz, B. (2001) Archaeological evidence of *Teosinte* domestication from Guila Naquitz, Oaxaca, *Proceedings of the National Academy of Science* 98(4): 2104–2106

Cámara Nacional del Maíz Industrializad (CNMI) (2003), Mexico http://www.cnmaiz.org.mx/industria/index.html (December 2004)

Dickerson, G. (2003) *Nutritional Analysis of New Mexico Blue Corn and Dent Corn Kernels*, (Guide H-233, Cooperative Extension Service), College of Agriculture and Home Economics, New Mexico State University, New Mexico

Doebley, J. (2003) *The Taxonomy of Zea*, University of Wisconsin-Madison (The Doebley Lab., Department of Genetics, Laboratory of Genetics) http://www.wisc.edu/teosinte/taxonomy.htm (December 2004)

Durham, S. and McGraw, L. (2001) Cooking process reduces toxin in corn, *Brief Article Agricultural Research*, August http://www.findarticles.com/p/articles/ mi_m3741/is_8_49/ai_77704440 (December 2004)

Fernández, J., San Martín E. and Rodríguez, M. (2004) Study of calcium ion diffusion process in maize kernels during the traditional nixtamalization process. In García, J., Rodríguez, M., Gómez, C. and Cornejo, M. (eds), *Memorias del Primer Congreso Nacional de Nixtamalización. Del Maíz a la Tortilla*, Universidad Nacional Autónoma de México, Universidad Autónoma de Querétaro, Querétaro

Food and Agriculture Organisation (2005) Statistical Databases. http://faostat.fao.org/faostat/default.jsp?language=EN&version=ext&hasbulk=0 (September 2005)

Gutiérrez, E., Rojas, I., Pons, J., Muñoz, C. and Rodríguez, M. (2004) Estudio de la difusión de calcio en maíz qpm, durante el proceso de nixtamalización, en función del tiempo de reposo. In García, J., Rodríguez, M., Gómez, C. and Cornejo, M., (eds) *Memorias del Primer Congreso Nacional de Nixtamal ización. Del Maíz a la Tortilla*, Universidad Nacional Autónoma de México, Universidad Autónoma de Querétaro, Querétaro

Mejía, D. *Post-Harvest Operation Chapter XXIII: Maize*. Food and Agriculture Organization of the United Nations (FAO), Rome, Italy (Edited by AGST/FAO, HTML transfer) http://www.fao.org/inpho/content/compend/text/ch23_02.htm (Post Harvest Compendium. Information Network on Post-harvest Operations Inpho (October 2004)

Millán Fuertes, A.A., Cantarero, L., Medina, F.X., Montejano, M. and Portalatín, M-J. (2004) *Arbitrario Cultural: Racionalidad e irracionalidad del comportamiento comensal: Homenaje a Igor de Garine,* La Val de Onsera, Huesca

Palencia, E., Torres, O., Hagler, W., Meredith, F., Williams, L. and Riley, R. (2003) Total fumonisins are reduced in tortillas using the traditional nixtamalization method of Mayan communities, *Journal of Nutrition* 133(10): 3200–3203

Pless, R., Ramos, G. and González, E. (2004) Estudios a nivel de grano individual de la entrada del ión de calcio y del agua al grano de maíz en condiciones relevantes para la nixtamalización. In García, J., Rodríguez, M., Gómez, C. and Cornejo, M., (eds) *Memorias del Primer Congreso Nacional de Nixtamal ización. Del maíz a la tortilla,* Universidad Nacional Autónoma de México, Universidad Autónoma de Querétaro, Querétaro

Salvador, R. (2001) *Maíz,* Publicaciones del Programa Nacional de Etnobotánica, Chapingo, Mexico (Serie Traducciones, Nº 15)

Sánchez, S. and Durán, C. (2004) Efecto del calcio en las modificaciones de los almidones de maíz sujetos a extrusión y nixtamalización. In García, J., Rodríguez, M., Gómez, C. and Cornejo, M. (eds), *Memorias del Primer Congreso Nacional de Nixtamal Ización. Del Maíz a la Tortilla,* Universidad Nacional Autónoma de México, Universidad Autónoma de Querétaro, Querétaro

Souza, N. *El Maíz, la Milpa,* Biblioteca Virtual de la Yucataneidad, Universidad Autónoma de Yucatán http://www.uady.mx/sitios/editoria/biblioteca-virtual/ (December 2004)

Vásquez, C. (1997) *¿Cómo Viven las Plantas?,* Fondo de Cultura Económica, Mexico

10. SALT AS A 'NON-FOOD'
TO WHAT EXTENT DO GUSTATORY PERCEPTIONS DETERMINE NON-FOOD VS FOOD CHOICES?

Claude Marcel Hladik

Most physiologists believed for several years – and some of them still believe – that taste perception is limited to four or five primary taste perceptions (salty, sweet, sour, bitter and finally umami), with the implicit idea that a pure chemical such as sodium chloride does elicit what could be named a 'pure taste'. However, the hypothesis of a small number of basic tastes does not fit with recent electrophysiological records on the taste nerves of primates and on the neurones of the primary and secondary taste cortex (Rolls 2004; Scott and Plata-Salamán 2004). The taste signals transmitted by taste nerve fibres are complex and involve, in the brain, a combination of various neurones flashing simultaneously, even in the case of the response to a solution of a simple compound such as sodium chloride.

In the same vein, the present utilisation of salt in cooked foods throughout the world led several scientists to consider that salt is a basic and compulsory part of the human diet and that our ability to perceive the salty taste is an adaptive trait that evolved from our primate ancestors. Of course, the nutritional requirements for a balanced diet include sodium chloride (Randoin *et al.* 1985), as well as several other salts, most of them in a small but compulsory proportion of the global food intake. But the evolution of the primate taste system must be understood, bearing in mind the fossil records, with the help of the observations and experiments on the extant primate species, and according to adaptations to various environmental conditions (Hladik *et al.* 2003; Hladik and Pasquet 2004). Such considerations as I am going to present here, shed a new light on taste perception, and especially on salt perception that can be considered as a side effect of taste evolution.

These considerations are also related to the issue about the boundary between foods and 'non-foods' for humans. From field observations by both anthropologists and primatologists, the practice of geophagy (eating earth) has been described and often explained as a search for sodium chloride. However, the analysis of the clay or other types of earth eaten by non-human primates has shown that, in most instances, the salt or the salty taste is not a relevant parameter determining the intake. Nevertheless, clay could be a complementary part of the vegetarian diets of non-human primates because of its role in plant detoxification (Johns and Duquette 1991). In humans, further considerations (presented by other authors of this volume) show evidence of non-nutritional factors determining geophagy. Accordingly, while clay is a true part of the diet of non-human primates, it is a 'non-food' for humans, and in this context, sodium chloride could also be considered as a kind of 'non-food' for the humans, who currently consume salt in such large and nutritionally useless amounts, that the risk of cardiovascular diseases has apparently been significantly increased.

The Salty Taste and the Status of Salt for Humans

Since I am not a cultural anthropologist, my own data, related to the status of salt in various populations, are limited to a few studies for which I was working in an interdisciplinary programme together with my colleague anthropologists. These studies, however, which focussed on the variability of taste sensitivity, provided the opportunity to investigate the perception of peoples adapted to contrasting environments, such as the Inuit of Greenland and the Aka Pygmies of the equatorial rainforest.

Interestingly, salt can be perceived either as a distasteful or as a very pleasant taste, when comparing two populations living in drastically different environmental conditions, but who share a quite comparable diet including the highest proportion of animal protein observed throughout the world. For the Inuit, who make their living by hunting seals and other large marine mammals along the coast of Greenland, the preferred food is boiled meat with the lowest salt concentration (using melted ice carefully selected from freshwater icebergs). When a European explorer at the beginning of the twentieth century offered salted fish to the Inuit, they tried to eat a piece but immediately spat out the bite with surprise and disgust (Robbe 1994). By contrast, in the African rainforest, salt has been a classical gift from early explorers, and still is appreciated by Pygmies who crave salty foods. For the Aka and Baka Pygmies, besides meat of wild game, both salt and sugar are prestigious foods. They do like salt as much as all sweets, especially the honey from wild bees, which is one of the highest ranking gifts (Robbe and Hladik 1994). Thus, it is not very surprising, in this cultural context, that the same word can be used for the taste of sugar and for that of salt (Hladik 1996).

We recently had the opportunity to compare taste perceptions in another cultural context, that of the Susu of Guinea who live along the coast, where they devote a large part of their activity to extracting salt out of the salty mud of mangrove swamps, using a sophisticated technique of boiling concentrated salty solutions (Geslin 2002). The process of extraction leads to a soft white powder, designated as 'female salt' and to crystalline concretions named 'male salt'. Both female and male salts, which may contain various salts besides sodium chloride, are perceived as different in regards to their tastes and their qualities. We only carried out a few taste tests to get comments about these salty tastes and those, for example, of very acidic fruits (*Salacia senegalensis*) or of the strongly astringent, immature yellow fruits of *Phenix reclinata*, and all other known tastes. In this Susu cultural context where salt is so important, when the taste of pure salt was compared to other tastes, in order to find differences and partial similarities, it appeared to be perceived as a very strong taste as strong as that of the hot pepper.

Thus, such cultural contexts may drastically influence the perceptions and appreciation of the various compounds of foods and non-foods. However, to show how far this can determine a boundary between foods and non-foods, we have to consider some of the functional aspects of the taste responses, especially according to the activation of taste bud cells on the tongue's surface, the connections of peripheral taste nerve-fibres to brain taste-areas, and the links to other brain parts, as described by Rolls (2004).

Salt among Other Taste Stimulations

In humans, the level of taste sensitivity – allowing comparisons between individuals and population – can be assessed through simple and reliable tests (Simmen *et al.* 2004). In our research we have measured taste recognition thresholds with diluted solutions of sugar, bitter substances, organic acids and tannins, together with salt solutions, allowing us to determine what is the dilution actually perceived during blind tests. Each of the series of solutions of these purified substances is not devoted to a 'basic taste'; rather, it can be considered as a kind of probe, allowing us to find the limits of efficiency of the complex taste signals in relation to genetically determined capacities of individuals within each population.

According to the results of such measurements, we could compare the responses to salt of the Inuit to that of various groups of Pygmies, as well as to those of sub-samples of the populations of Africa, Europe and Asia. The extreme sensitivity to salt of the Inuit (Hladik *et al.* 1986) was quite remarkable as compared to that of other population sub-samples, especially those of various countries of Europe, investigated during a programme of the European Union which focussed on health and food choice (Gerber and Padilla 1998). Although most aversive responses to salt of the Inuit are obviously culturally learned, the biological peculiarity of this population in terms of taste sensitivity appears to be an adaptive trait, as it helps prevent the excessive intake of sodium which could result from drinking large quantities of water (5 to 6 litres per day), characteristic of the protein-rich diet that triggers renal elimination of the products of catabolism. If the ice collected from icebergs (melted for drinking water) had been polluted by seawater, the excess of sodium intake would have been hazardous, in terms of cardiovascular risk, hence the advantage of a trend towards a high sensitivity to sodium chloride (Robbe and Hladik 1994).

These measurements of the taste responses could also show the relationships between taste responses to various compounds as a global shaping of the taste system of *Homo sapiens* (Hladik and Pasquet 2004). Figure 10.1 shows this global result after using all individual data in a paired-sample correlation analysis: the correlation between the perception of two compounds shows a partial similarity between the signals (i.e. a part of the taste receptors and taste fibres are common to both perceptions). As regards the sugars fructose and sucrose, there is an obvious similarity shown by a short distance in this diagram. As regards sodium chloride, as well as citric acid, the distance to sugars is fairly long, but this diagram shows that a part of the receptors and fibres are common to these perceptions. Finally, for bitter substances, such as quinine, and the strongly astringent plant secondary compounds, such as the tannins, the distance to sweet perception is large, thus implying a quite different set of taste receptors.

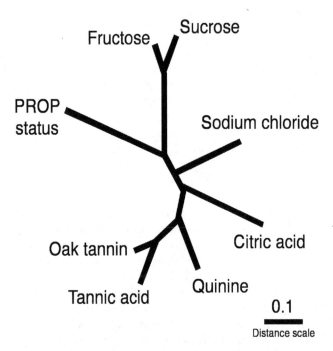

Figure 10.1 Additive tree, showing correlation among recognition taste thresholds for various compounds (including the propylthiouracile, PROP), in a total of 412 human subjects from population sub-samples of Europe, Asia and Africa

However, the intermediate place of salt perception, sharing in this way some of the taste fibres involved for sweet and bitter substances, involves a peculiar status, and may partly explain why a salty taste is considered either as pleasant or as distasteful.

The Evolutionary Background of Taste Perception

In order to understand the origin and the evolution of the ability to perceive the tastes of various compounds of the foods available in different environments, it is useful to compare the taste sensitivities of human and non-human primates, although the measurement of taste responses with lemurs, monkeys and apes necessitates a quite different technique (Simmen *et al.* 2004). It is remarkable that, using such totally different techniques (especially recording signals on the taste nerve), a global pattern of the primate taste

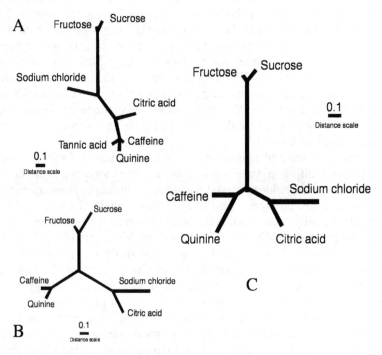

Figure 10.2 Additive trees, showing the correlation among responses of isolated taste fibres (data from Hellekant *et al.*) after stimulation with solutions of various compounds applied to the tongue of non-human primates:
A – The marmoset (*Callithrix jacchus*)
B – The rhesus macaque (*Macaca mulatta*)
C – The chimpanzee (*Pan troglodytes*)

system appears to be quite similar to that constructed with the human-responses. When constructing a tree of correlation (Figure 10.2), using the signals recorded on taste-nerve isolated fibres by Hellekant and Danilova (2004), the analogy with the previous tree constructed with correlation between the human taste thresholds, the dichotomy appears between the responses to beneficent compounds (mostly sugars) and the responses to potentially harmful compounds such as tannins and alkaloids. Some variations between primate species concern salts, especially the response to sodium chloride for which perception might be closer to that of acids, tannins and quinine, most of them potentially harmful. In most instances, if concentration of the tested solution is high enough, salt is avoided by non-human primates and perceived by humans as a bad taste.

In all primate species, including humans, the gusto-facial reflexes reflect this dichotomy of the taste system. In newborns, whereas the contact with the tongue of sugar solutions elicits relaxation of all facial muscles and facilitates swallowing, the contact with bitter compounds, such as quinine, triggers an immediate contraction and spitting (Steiner *et al.* 2001). Such reflexes, obviously adaptive, are most probably the result of the long lasting co-evolution history (during the Cenozoic Era) of the primates and the angiosperms which provide fruits with a pulp rich in sugars, in various environments, where previous selective pressures had maintained plant species which were resistant to herbivorous invertebrates and vertebrates, thanks to the presence of secondary compounds such as alkaloids and tannins (Janzen 1978). The taste thresholds for all these beneficent or potentially toxic compounds vary among primate species, in relation to the content of the plant species in the various environments (Simmen and Hladik 1993).

As regards the taste of salts, especially that of sodium chloride, the natural setting is totally different, since salt concentrations in food plants are far below the recognition thresholds of primates species, including humans. Accordingly, most primates (except some rare species living along the seashore) never experience the salty taste; thus, there is no evidence of any selective pressure allowing selection of food plants, or non-foods such as pieces of earth, according to sodium content. If we consider the data available on various natural environments, this is true for forest primates as well as for the first human populations. For instance, in the diet of a leaf-monkey, the grey langur (*Semnopithecus entellus*), the mineral content of their plant foods is enough to supply their nutritional requirements, but at a very low concentration (generally below 1 millimole in the juice of most plants). When we compared this content to that of the clay which is often ingested (especially in pieces of termite mounds), we found an even lower salt mineral content in the clay (Hladik and Gueguen 1974), showing that, in that case, geophagy was not determined by the presence of salt. Most salts nutritionally available (especially sodium chloride) are not detectable by primates at such a low concentration.

Our hypothesis was that the clay eaten by leaf-monkeys – and by most primates extensively feeding on foliage – could play a role in detoxification by its adsorbing activity. This activity of clay, especially adsorption of the tannins and other anti-feedants or toxic substances, has been experimentally demonstrated by Johns and Duquette (1991). Accordingly, the ingestion of pieces of earth rich in clay could be essential for providing a useful supplement of the diet, at least for several species of non-human primates.

Considering that there is no craving for salt, and that sodium chloride is not detectable by the primate taste system in the foodstuffs of most natural environments, we may wonder why we can actually perceive a salty taste. Obviously, the extant species of non-human primates have no experience of the taste of salt and there is no evidence of a selective pressure exerted during the whole Cenozoic Era that could have selected the primates best responding to sodium chloride. The concentration of salt eliciting a response in a lesser mouse lemur, or in a macaque are in the same range as the median thresholds that we found in various human populations (Hladik and Simmen 1996), reaching about one hundred times the concentrations observed in food plants.

However, everyone knows that salt can be licked by mammals, including primates such as *Lemur catta*, which we observed in the south of Madagascar. But this always occurs in peculiar conditions: locally it could be due to the presence of a wall with salt exudates. Why do primates actually perceive salts when the concentration is higher than in food plants?

We have indeed to consider the evolutionary history of vertebrates, which is not restricted to the relatively recent co-evolution of the Primate Order in parallel with the angiosperms that evolved the juicy fruits rich in sugars. The positive taste response to sweetness benefitted plant seed dispersal, and we are among the primates for which sweetness has been selected. However, before this evolutionary venture, the first vertebrates were fishes that had to cope with salt or freshwater (as illustrated in Figure 10.3). Some of the extant fish species (such as the minnow, *Phoxinus phoxinus*) are still able to perceive sodium chloride and other salts through their skin, which is covered with taste buds quite similar to those lining our human tongues. And they are able to detect very low concentrations (less than 1 millimole).

The taste buds responding to various substances, notably to the tannins, that evolved with the first terrestrial plant species, have been restricted to the inside of the mouth of reptiles, then birds and mammals. Complex combinations of the taste receptors allowing a response to substances more sophisticated than pure salts, led to the complex taste signals, due to some genome 'tinkering' with old genes during the various phases of vertebrate (and primate) evolution. Finally, during the period of co-evolution of primates and angiosperms, taste responses have been adapting to sugars and other more complex substances, but, of course, several taste receptors have kept their original ability to respond to salt.

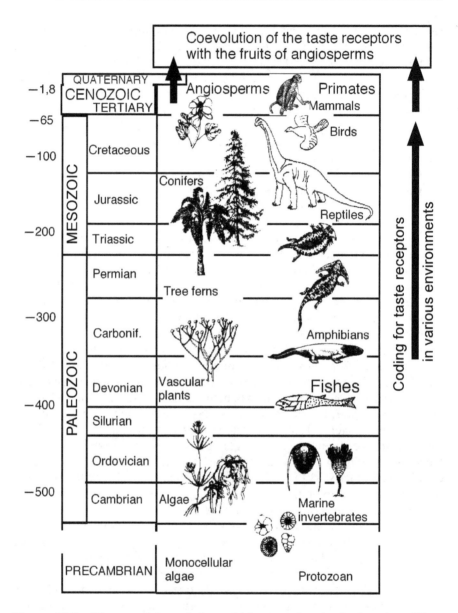

Figure 10.3 The parallel evolution of plants and animals (age in million years), showing co-evolution between the primate taste system and fruit composition of the angiosperm species during the Cenozoic Era. Primate taste receptors are derived from those of aquatic vertebrate ancestors which evolved as amphibian reptiles and mammals, with chemoreceptors being exclusively located inside the oral cavity. Genes coding for taste receptors were selected according to successive changes in the biochemical environments in which terrestrial vertebrates evolved

Is Salt a Non-food?

Tastes of astringent or bitter compounds, even though the content is low, are actually perceivable by all primates in several non-foods such as the barks consumed by the chimpanzees observed in Uganda by Krief (2004). When these non-foods are used, there is a reversal of the normal behaviour that can have a beneficial effect, due to the activity against parasites of low amounts of active compounds. This is exactly the opposite of pica, being a maladapted use. All these types of non-foods can thus be considered as a useful part of the diet.

Conversely, the utilisation of cooked salted foods is a very recent one in evolutionary terms. It was a great discovery of early *Homininae*, and humans now enjoy cooked salted foods. However, we know that we do not need so much sodium chloride in our food; it could be considered as an addiction, since, in terms of epidemiology, the present amount of salt consumption (Anonymous 2003) is almost as bad as eating some of the toxic non-foods (pica). Therefore, from this viewpoint, salt is a non-food.

References

Anonymous (2003) *Salt and Health*, Scientific Advisory Committee on Nutrition, www.sacn.gov.uk

Gerber, M. and Padilla, M. (Coord.) (1998) *Consommer Méditerranéen, une Action Préventive au Cancer,* Final Report of Contract SOC 97 200420 05F02. Brussels, CCE DG V

Geslin, P. (2002) 'L'amitié respectueuse': production de sel et préservation des mangroves de Guinée, *Bois et Forêts des Tropiques*, 273(3): 55–66

Hellekant, G. and Danilova, V. (2004) Coding of sweet and bitter taste: lessons from the common marmoset, *Callithrix jacchus, Primatologie*, 6: 47–85

Hladik, C.M. (1996) Perception des saveurs: aspects méthodologiques de l'acquisition et de l'interprétation des données. In Froment, A., Garine, I. de, Binam Bikoi, C. and Loung, J.F. (eds) *Bien Manger Et Bien Vivre. Anthropologie Alimentaire et Développement en Afrique Intertropicale: du Biologique au Social,* L'Harmattan/ORSTOM, Paris, 99–108

—— and Gueguen, L. (1974) Géophagie et nutrition minérale chez les primates sauvages, *Comptes-Rendus des Seances de l'Academie des Sciences*, série D, 279: 1393–1396

—— and Pasquet, P. (2004) Origine et evolution des perceptions gustatives chez les primates non humains et chez l'homme, *Primatologie*, 6: 193–211

—— and Simmen, B. (1996) Taste perception and feeding behavior in non-human primates and human populations, *Evolutionary Anthropology*, 5: 58–71

——, Simmen, B. and Pasquet, P. (2003) Primatological and anthropological aspects of taste perception and the evolutionary interpretation of 'basic tastes'. *Anthropologie*, 41: 9–16

Janzen, D.H. (1978) Complication in interpreting the chemical defences of trees against tropical arboreal plant-eating vertebrates. In Montgomery, G.G. (ed.) The

Ecology of Arboreal Folivores. Smithsonian Institution Press, Washington, D.C., 73–84

Johns, T. and Duquette, M. (1991) Detoxification and mineral supplementation as function of geophagy, *American Journal of Clinical Nutrition*, 53: 448–456

Krief, S. (2004) Effets prophylactiques et curatifs de plantes ingérées par les chimpanzés et rôle de la perception gustative: La notion d'"automédication" chez les chimpanzés, *Primatologie*, 6: 171–191

Randoin, L., Le Gallic, P., Dupuis, Y. and Bernardin, A. (1985) *Table de Composition des Aliments*, Editions Jacques Lanore, Paris

Robbe, B. and Hladik, C.M. (1994), Taste responses, food choices and salt perception among the Inuit of Greenland. In Thierry, B., Anderson, J.R. and Herrenschmidt, J.J. (eds) *Selected Proceedings of the XIVth Congress of the International Primatological Society*. Vol.I Editions de l'Université Louis Pasteur, Strasbourg, 151–154

Robbe, P. (1994) *Les Inuit d'Ammassalik, Chasseurs de l'Arctique*. Mémoires du Muséum National d'Histoire Naturelle, Tome 159, Ethnologie, Editions du Muséum, Paris

Rolls, E.T. (2004) Taste, olfactory, texture and temperature multimodal representations in the brain, and their relevance to the control of appetite, *Primatologie*, 6: 5–52

Scott, T.R. and Plata-Salamán, C. (2004) Les goûts des sels chez le macaque, *Macaca fascicularis*, et leurs relations avec les perceptions chez l'homme, *Primatologie*, 6: 33–45

Simmen, B. and Hladik, C.M. (1993) Perception gustative et adaptation à l'environnement nutritionnel des primates non humains et des population humaines, *Bulletins et Mémoires de la Société d'Anthropologie de Paris*, n. s. 5: 343–354

Simmen, B., Pasquet, P. and Hladik, C.M. (2004) Methods for assessing taste abilities and hedonic responses in human and non-human primates. In Macbeth, H. and MacClancy, J. (eds) *Researching Food Habits: Methods and Problems*, Berghahn Books, Oxford, 87–99

Steiner, J.E., Glaser, D., Hawilo, M.E. and Berridge, K.C. (2001) Comparative expression of hedonic impact; affective reaction to taste by human infants and other primates. *Neuroscience and Behavioral Reviews*, 25: 53–74

11. NON-FOOD FOOD DURING FAMINE
THE ATHENS FAMINE SURVIVOR PROJECT

Antonia-Leda Matalas and *Louis E. Grivetti*

Food Choice during Shortage

Food choice is determined by a number of factors that include environmental, psychobiological and cultural factors (Katz 1987; Rozin 1986). Every society adopts a varied diet based on available plant and animal food; however, many of the available edible species remain unexploited. Moreover, it is generally accepted that what species societies judge as edible is largely dependent on cultural traditions (Fieldhouse 1986). In the events where normal availability of food is disrupted, societal mechanisms are fundamentally challenged and the need for survival becomes paramount. The coping strategies employed by populations faced with regular or occasional deficits of food supply have been studied primarily within the context of developing societies (Garine and Koppert 1988; Huss-Ashmore and Katz 1989). In this context, the term 'famine foods' has been used to describe foods that serve as a food basis during critical periods of shortage, either during the pre-harvest 'hungry-months' or during acute shortages. Wild plants are among the most significant famine foods, being exploited extensively by traditional societies as an alternative source of nutrients (Grivetti 1999). The behaviour that urban populations exhibit when faced with starvation has also been described on a few occasions. In Salisbury's 1969 account of what happened during the Leningrad siege the author describes alternative sources of nourishment procured by the trapped citizens; foodstuffs were consumed that included meat from 'taboo' animals, such as dogs, cats and birds, as well as inorganic substances such as tree bark and sawdust, that were added to flour as extenders. The present study aimed to investigate further, with the aid of personal memoirs, the behaviour and food choices of an urban, 'Western' population when threatened by famine and starvation.

The Athens Famine of 1941–42

The fighting of 1940 with the Italians disrupted the autumn planting in Greece and created an acute shortage of farm workers as well as of horses, tractors, gasoline and insecticides. Railroads, highways and roads were disrupted, bridges destroyed and irrigation systems damaged. The summer of 1941 was very hot and the winter of 1941–42 exceedingly cold. In the spring of 1941 the Germans and Bulgarians invaded Greece to support the faltering Italians. The result was more privation and more refugees as the Bulgarians occupied a rich agricultural area, while the Germans used Greece as a supply base for Rommel's army in North Africa. Food shortage was acute and famine struck Greece, in the urban centres in particular. It was the worst famine that Greeks had endured since ancient times (Mazower 1993).

The inhabitants of the greater Athens area suffered the most, as they were not allowed to move freely, even within the city itself. According to (conservative) official statistics, a great increase was observed in the number of deaths in Athens and Piraeus during the winter months of 1941–42 (Skouras *et al.* 1991). The number of registered deaths in November 1941 was four times higher than the mean number of deaths for the decade 1931–40. The following month, as well as in the first three months of 1942 (January-March) the number of deaths was six times higher than the mean for the previous decade, while in April 1942 and May 1942 it was four times and three times higher, respectively.

A great number of the deaths that occurred during the famine period, however, were never registered and the real numbers are generally believed to be far more dramatic than those presented by official statistics (Hourmouzios 1943; Mazower 1993).

Study Questions and Design

The Athens famine provided an opportunity to study the methods that urban people adopt in order to cope with acute food shortage. More specifically, our study aimed to investigate:

1. techniques that Athenians used to secure food when threatened by starvation and famine; and
2. the use of *unfamiliar* foods and novel food items.

For this purpose we designed and conducted a field study among survivors of the famine, i.e. older Athenians who had been living in the city during the famine period.

Subjects and Methods

All fieldwork was conducted in 1998 among older men and women who had been residing in Athens during the entire occupation period of 1940–44. Participants were recruited from among attendants of nine Senior Citizen Centres in the central, north, south, east and west zones of the greater Athens area. Ninety-eight subjects were recruited and interviewed, with the aid of a structured-interview scheme, by two trained nutrition students. Interviews were then conducted at eight of the nine Senior Citizen Centres and were all tape-recorded. Participants were asked to provide basic demographic and social data about the famine period, including all professional activities, family status and income sources. They were asked to report all foods they were deprived of during the famine, the foods they were consuming on a daily basis and any new foods they consumed. Information was also collected on the techniques used by the respondents for securing food. Finally, participants were asked to report any health complications, such as weight loss, symptoms of nutritional deficiency (skin lesions, gum bleeding and alopecia) and any infectious diseases that they or their family members experienced. Respondents were generous in their time, willing to discuss the hardships they experienced.

Additional data were derived from the inspection of newspapers, literary works, various historical essays and photo documents to help clarify some of the information collected via the fieldwork, such as the composition and use of novel foodstuffs and food additives used during the famine.

Demographics

The mean age of the participants at the time of data collection in 1998 was 74.8 years, and was 17.8 when the famine began in 1941 (within an age range of 6 to 36 years). About two-thirds of the sample (63 people) were comprised of elderly men and one-third (35 people) of women. Approximately 40 per cent of our sample was comprised of 'youngsters' who prior to the German occupation were perhaps school children. Most of the participants were of medium and low socio-economic status and more than a third were living in households of more than six members.

Reported Health Consequences

The majority of the respondents (74.5 per cent) recalled experiencing a serious weight loss. When asked how much their body weight was reduced, most reported a loss of 6 to 10 kilograms; overall however, the reported weight losses ranged between 3 and 38 kilograms. A relatively small proportion (7.1 per cent) reported to have suffered symptoms of a nutritional deficiency, mainly skin lesions and gum bleeding, while 8.2 per cent became sick with an infectious disease, such as malaria. Finally, 13.3 per cent of the participants had at least one famine-related death in their family.

The Staple Foods of Famine

Most of the familiar staple foods were not available to the people of Athens. The vast majority (90 per cent) of the respondents stated that they could not obtain any wheat bread, 83 per cent had no access to any dairy products, while more than half were deprived of olive oil, a basic foodstuff for the Greeks. Furthermore, when asked about the frequency of their meals, 30 per cent of the participants replied that they had no regular mealtimes and ate according to food availability in their home.

Instead of wheat bread, Athenians ate the maize bread that they obtained with their ration cards. Almost all of the study participants (92 per cent) used ration cards during the famine period and received 110 grammes of maize bread daily, a quantity that supplied them with almost 200 calories. The maize bread of the famine became known as *bobota*, and as maize has been traditionally looked down upon with disregard in most Greek regions and thought to represent an animal fodder, the term *bobota* in modern Greek became a synonym for food of poor quality. Dried beans were the staple food next to maize. Bean soup was served at the food 'mess', organised with the assistance of the Red Cross during the year 1942 (Pantazidis 1987). More than half (59 per cent) of our participants were eligible for participating in the 'mess' and thus derived an extra 220 calories daily.

Quite a few food items could be obtained in the markets, but prices were exceedingly high. Nuts and raisins were among the items that Athenians purchased at dear prices (Gatopoulos n.d.) Pine nuts were the nut variety most commonly consumed by the Athenians and came from harvesting the pine trees in the proximities of the city and were put out for sale in the central market. Wild greens represented one more precious source of nutrients for many of the Athenians. Wild greens were sold at the market at outrageous prices, which according to evidence found in the newspapers of the time, were a hundred times higher compared to the prices one year earlier (Akropolis 1942). Nearly half of our respondents (42 per cent) stated that they were personally collecting wild greens in every possible location around Athens, even by the railway tracks (Table 11.1). While describing her endeavours in securing food, one elderly woman stated: '... it was great luck if I found a few nettles.'

Unusual Food Procurement Techniques

In an effort to alleviate their hunger, Athenians resorted to food procurement techniques that they previously regarded as unacceptable, such as the use of discarded food, stealing and begging. According to our results, one-fourth (26

Table 11.1 Unusual food procurement techniques

	Per cent Respondents (n=98)
Collection in an urban environment	41.8
Use of discarded food	26.0
Stealing	17.3
Begging	3.1

per cent) of the study participants regularly consumed food collected from garbage bins (Table 11.1). In fact, food leftovers were often the sole means of survival for the Athenians. In a novel written in the 1970s (Panselinos 1972: 338) we find the following extract that illustrates how children exploited the discarded food:

> ... children were looting the garbage bins outside the Athenian and the Averof, the restaurants where German soldiers were dining ... potato peels, onion peels, cabbage roots, rotten apples, bones, leftovers, and whatever else could be possibly chewed, was placed into a tin and boiled over a fire of garbage and waste papers. The leader of the group tasted the food once in a while. Then, they passed it out to be eaten.

The scene of hungry children fighting over the olive stones that German soldiers had thrown away was also common (Gatopoulos n.d.: 51). They collected and chewed them for as long as it was possible.

A substantial portion of our respondents (17.3 per cent) recalled having stolen food to sustain themselves and their families. Most of the time they stole German supplies, risking their lives; it was not uncommon for children to be shot to death while stealing a handful of raisins (Tsatsou 1965). Begging was not as widely practised, as only a small number of participants, 3.1 per cent of our sample, reported that they begged to obtain a piece of bread.

Consumption of Unfamiliar Foods

Animal Foods

Most of the study participants (80 per cent) reported that during the famine year they had consumed one or more 'food-item' for the first time. In answer to the question, 'Which food or non-food item did you eat for the first time during the famine period?' a great portion of our respondents pointed out the consumption of meat that came from unfit animals (Table 11.2). The meat of donkeys and horses was consumed by 6.1 per cent of the study participants,

Table 11.2 Deliberate consumption of unfamiliar animal foods

Type of meat	Per cent Respondents (n=98)
Tortoise	8.2
Horse	6.1
Donkey	6.1
Dog	4.1
Hedghog	1.0
Blood pudding (*matsita*)	3.0

while dog meat was deliberately eaten by 4.1 per cent. A man recalled that the day he was released from jail, hungry as he was, he ate raw the head of a dog which was given to him by a herder. The consumption of dog, horse and donkey, however, was a practice highly disapproved of by the majority of the Athenians, even those who had yielded to their hunger and ate such meats. A man witnessed: 'From time to time I purchased one of those hamburgers made of dog meat, but always threw it up afterwards ...' The disapproval of killing for consumption these taboo animals is also evident in the initiative taken by the Greek authorities to prosecute people for killing these animals. A piece of news in an Athenian newspaper (Proini 1942) describes the arrest of a citizen who killed and ate a donkey. A commonplace found among the personal memoirs we recorded was the belief that the ingestion of dog meat was the cause of health complications experienced by either themselves or their family members.

Two more unfamiliar animals were reported to have served as alternative foods during the famine: tortoise and hedgehog. Tortoise was the animal species reported most frequently among all unfamiliar animal species. Tortoise had been eaten by 8 per cent of the respondents and, though unfamiliar, it was not generally viewed as a taboo animal. A man characteristically pointed out: 'Tortoise was the best of the foods I could get.' Hedgehog, on the other hand, was mentioned only once. Finally, few of the respondents (3 per cent of our sample) ate the blood pudding (*matsita*) that was sold in the market during the famine.

It is noteworthy that no mention was recorded for consumption of either cat or insects. For the cats, Athenians believed that the Italian invaders had already eaten them all during the year that preceded the famine (Pirpassos 1977).

Plant Foods

The analysis of the personal memoirs revealed a number of previously unfamiliar or unknown plant foods, which the Athenians became acquainted with during the famine (Table 11.3). Carob was an item that played the role of a staple food for many: one out of three of the survey participants consumed

Table 11.3 Deliberate consumption of unfamiliar plant foods

Type of food	Per cent Respondents (n=98)
Carob, pods and seeds (*Seratonia siliqua*)	33.7
Broom corn (*Sorghum scoparium*)	12.2
Breadfruit (*Artocarpus insisus*)	12.2
Nettles (*Urtica dioica*)	10.2
Tree blossoms	2.0
Acorn (*Quercus*)	1.0

regularly either whole carobs, or carob seeds (in the form of flour, known as *koukoutsalevro*), or both. A good portion of the respondents (12 per cent) mentioned the use of breadfruit, an item that was imported to Greece from Africa by the Italian invaders. 'Broom corn' (*Sorghum scuparium*) was also reported by 12 per cent of the respondents. The seeds of broom corn, known for its use as an animal fodder (Vezpaly 1984), were consumed by the participants in the form of flour for making pies and a type of raisin-cake. Nettles were the most common wild green species, consumed regularly by 10 per cent of the participants, while a few recalled the use of tree blossoms and acorns.

Consumption of Inorganic, Novel, and Toxic Ingredients

Salt becomes a non-food food when taken in large quantities to suppress hunger. An elderly man described how he used it to substitute for lack of food: 'I ate a whole handful of salt, in the hope it would fill me up ... ' *Zithamine*, the greyish precipitate that is formed at the bottom of the beer barrels was also exploited as food: Athenians ate it with the scarce bread they could secure, as a butter substitute.

Food adulteration was common during the famine period. Given the fact, however, that no food inspections were effected during this period, the information we have on the substances used as adulterants are limited to personal witnesses and descriptions in the newspapers of the time. The survey respondents referred to the use of improper ingredients, such as sawdust and soapwort, by bakers, confectioners and other professionals. Many of our respondents were convinced that the maize bread of the ration was adulterated with sawdust. Furthermore, they were aware of the adulteration of desserts with soapwort, the root of the plant *Saponaria officinalis*, known in Greek as *tsoueni* (Gennadios 1959). *Saponaria* contains saponine, a substance that induces hemolysis. It is used in cloth cleaning and for the esterification of lipid materials. In food adulteration, *Saponaria* was substituted for whipping cream in confectioneries as, due to the saponine it contains, it provides good foaming properties. The use of soapwort in confections during the famine is also recorded in a newspaper issue (Proia 1942). This practice was denounced by the head of the Association of the Greek Confectioners, who on 26th April 1942, via a newspaper advertisement, asked members to report cases of desserts prepared with prohibited ingredients (Kathemerini 1942).

Conclusions

Athenians resorted to new food procurement methods and exploited a variety of previously unfamiliar foods in order to secure some nutrition. They overlooked many inhibitions and embedded food taboos. Discarded foods, taboo animals, and several improper items contributed to their poor daily regimen.

The elderly people who took part in this survey belong to the fortunate Athenians who managed to survive the famine of 1941–42. A question can be posed of whether or not these particular respondents had an advantage by being less restricted and more adventurous in their quest for food compared to others, who failed to survive. Though this question cannot be resolved in a definitive manner by the present study, we may conclude that the willingness of many Athenians to try unfamiliar and even aversive foods sustained them in the harsh time of the famine.

References

Akropolis, Issue of February 12, 1942

Fieldhouse, P. (1986), *Food and Nutrition and Customs and Culture*. Chapman and Hall, London

Garine, I. de and Koppert, G. (1988) Coping with seasonal fluctuations in food supply among savannah populations: the Massa and Mussey of Chad and Cameroon. In Garine, I. de and Harrison, G.A. (eds), *Coping with Uncertainty in Food Supply*, Clarendon Press, Oxford, 210–260

Gatopoulos, D. (undated) *The History of Occupation*, (*Istoria tis Katohis*) Vol 2, Petros Dimitrakakos A.E., Athens, 59–64

Gennadios, P. (1959) *Lexicon of Plants*, Private publication, Athens

Grivetti, L.E. (1999) Sound nutrition in the midst of poverty. The Otomi revisited. In Kelsey, M.W. and Holmes, Z.-A. (eds), *Cultural and Historical Aspects of Foods. Yesterday, Today, and Tomorrow*, Oregon State University, Corvalis, 90–98

Hourmouzios, S.L. (1943) *Starvation in Greece*, Harrison and Sons Ltd., London

Huss-Ashmore R. and Katz S. H. (eds) (1989) *African Food Systems in Crisis, Part One: Microperspectives*, Gordon and Breach, New York

Kathemerini, A good initiative (Kalin prwtovoulia), 26 April, 1942

Katz, S. H. (1987) Food and biocultural evolution: a model for the investigation of modern nutritional problems. In Johnston, F.E. (ed.) *Nutritional Anthropology*, Alan R. Liss, New York, 115–140

Mazower, M. (1993) *Inside Hitler's Greece. The Experience of Occupation, 1941–44*, Yale University Press, New York

Panslelinos, A. (1974) *Then, When we Lived (Tote pou Zousame)*, Kedros, Athens

Pantazidis, X. (1987) *History of the Greek Red Cross* Vol. 1, Editions of the Greek Red Cross, Athens

Pirpassos, C. (1977) *The Time of the Maize-Bread (Ton Kairo tis Bobotas)*, Grammata, Athens

Proia, Pre-war memories (Propolemikai anamniseis), 22 April, 1942

Proini, Arrests (Syllipseis), 9 April, 1942

Rozin, P. (1986) Psychobiological perspectives on food preferences and avoidances. In Harris, M. (ed.) *Food and Evolution*, Temple University Press, Philadelphia, 181–205

Salisbury, H.E. (1969) *The 900 Days – The Siege of Leningrad*, Harper and Row, New York

Skouras, F., Hatzidemos, A., Kaloutsis, A. and Padimetriou, G. (1991) *The Psychopathology of Hunger, Fear and Stress*, Odysseas/Triapsis Logos, Athens

Tsatsou, I. (1965) *Phylla Katoxis*, Estia, Athens

Vezpaly, I. (1984) *Les Plants Cultivees an Afrique Occidentale*, Mir, Moscow

12. EATING GARBAGE
SOCIALLY MARGINAL FOOD PROVISIONING PRACTICES

Rachel Black

Introduction

Hunger can still be observed despite the abundance of food in Western cities. Perhaps we have just chosen to turn a blind eye. Where do the hungry find food when their pockets are empty and there are few charitable institutions? What strategies do the poor and socially marginalised engage in to keep their stomachs full? Food banks and charitable (often religious) organisations (providing facilities such as soup kitchens and night shelters) are one solution. However, the idea of charity, in particular non-state charity, is often seen in a negative light: an affront to dignity. The recipients of charity often feel disempowered and humiliated for accepting handouts. To be self-sufficient one usually has to have an income or be the producer of goods that are consumed. However, the act of foraging is often overlooked in complex societies and often associated only with primitive societies.

This paper looks at the practice of foraging for food in urban refuse, focussing on the social and cultural aspects of 'eating garbage'. What is rubbish and what is good to eat are often culturally determined, but this paper will argue that what is considered edible is also often shaped by economic circumstances in the Western world. Foraging can be defined as wandering in search of food or provisions. Urban foraging, in my own definition, is the act of searching for and gathering food in the city without exchanging goods or money. This activity is an expression of resourcefulness and suggests the need to search. The act of foraging in urban environments goes against mainstream social behaviour and can even be considered antisocial behaviour. In societies where abundance reigns and consumption is essential to the functioning of the economy and the creation of identity, urban foraging can seem like an affront to cultural norms and may even be declared deviant behaviour.

I will look at two cases; one in France and one in Italy, where socially and economically marginalised people look for their next meals in what most would consider to be rubbish. More specifically, I will look at young people who do the *récupe* (foraging through market waste) in French markets and how their actions are a reaction to a society of excess. The same practice can be found in Italian market places but in this case with a very different group of actors: the elderly scavenge through heaps of market waste looking for their next meal. This is a public display of the striking poverty amongst Italy's growing population of pensioners. These foraging activities, which mainly occur after market hours, are expressions both of hunger and of human resourcefulness for provisioning in a consumer-oriented urban foodscape.[1]

There is very little literature about this type of recovery of food waste in Italy and France; this may be due to the general taboo about such topics in countries where food waste was an extreme rarity until recently. Scarcity of food during the First and Second World Wars taught an entire generation of Italians and French to be extremely frugal and efficient with food preparation (Helstosky 2004; Counihan 2004). Waste and excess concerning food are recent developments that have not yet touched parts of Southern Italy, where this type of abundance is still unknown (Teti 1999). In the case of France, food that was discarded at the end of markets was traditionally collected by charities and religious organisations, who used these 'leftovers' to make soups to feed the poor and needy (Black 2005).

Market foraging can also be compared to the North American practice of 'dumpster diving'. This is the activity of looking for foodstuffs and salvageable clothing and household items in the large rubbish bins that are usually located in back alleys in urban areas. This is a topic that has been explored by North American scholars from economic and cultural perspectives and which has been put into juxtaposition with consumer culture and a culture of abundance (Eikenberry and Smith 2005; Hopkins 2004; O'Malley 1992). In Padraig O'Malley's book on homelessness in New England, one dumpster diver, Lars Eigner, expresses his opinion on his activities: 'I live from the refuse of others. I am a scavenger. I think it is a sound and honourable niche, although if I could I would naturally prefer to live the comfortable consumer life ... ' (O'Malley 1992: 87). Eigner is particularly articulate and goes on to express his dislike for the term dumpster diving, since it suggests an athletic activity, and he also rejects the term foraging, which is something he associates with gathering foodstuffs provided by nature. He goes on to tell how he supplements his 'garbage' diet with seasonal nuts and berries that he collects. Eigner demonstrates the agency and self-sufficiency that dumpster diving gives to the people who practise this method for obtaining food. However, he is careful not to express romantic notions about this practice; Eigner still has a desire for a more comfortable lifestyle. This paper will look at how urban foraging can be motivated by hunger, rejection of wasteful social practices and as an expression of resourcefulness.

This study of urban foraging is part of a larger project on open-air markets for which I carried out two-and-a-half years of fieldwork from 2000 to 2003 in the Croix-Rousse market in Lyon, France, and the Porta Palazzo market in Turin, Italy. This research focusses on the role of markets as important sites for sociability in the increasingly 'private' social fabric of these two cities. While I was doing my fieldwork, I noticed that in both markets people would sift through the waste left at the end of the market. I started to observe these people and think about this practice. I began to notice that these foragers were going home with trolleys and bags of edible produce. At this point, I decided it was time to investigate this through participant observation and I tried foraging myself. At the end of the market, I participated in the *récupe* or talked to the foragers and the vendors cleaning up. It did not bother me sifting through half-rotten fruit and vegetables, as I had thought it might, and I did find that there was a lot of what I considered edible produce to be had. People walking down the street did not stop and look at me or make comments. The other foragers were not at all territorial or competitive, as I thought they might be. In fact, the other foragers were readily available to answer my questions; they were quite helpful and some even suggested recipes for seasonal vegetables or handed over some fruit if they felt they had too much for themselves. The people who were rather unkind were the market vendors. If I started picking through the rejected produce from their stall and they were still there packing up, they often made snide remarks about freeloading and not wanting to work to buy food. The vendors did not like the fact that they had to throw away perfectly good produce but they also knew customers were not going to buy slightly bruised or overripe produce and they resented the waste. Often they took home this produce for themselves but there was just so much. The vendors also resented the foragers who were getting their produce without paying: they saw it as an injustice, and charity seemed to be far from their minds. They did not hesitate to hurl insults and derogatory comments as well as suggesting that sexual favours be given in exchange for food. The bottom of the urban food chain is not all about sharing and can be animalistic and rough.

The *Récupe*: Youthful Foragers at the Croix-Rousse Market in Lyon

The *récupe* at the Croix-Rousse is generally practised by young people, such as students, low-income individuals, and artists. It was interesting that the homeless, who often sheltered in passageways between buildings adjacent to the market, did not participate in the *récupe*, nor were there any elderly participants. This is perhaps due to the numerous charitable organisations that offer meals to the needy, such as Restos du Coeur, and the fairly well organised social security system. Many of the foragers, whom I got to know and interview, expressed the feeling that society was wasteful. They did not want to participate in wasteful consumption: this was one of the many lifestyle choices that these people made as a conscious effort to opt out of mainstream society. The actual 'performance' of the *récupe* is also a way in which these people publicly display their lifestyle and affirm an alternative lifestyle.

'Look at this; they have thrown away a perfectly good piece of squash. I'll just cut away the black part and make soup out of it, and, look, there are even some carrots over there! What a waste!' (Cecile, 22–year-old student). Young French people doing the *récupe* at urban markets challenge the defining line between garbage and food. In *Fast Cars, Clean Bodies: Decolonization and the Reordering of French Culture* (1996) Kristin Ross underlines that the French nation went through what one could call a fetish for hygiene, which was essentially a reordering of society after the Second World War, in which hygiene was directly related to ideals of modernity. For this reason the récupe is quite remarkable, since it is an outright rejection of socially constructed hygiene standards and of supermarket culture, a bastion of hygiene and order. There is something primitive about this gathering activity that stands in direct contrast and refutation of the urban environment. The city is a place where people are not supposed to be able to collect or grow their own food; yet, urban foragers and farmers subvert these constraints that force most individuals into mainstream provisioning practices. My informants also expressed outright defiance and pushed off social criticism of their actions: 'I do not care what people say or think of the *récupe*. They are the fools who waste and throw perfectly good food away while people are starving. I am the one who is laughing: I am eating for free' (Sébastien, local artist, 31 years old). Sébastien's comment also contains an element of morality: it is wrong to waste and it is particularly immoral to waste food when there are people who are needy. Although it is a rather idealistic way to justify urban foraging, Sébastien expresses a social consciousness that many people in the Western world lack or do not consider as they throw their leftovers in the bin. At the Croix-Rousse market in Lyon, the *récupe* is a political and defiant act that rejects the waste of mainstream society. Unlike other cases of urban foraging, the *récupe* does not have much to do with hunger; it is rather an expression of resourcefulness and social identity.

The term *récupe* comes from *récuperation* (recovery). In this sense, recovering means salvaging, saving the good or useful elements from refuse or something that has been lost. By participating in the *récupe* at the market, I was learning how to see what could be salvaged and what was still good in the masses of food that were thrown away at the market each day. What is good or not to eat becomes relative and subjective. As I sifted through rotten apples and wilted lettuce leaves, I overcame my own threshold of disgust and began to see edible food mixed in with the heaps of what was deemed rubbish.

The *récupe* participants are not the only socially conscious people who are beginning to consider contemporary food distribution and the waste that it produces; they can be compared to the 'freegans' in North America.[2] Freegans are a group of people who are attempting to boycott the capitalist economic system through a number of strategies such as waste reclamation (Flanagan 2003). Recovering food that has been thrown away by supermarkets, restaurants or private individuals is one of these activities. Like the people doing the *récupe* at the Croix-Rousse market, Freegans are reconsidering what is considered edible or inedible as a way of protesting against and challenging social and economic structures that thrive on waste.

Scavenging Pensioners at the Porta Palazzo Market, Turin, Italy

At Porta Palazzo in Turin, Italy, the situation is somewhat different. The majority of people foraging are elderly. This is a reflection of the current social reality in Italy: an aging population with a low birth rate and a failing pension system. 19.4 per cent of the Italian population is over 65 and the growth rate is forecast at 0.07 per cent for 2005, compared with 0.28 per cent for the UK. The minimum pension was recently raised to 543.79 euros/month.[3] Many elderly Italians, often living on their own, find it hard to make ends meet with such a limited income. Hunger and necessity are the biggest motivations behind foraging at markets. The Porta Palazzo market draws the most foragers because of its size, the amount of waste it produces and due to the fact that the neighbourhood is home to a large number of pensioners who live in low-income housing in one of the most rundown areas of the city.

Figure 12.1   Woman scavenging for food at the Porta Palazzo market, Turin, Italy (Photograph: Alice Massario)

While conducting my research I noticed that the number of foragers increased greatly. In 2000 there were maybe two or three individuals on any given market day; by 2003 there were perhaps five or six. This is largely due to increased inflation and the massive rise in prices after the introduction of the Euro. Italians, and in particular pensioners, found that their fixed incomes were not going as far each month. Most foragers did not speak of hunger *per se* but complained of economic hardship. A few people came out after each market day and others only foraged once or twice a week to supplement the food that they bought at the market and small nearby grocery stores.

Some informants told me that they liked foraging because it gave them independence; they did not have to beg for charity; they enjoyed the activity and saw it as a form of entertainment (*divertimento*). Many expressed enjoyment in cooking and preparing their own food, another sign of independence in old age. None of the people I spoke with found it disgraceful or shameful to look for food in what most people saw as garbage and waste. Unlike in France, no one gave foragers a hard time at Porta Palazzo. In fact, a few times I saw vendors slip some produce to the elderly foragers who were searching through the rubbish behind a stall. Other vendors even left produce to be discarded in crates for foragers so they would not have to pick through the other refuse on the ground. The workers who clean the square are considerate of foragers; they do not seem to be bothered by their presence. In addition, the cleaning of the square usually occurs later in the afternoon, after the market has been officially closed for several hours. The open nature of the square (no walls or gates) allows for easy access to waste, and foragers can come and go as they please without much hurry.

Although the foragers themselves did not find their activity shameful or distasteful, market vendors and shoppers found it to be a sad comment on the state of Italian society. 'How can we let our elders pick through heaps of garbage? Where are these people's families?' (Giuseppe, 45-year-old blue-collar worker and Porta Palazzo shopper). Giuseppe's comment insinuates that it is the role of the family to look after its elders. There is no mention of state responsibility, in contrast to French informants who frequently blamed the State for poverty. In Italy, the family has largely acted as the prime social security net until the post-war period when women began to enter the workforce on mass (Saraceno 2004). In fact, the traditional structure of the Italian family has begun to crumble and the presence of elderly foragers is just one of the many signs of a new type of poverty that affects the elderly in particular.

The foragers at Porta Palazzo do not frequent the nearby soup kitchens run by religious organisations and the soup kitchen crowd, mainly immigrants and middle-aged unemployed men, do not go out to forage at the market. I started to wonder why it was exclusively the elderly who foraged? One reason could be that amongst this elderly generation of Italians, there are many who experienced hunger during the Second World War. Hunger pushes people's boundaries for defining what is edible (also see the chapter by Matalas and Grivetti, this volume). Many informants expressed their dismay and shock at the amount of waste that is produced these days. 'Today they throw away things that we never even dreamt of eating at Christmas when I was a child. You can find a feast amongst the *scarti* (scraps) here at Porta Palazzo' (68 years old, forager and retired FIAT factory worker).

Discussion

Both cases of foraging at markets in France and Italy raise questions about what is edible and what is inedible. How do individuals and groups decide what is food and non-food? It would seem that these categories may not be entirely based on gustatory factors or physical constraints (things that can make you potentially ill). The amount of waste that is produced at markets is largely due to consumer demand for aesthetically pleasing foods. If an apple is bruised or a head of lettuce is wilting, it will not be easy to sell. At the end of the market these goods are discarded even though they are perfectly edible. For example, I found several kilos of oranges on the ground one day and many of them were still edible but the fact that a few in the lot were rotten had turned them into waste. What is the logic behind this idea of contamination: if one rotten object touches an edible object, the latter somehow becomes contaminated in the minds of many shoppers and vendors. According to Rozin and Fallon (1987: 23), 'The offensive objects are contaminants; that is, if they briefly contact an acceptable food they tend to render that food unacceptable.' Also, if 'food' is thrown or placed on the ground it becomes contaminated, '*sporco*' (dirty), and is considered no longer good to eat. For most market shoppers, food that hits the ground becomes non-food, although it may be perfectly edible despite minor imperfections. Applying Mary Douglas's concept of hygiene from *Purity and Danger* (1966), we can see how dirt and refuse are associated with disorder. Food that has been discarded is no longer considered to be part of the socially constructed classification of 'edible'. This is perhaps why many find it repulsive to look for food in the rubbish; it is something that is polluted and disorderly but that is later ingested and integrated into the body. In addition, urban foraging can be seen as going against the social order because it delves into the world of 'disorder', rubbish. Repulsion as a reaction to potential contamination is not only a physical reaction; in this case, it is socially constructed and imposed. As the reaction of the vendors in the Croix-Rousse market showed, foraging through refuse was seen as a socially unacceptable practice. There it is frowned upon, mainly by market vendors, but in some cases market shoppers also expressed their disdain. Once again dirt and refuse can be associated with disorder, but in this case social disorder. By foraging, individuals are acting outside of the accepted Western political economy: they are not working to produce goods or capital with which to buy goods. Urban foraging challenges social order because getting something for nothing destabilises the culture of consumption.

I addressed the issue of dirt, pollution and rottenness with a number of my informants. Many of them told me they were not bothered by dirt because in many cases food was made edible by cooking. This fits in well with Lévi-Strauss's conception of raw and cooked and the transformation of food from nature to culture through cooking (Lévi-Strauss 1945). Pollution is avoided by cooking and food that was made rubbish is turned into food fit for human consumption through cooking. None of my informants ate any rotten food because there was so much to choose from; so, it was not necessary. Sometimes they would cut rotten bits away and salvage the edible parts of fruits and vegetables. It should be added that meat was rarely consumed. This probably greatly helped reduce the risk of food poisoning. However, I did witness people drinking eggs that were discarded because they had been broken that day and others who were given bits of cheese and other packaged foods that had reached their expiry dates. It could generally be said that there was less regard for food safety than in most provisioning scenarios.

There is little risk of eating rotten food because of the basic human reaction of disgust (Curtis and Biran 2001). Paul Rozin has explained that this reaction helps protect humans from the possible ingestion of dangerous micro-organisms in decaying food (Rozin and Fallon 1987). In addition, disgust is a response to an actual or possible threat, perhaps reminding humans of their animal origins. This response helps people avoid confronting fears of morality (Rozin *et al.* 1999). Perhaps the reactions of people viewing the *récupe* and urban foraging can be explained in this way: by expressing disgust these onlookers feel freed from further moral reflection on poverty, waste and over-abundance. However, I noticed that these different groups of people at these two markets had very different 'disgust thresholds' and this was often determined by the person's age, their socio-economic situation or their socio-political convictions. The elderly were far less disgusted by rotting food compared to middle-aged Italians. This did not hold true in France where young people used their political ideals to broaden their views on rotten food and waste.

No matter how normal my informants made it seem, urban foraging remains a socially marginalised practice. My observations led me to believe that most people do not want to see hunger or waste: they turn away from it quite naturally, perhaps as a reaction of disgust. Strangely enough, throwing away edible food *is* socially acceptable but eating garbage is not. People who do the *récupe* and who forage at the Porta Palazzo market are aware of this taboo but they consciously reject social norms and make judgments based on their hands-on experience.

Conclusion

In conclusion, by looking at urban foraging practices, we become more aware of the social realities of people who are faced with hunger, those who reject social norms and individuals who condemn wasteful consumer societies. These provisioning practices challenge us to reconsider conceptions of what is edible and inedible by looking at how these terms are socially constructed. As these practices of urban foraging show, the lines drawn between food and non-food are subjective and mutable.

Notes

1. I use the term 'foodscape' as the overall ability of food in an area or city.
2. http://freegan.info
3. European Union Statistics, http://www.europa.eu.int

References

Black, R. (2005) Feeding the city: social welfare, food supply and urban markets in Lyon, France, *Journal of the Oxford University History Society*, Vol. 3: http://users.ox.ac.uk/~jouhs/michaelmas2005/Black03.pdf

Counihan, C. (2004) *Around the Tuscan Table: Food, Family and Gender in Twentieth-Century Florence,* Routledge, New York

Curtis, V. and Biran, A. (2001) Dirt, disgust and disease: is hygiene in our genes?, *Perspectives in Biology and Medicine,* Vol. 44(1): 17–31

Douglas, M. (1966(2004)) *Purity and Danger: An Analysis of Concept of Pollution and Danger,* Routledge, London

Eikenberry, N. and Smith, C. (2005) Attitudes, beliefs and prevalence of dumpster diving as a means to obtain food by Midwestern, low-income, urban dwellers, *Agriculture and Human Values,* Vol. 22(2): 187–20

Flanagan, B. (2003,) The sell-by foragers. *The Observer.* Retrieved June 2, 2006, from http://observer.guardian.co.uk/cash/story/0,,1091014,00.html

Helstosky, C. (2004) *Garlic and Oil: Food and Politics in Italy,* Berg, Oxford

Hopkins, J. (2004) *Extreme Cuisine: The Weird and Wonderful Food People Will Eat,* Periplus Editions, Singapore

Lévi-Strauss, C. (1945(1964)) *Le Cru et le Cuit,* Librarie Plon, Paris

O'Malley, P. (1992) *Homelessness: New England and Beyond*, University of Massachusetts Press, Boston

Ross, K. (1996) *Fast Cars, Clean Bodies: Decolonization and the Reordering of French Culture,* MIT Press, Cambridge, Mass

Rozin, P., Lowery, L., Imada, S. and Haidt, J. (1999) The CAD Triad hypothesis: a mapping of three moral emotions (contempt, anger, disgust) and three moral codes (community, autonomy, divinity), *Journal of Personality and Social Psychology,* Vol.76: 574–586

Rozin, P. and Fallon, A. (1987) A perspective on disgust, *Psychological Review,* 94(1): 23–41

Rozin, P. and Vollmecke, T.A. (1986) Food likes and dislikes, *Annual Review of Nutrition,* 6: 433–456

Saraceno, C. (2004) The Italian family from the 1960s to the present, *Modern Italy,* 9(1): 47–57

Teti, V. (1999) *Il Colore del Cibo: Geografia, Mito e Realtà Dell'allimentazione Mediterranea,* Meltemi, Rome

13. EATING CAT IN THE NORTH OF SPAIN IN THE EARLY TWENTIETH CENTURY*

F. Xavier Medina

Introduction

The origin of this article was the somewhat surprising discovery I made towards the middle of the 1990s, while I was doing fieldwork for my doctoral thesis[1] on identity and Basque immigration in the city of Barcelona. I was interviewing a woman in her fifties, born in an inland area of the province of Vizcaya, near the border with the province of Álava, in the southernmost part of the Basque country.[2] We were at her home and as the conversation moved on to cookery books and old traditional recipes, she proudly showed me a very dear possession of hers: a handwritten notebook with recipes that had belonged to her mother. Among the many recipes noted down in the book, of which there were probably more than forty, one in particular caught my attention: its title was 'Cat Stew'.

Curious about the presence of such a dish in a family recipe book, I asked the woman about its history and whether she and her family had actually tried it. The answer was categorically negative: no one had ever eaten cat in her family, despite the fact that the recipe appeared in her mother's notebook. She attributed the presence of that recipe in the book to the fact that food had been scarce during the Spanish Civil War (1936–39) and the first years of the post-war period. Even so, she was not aware of having ever eaten cat meat (the very idea disgusted her, as she remarked on that occasion), neither prepared according to that recipe nor cooked in any other way, and she did not know how the recipe had ended up in the family cookery book. Yet, when asked whether she knew of any cases of other families or people who had consumed this meat, she gave a different answer: she had heard of people actually eating cat meat, especially during the war years, although she herself had not witnessed it.

In this article I will try to provide some answers to the questions arising from the situation I have just described: what food status is given to animals like cats by the peoples of Spain in their cuisine? What history is there, if any, of cat-meat consumption in modern or contemporary Spain? What might have been the reasons for its consumption, if it ever occurred?

The Cultural Construction of Animal Status

As Amado Millán (1998) points out in an engaging article, human beings establish different cultural statuses for the different members of the animal kingdom. In this sense, Millán observes, a symbolic relationship is created between man and meat consumption based on such dualities as desire/revulsion or object/subject and in relation to the role that the various animals play in the human imagination. All this is regulated by sociocultural norms that determine what *can* or *cannot* be eaten.

Thus, throughout history, certain animals have been turned into 'subjects' and their status has changed according to the possibility or impossibility of them being consumed as meat. This is also the case with the animal in question: the cat. As Millán points out, cats and other animals with a similar status, such as dogs, canaries, parrots, etc., are nowadays considered members of the family (Millán 1998: 139). As this author goes on to explain, under normal circumstances, animals that belong in one category cannot carry out functions that are typical of another category. For instance, pets cannot serve as food (Millán 1998: 141; cf. Simoons 1994: 201).

Therefore, the status of animals may vary in time and space. In addition, within these parameters, it appears that their status may vary according to the different stages of a person's life. A passage from a famous novel by Donna Leon (2003: 222–223), a Venice-based North American writer, is an illustrative example of this. The context is that of a family dinner, involving a married couple, their teenage daughter and her friend of the same age, who has been invited over for the meal. They engage in a conversation that runs as follows:[3]

While she was speaking, Michela had eaten all the food on her plate and she did not stop until Paola gave her another piece of rabbit and sauce and then she said:
'This chicken is very good, signora.'
Paola thanked her with a smile.
After dinner, Chiara and Michela went to Chiara's bedroom (...)
'Why doesn't she want to eat rabbit?' Brunetti eventually asked.
'Children's stuff, you know. They don't like eating animals that strike a sentimental chord,' explained Paola sympathetically.
'This does not prevent Chiara from eating beef,' Brunetti said.
'Or lamb,' Paola agreed.
'Why wouldn't Michela want to eat rabbit?' Brunetti asked.

'Because a rabbit is cute. It's an animal that a child from the city can see and touch, even if only in a pet shop. In order to touch other animals we must go to a farm, for this reason they don't seem so real to us.'

'Do you think this is the reason why we don't eat either cats or dogs?' asked Brunetti, 'Because they are always around us and become our friends?'

'We don't eat snakes either.' Paola observed.

'Yes, but that's because of Adam and Eve. There are a lot of people who eat them without any problem, the Chinese, for example.'

'And we eat eels,' she added (...)

'Why did you lie to her?'

'Because I like that child and didn't want to force her to eat something against her will or cause her to feel embarrassed about rejecting it.'

'Well, it tasted wonderful.' he remarked.

'Thank you (...), besides, she will get over it, or give up her scruples when she grows up.'

'And will she eat rabbit?'

'Probably.'

This dialogue created by Leon gives rise to an interesting debate about the various statuses given to different animals: cats and dogs, for instance, are not eaten in the West (although they are in other societies) because, as one of the protagonists points out, 'they are always around us and become our friends'. In other words, whenever animals are granted the status of 'friends' (or 'subjects'), they are not included in the category 'edible'.

A particular case is that of the rabbit: an animal whose status lies between that of a domestic pet and of edible meat (although in societies like those of the Mediterranean it is most commonly regarded as meat). As mentioned in the novel, to children the rabbit is 'cute'. 'It's a little animal that a child from the city can see and touch, even if only in a pet shop'. Besides, children (and adults, too), 'don't like eating animals that strike a sentimental chord'. Rabbits thus fulfil some conditions that bring them closer to the status of pets. On the one hand, they may become a pet (and may even be purchased from a pet shop) and therefore enjoy a certain proximity to humans, which removes from them the impersonal quality of edible meat. On the other hand, however, the rabbit as a herbivorous animal has been bred for consumption ever since ancient times; its meat has always been popular[4] and it is used in a wide variety of recipes, like those in Spanish, French and, as may be inferred from the dialogue above, Italian cuisine. In this sense, it fully qualifies as edible meat. This transitional status creates a difficult balance for the socially constructed identity given to the animal and is responsible, for example, for situations like that described in Leon's novel.

As far as cats are concerned, their socially constructed status places them more clearly among domestic animals, or at least in a position which is 'close' to humans.[5] Besides, cats possess characteristics that exclude them from human meat preferences. In addition to being pets and thus 'subjects' with their own names and specific identities[6] that share the privacy of the home; they are also carnivorous, a characteristic that humans do not regard as positive when it comes to the meat they consume. Moreover, they are useful because they hunt smaller animals that are considered harmful and are disliked by human beings, such as rats. The problem with cat consumption in Western Europe is, therefore, that it transgresses the cultural classification system which draws a line between what is edible and what is not. This system operates under normal circumstances; however, it may be suspended in exceptional circumstances like, for example, famine.

The Memory of Hunger

As Catalan writer and politician Ignasi Riera (1996: 429) argues in one of his articles, our childhood memories revolve around our parents' and grandparents' sayings: 'they used to say things like "you have obviously not experienced a war!" because they believed that it was a shame to waste the already scarce food during a harsh post-war period characterised by ration cards and "bribes" consisting of a simple piece of bread ... Later on, we ourselves have repeated the same to our children, telling them things such as "it's evident that you have not experienced post-war scarcity".'[7]

The same author observes that 'hunger is one of the constants' of Southern European and Mediterranean cultures in general. Over the centuries and well into the twentieth century, different generations had to fight against food scarcity and struggle for the survival of their families.

To Sell Cat as Hare

There is an old Castilian saying that goes 'to sell cat as hare', which means 'to deceive'[8] (or rather, to give somebody something which is different or less valuable than what was expected). Cat meat is certainly regarded as the meat of an animal whose status is that of a domestic pet, but this has only been true for a relatively short period of time, in historical terms. Over the centuries cat meat has not been generally considered very suitable for consumption for various reasons. Firstly, the cat is a carnivorous animal, a fact that in most Western societies prevents it, in principle, from being eaten. Secondly, the cat is considered 'useful' to humans since it consumes animals (mainly rats) that cause not only disgust, but also economic damage and illness. Only in the last two centuries, as it has gradually lost its other uses, has its status progressively shifted towards that of a pet.

Cat Recipes

Throughout history, cat meat has not been commonly used in Europe in general, or in Spain in particular; in fact, rather the opposite. This does not mean, however, that it has never been consumed. There are, for example, references to the sale of the fur of both wild and non-wild cats (Banús 1963: 107–10) as well as references to their meat. In this respect, and as far as the cuisine of the Iberian Peninsula is concerned, it is worth noting that a recipe for roast cat appears in the first cookery book known in the peninsula (one of the first in Europe), the *Llibre de coch*, by Robert [or Rupert] de Nola. It was originally written in Catalan towards the middle of the fifteenth century and was later translated into Castilian in 1525 under the title: *Libro de Guisados, manjares y potajes intitulado Libro de cocina*. The roast cat recipe (also called 'Cat as it should be eaten') was quite well known and reads as follows:

> Take a fat cat; slit its throat and once it is dead cut off its head and throw it away because it is not to be eaten, for it is said that he who eats the brains might lose his own sense and judgment.[9] Then, skin it very cleanly, open it and clean it well; wrap it in a clean linen cloth and bury it in the earth where it shall remain one day and one night; then take it out and put it on a spit; roast it over the fire and when it begins to roast baste it with good garlic and oil, and when you have finished basting it, beat it well with a green branch; this must be done until it is well roasted; basting and beating; and when it is roasted carve it as if it were rabbit or kid and put it on a large plate; and with garlic and oil make a coarse sauce (not very thick), pour it over the cat and you can eat it because it is a good dish.[10]

Cat (despite Robert de Nola's last words in the recipe) has never been a popular meat, although one can deduce that it has not always been completely ignored in the past. The recipe above is the only one known (therein lies its importance) which was published in a mediaeval cookery book[11] and was probably the only one in existence until the modern era. Antoni Riera[12] points out that, in this specific case, we are dealing with a recipe of a certain exoticism, unusual and aimed at neophiles (people who love new things) and which neophobics would never taste anyway. Likewise, its presence in a book like Nola's indicates that cat meat was not, to say the least, *repugnant* to the upper, literate, classes of this period, to which such books were addressed.

Another aspect to take into account in relation to cat-meat consumption concerns health. Robert de Nola himself specifies that the cat's head must be cut off and thrown away because 'it is not to be eaten; it is said that he who eats the brains might lose his own sense and judgment'. This instruction is significant since it does not appear in relation to any other animal mentioned in the same cookery book. A similar warning appears in French folklore at the turn of the twentieth century: in order to avoid paralysis and madness, one must 'abstain from eating the cat's head and meat'.[13] However, in certain regions of France folklore has it that the meat of black cats can cure various diseases.[14]

Further references or recipes concerning cat consumption are not found in Spain until several centuries later. At the end of the nineteenth century a poem was written by José Fernández Bremón,[15] which upon close reading can be considered a variation of de Nola's recipe. Despite the subtle humour which permeates the whole passage reproduced below, the poem is, after all, a roast cat recipe:

Choose a young cat/ it must have a good appearance,/ call the waterman/ and he will provide you with one./ Fatten it with kidneys,/ liver, sweetbread and pigeons;/ forbid everyone to scare,/ bother or punish it/ and after a year or more/ the pussycat will have a broad neck and a fine fur./ Once it is fat and shiny,/ caressing it,/ you will slit the cat's throat gently/ as you would with a brother./ Skin it skilfully,/ clean it well and air it in the wind./ Run a spit through it/ and roast it over slow fire./ Slowly and carefully/ baste it with a mixture of oil/ lemon and chopped garlic: meanwhile, turn it round/ and only when it is half roasted, for that is the right time/ will you sprinkle it with salt;/ never taking your eyes off the cat/ until its rind is brown,/ and once the animal is roasted and has been long enough over the fire/ its sharp aroma will force you to remove it and eat it;/ if you followed my advice when roasting it,/ you will laugh at hares and rabbits:/ only a fool/ to whom you are trying to sell cat as hare/ will ask to be sold hare as cat.[16]

The poem's sly humour and shocking quality are apparent; as a matter of fact this 'recipe' would rarely be taken seriously. Yet, literally speaking, we cannot ignore what the recipe (shocking or not) actually says.

As Luján (1994: 130–31) argues, until the beginning of the twentieth century, inns, taverns and popular boarding houses traditionally had a dubious reputation as far as the quality of their food was concerned. Such places were so notorious that according to Luján, it became common practice for those about to eat together to recite a popular spell before the meal: the guests, with the recently roasted meat in front of them, repeated the following words: '*Si eres cabrito, mantente frito; si eres gato, salta al plato*' (If you are kid, stay still; if you are cat, jump on the plate).[17] Obviously, this spell could never shed any light on the reputation of the tavern, but possibly reinforced the expression 'to sell cat as hare', which over time became integrated into popular Castilian language as meaning 'malicious deceit whereby something of inferior quality is passed off as something superior'.

In spite of the exoticism surrounding cat meat and the more or less well-grounded suspicions concerning the quality of food in such lower-class inns, it cannot be forgotten that cat meat is, above all, a *famine food*. During times of greatest scarcity – war and post-war periods – cat meat became a very common food, even among the lowest classes. French anthropologist Colette Mechin

(1992: 152 ff.) recorded the testimonies of French soldiers who had fought in the Second World War; these admitted to having eaten cat meat, and made observations on its culinary resemblance to rabbit. Likewise, British anthropologist Jack Goody (1995) admitted to having eaten cat, which had originally been presented to him as rabbit. A similar case can be observed in the film, *La hora de los valientes*, by Spanish director Antonio Mercero (1998), set during the Spanish Civil War. During the wedding banquet scene a great stir arises when the innkeeper is accused of having cooked and served cat meat instead of the rabbit which everyone thought they had eaten.

Much more recently, in 1996 – outside Europe but in a fully Western society – a case of cat consumption during a famine in the province of Rosario (Argentina) caused a sensation in the media. It was announced that 'in Rosario a real culinary scandal had taken place as a pet, the cat, had become food' among the poor inhabitants of Gran Rosario, in the middle of an economic and food crisis (Arribas *et al.* 2005).

As these examples suggest, the cat treads a fine line between the domestic and the culinary: as the quoted Argentine authors argue, it is inedible and even taboo in times of food abundance, but within the limits of a 'forced edibility' in times of food scarcity, when the range of foods available to the population is dramatically reduced. As a citizen of Rosario argued to the media, 'it's not denigrating to eat cat, if it keeps a child's stomach full' (quoted by Arribas *et al.* 2005).

More evidence of this 'fine line' is provided by the use of cat meat in some rites of passage or of 'virility', typical of rural Spanish societies in the first half of the twentieth century (in the Castile-Leon provinces of Soria and Zamora, for example). During one of the rituals whereby young boys move from the status of children to that of men, and in order for them to be accepted into the circle of young adults, they had to eat cat meat.[18] In this case this animal also occupies a position along a fine line, because socially it is defined as being between edible and inedible (and therefore as something that determines one's manliness).[19]

Cat Recipes in the Twentieth Century

As explained above, the cat has never been particularly appreciated for its meat, but has been consumed in Europe when necessary. Its absence from the recipes published so far does not mean that such recipes do not exist, either orally or in home cookery books which are not accessible to the public – as in the case mentioned at the beginning of this article shows. An example of the oral existence of cat recipes can be found in the Basque Country, in the province of Álava, in two cat-stew recipes from two different places in the province and by two different Basque women born at the turn of twentieth century. Such recipes were recorded by Basque cook and gastronomic writer José Castillo over the years and published in a book called *Recetas de la Cocina de las Abuelas Vascas (Álava-Navarra)* (Recipes of Basque Grandmothers) (1983).

The first one belongs to a woman from Acilu-Iruraiz (Álava) who was already ninety years old at the beginning of the 1980s. Her recipe 'Cat stew' (Castillo 1995: 13) reads as follows:

> Skin it, gut it and hang it in the open air for one night. The next day, cut it up, place the pieces into a pot and add some chopped garlic, salt, thyme, red wine, a cup of vinegar and a cup of oil. Leave the pot out in the open all night and the next day place it close to the fire and let the meat cook slowly, until it is tender.[20]

The second recipe belongs to a woman from San Román (also in Álava), aged eighty-two at the beginning of the 1980s. Her recipe called 'Cat in Sauce' (Castillo 1995: 66) runs as follows:

> Skin it, gut it and wash it well. Cut it into pieces and place these into a pot, with a couple of garlic heads, finely chopped, some thyme branches and a cup of vinegar. Leave it thus all night in the open air. The next day, add a kilo of chopped tomatoes, a spoonful of paprika, two apples, cut up, half an onion, chopped, and a cup of oil. Cook everything until the meat is tender. Afterwards sieve the sauce and pour it again over the meat in the pot. Let it simmer a little longer and it will be ready.[21]

It is immediately clear that despite the variations, these two recipes have important points in common. Firstly, marinating the meat in an aromatic vinegar mixture, which is meant to make it more tender. Secondly, the method, which differs only in a few of the ingredients used and in the presence of a sauce in the second recipe.

Unfortunately, the author of the book only transcribed the recipes, authenticating them simply by stating their exact source. His intentions did not go beyond recording and he never questioned his sources on aspects which might have been of great interest to us (or at least never published this information). For example, why these recipes exist; the period they belong to; their origin (whether they were handed-down family recipes, dishes invented by the informants themselves or heard in a local or distant area); if they had ever used them and why; how they had done so; if they had ever presented them as what they were or had 'disguised' them as rabbit or other kinds of meat, etc.

In the case of the family cookery book[22] found during my fieldwork, there is more information available, though it is 'second-hand' as it was provided by the daughter of the original owner of the book. Although we know that the author of the cookery book was our informant's mother and that the book was handed down from mother to daughter, we do not have first-hand information on the origin of the recipe, its possible use in a specific period or during the author's life, etc. All we have is our informant's comments that she had never tried this recipe and does not remember her mother having ever cooked it. As stated earlier, she expressed a strong feeling of disgust at this very idea[23] and had the impression that this recipe must have belonged to times of scarcity probably related to the Civil War. At the same time, she admitted to having heard about other cases, outside her family circle, of people who had actually consumed cat.

Conclusion

Finally, the point I would like to make is that the cat-meat recipes mentioned in this article do exist: two of them have even been published and can be accessed by the public. This brings us back to reflect on the sociocultural constructions that different European societies create in relation to the consumption of this kind of meat, as well as on the possible differences between such cultural constructions and their actual practice in specific historical moments.

Firstly, in the area studied (the Iberian Peninsula and in particular the north) cat meat has never been a popular or common meat. The sociocultural status of the cat is that of an animal belonging to the domestic environment, possessing an independent character (thus, it is close to human beings, though this does not rule out its possible consumption, especially in the rural world). It is carnivorous and useful in that it hunts small animals; furthermore, in the popular imagination cats, especially black cats, are frequently associated with evil and superstitious beliefs, a characteristic which makes them less likely candidates for consumption.

However, it can be inferred that eating cat has not been considered repugnant in all historical times (as in the Middle Ages, for instance), at least by the upper classes (and more so, we suppose, by the lower classes). To some extent it might also be seen as an 'exotic' or unusual food, which explains its presence in Robert de Nola's recipe book. Subsequently, as the above-mentioned cases indicate, despite the initial reluctance, cat meat was consumed in Europe during several periods of food scarcity. To the people involved, this represented no more than an anecdote to be told, and they commented on the resemblance between cat and rabbit meats, in some cases without even expressing disgust. The meat of this animal, as mentioned above, has also been present in some generational rites of passage, as a means to demonstrate valour and virility.

Family recipes that include cat meat are further proof of cat consumption. Little direct information can be gained about them, but it can be hypothesised that these were recipes used in times of scarcity (probably during the Civil War), which replaced other similar meats that were more difficult to access (rabbit and hare, for example). Thus, cat consumption was not frequent; it was limited to specific moments of one's life and abandoned once access to normal foods had been re-established.

From the perspective of today, the consumption of an animal like the cat may seem repulsive: more so, considering that the construction of its domestic status draws it closer to human beings; it is given a name, it is personified and becomes one more member of the family that would be impossible to consume, since this would be considered an act of 'cannibalism' towards a member of the family unit. Yet, the construction of animal status has not been the same in all ages, but has undergone various changes. Cat meat, just like any other food, is the object of a cultural statute under continuous construction, and which nowadays, more so than at other times in history, enjoys a status of 'inedibility'.

Notes

* Translated by Monica Stacconi.
1. Published some time later under the title *Vascos en Barcelona. Etnicidad y migración vasca hacia Catalunya en el siglo XX* (Medina, 2002).
2. The Autonomous Community of the Basque Country, or *Euskadi*, is a coastal community which borders France – the Basque regions of France – and whose culinary richness and variety are due to the combination of fishermen's tradition and a deep-rooted mountain culture. Euskadi is administratively divided into three provinces: Álava (or *Araba* in the Basque language), inland, and Vizcaya (Bizkaia) and Guipúzcoa (Gipuzkoa) on the coast.
3. Translator's version.
4. Rabbit meat is very popular and is widely consumed all over Spain. Rabbits are abundant and were eaten in prehistoric times. They were widely cited in classical Roman texts on Hispania, such as those by Catullus, Varro and Pliny, which reported the abundance of such animals (wild rabbits) in the wild areas of the Iberian Peninsula. Rabbit farming was practised in Roman Hispania; the culinary possibilities and fast breeding, and therefore, the ready availability of rabbit meat, were very much appreciated. Rabbit meat is best consumed during the winter, preferably when the animal is between three and nine months old. It is the base for various typical regional dishes and stews, such as braised rabbit with *allioli* (local garlic sauce), rabbit hunter-style, rabbit with garlic, etc. Rabbits share this culinary variety with hares, which are also small game, but much larger in size than rabbits and very common in the Iberian mountains. Unlike other meats, hare must be consumed fresh, soon after the animal has been killed, and the hare must be young; possibly between three and six weeks old. However, the meat keeps its quality until the animal is more or less one year old, and, in the case of female hares, up to their second year of age (cf. Medina 2005: 58).
5. Cats are regarded as domestic animals, but are often considered 'wild' animals within an urban environment. They are integrated into it to the extent that, for example, in the city of Rome they are protected as part of the city's 'biocultural' heritage. In any case, despite not having any owners, they are still very close to humans.
6. Arribas, Cattaneo and Ayerdi (2005) compare today's cat meat consumption to a kind of 'cannibalism'. 'Eating cat is *like* eating a human subject, but it is not eating a human subject' [see also Millán's observations in this respect (1998: 147) about the upward mobility of animal status and the approximation to *human nature*.]
7. Translator's version.
8. Translator's note: an equivalent expression in English could be 'to sell a pig in a poke'.
9. On the idea that eating brains (not only those of cats, but of other animals as well) may cause madness, see Ife (1999).
10. Quoted in the book edited by Cruz (1997).
11. Riera, Antoni, Chair of Mediaeval History at the University of Barcelona. (personal communication, 2 May 2005).
12. Ibid.
13. Recorded by Paul Sébillot in 1906 in his *Folklore de la France*, with reference to the Évangiles

de Quénilles (quoted in Mechin 1992: 52).

14. Noted by Westphalen in the French area of Metz and quoted in Mechin (ibid.). It is worth recalling, in this respect, the characteristics popularly attributed to cats, especially black ones, as embodiments of evil.

15. Published in 1891 in the *Almanaque de conferencias culinarias* by Ángel Muro (quoted in Luján 1994: 130–131).

16. Translator's version.

17. Translator's note: The Spanish word 'frito' is used as a pun for its double meaning of 'fried' and 'stiff like a dead body'.

18. María del Carmen García Herrero, lecturer at the University of Zaragoza. (personal communication, 9 December 2004).

19. Another source explains that cat meat has been eaten in central Aragon, as a kind of joke (M. Jesús Portalatín, EIMAH, University of Zaragoza (Personal Communication, 8 May 2005).

20. Translator's version.

21. Ibid.

22. Despite knowing the recipe in question, I have not got the family's permission to make it public. I can say, however, that its preparation shares some elements with the two recipes mentioned previously.

23. There is, in this respect, an aspect to which I am not going to refer directly in this article, but which is worth noting. It is a topic that has been dealt with more extensively elsewhere (Medina 2004: 55–62), and that concerns the relationship between researcher and informant with reference to food issues. The information that may be extracted and processed is one of the researcher's main assets when it comes to the sociocultural study of human food. Such knowledge, however, due to the very fact that it is obtained by informants, may be subjected to limitations and bias that should always be taken into account, depending on the kind of reality that the anthropologist is seeking to capture. Certain pieces of information may be concealed or transformed by the informants according to the image they wish to show to the researcher and to the kind of interaction existing between the two of them. We cannot forget that, in certain cases, conducting food research in a family unit means stepping into the private life of the people under study.

References

Arribas, V., Cattaneo, A. and Ayerdi, C. (2005) *Canibalismo y pobreza.* Universidad de Naciones Unidas, Foro Latinoamericano de Nutrición, Santiago de Chile, http://latinut.net/documentos/antropologia/articlin/Canibalismoypobreza.pdf (viewed 22 February 2005)

Banús, J.L. (1963) *El Fuero de San Sebastián*, Ayuntamiento de San Sebastián, San Sebastián

Castillo, J. (1995) *Recetas de la Cocina de las Abuelas Vascas (Álava-Navarra)*, Ttarttalo, Donostia/San Sebastián

Cruz, J. (1997) *La Cocina Mediterránea en el Inicio del Renacimiento*, La Val de Onsera, Huesca

Goody, J. (1995) *Cocina, Cuisine y Clase. Un Estudio de Sociología Comparada*, Gedisa, Barcelona

Ife, B.W. (1999) 'Mad cats and knights errant: Roberto De Nola and Don Quixote', *Journal of the Institute of Romance Studies*, 7: 49–54. *Research at King's College, London. Early Modern Spain, http://www.ems.kcl.ac.uk/content/pub/b015.html* (viewed 25 April 2005)

La hora de los valientes (1998), motion picture, Spain, A. Mercero (dir.)

Leon, D. (2003) *Malas Artes*, Seix Barral, Barcelona

Luján, N. (1994) *Como Piñones Mondados. Cuento de Cuentos de Gastronomía*, Folio, Barcelona

Mechin, C. (1992) *Bêtes à Manger. Usages Alimentaires des Français*, Presses Universitaires de Nancy, Nancy

Medina, F.X. (2002) *Vascos en Barcelona. Etnicidad y Migración Vasca Hacia Cataluña en el Siglo XX*, Eusko Jaurlaritza/Gobierno Vasco, Vitoria-Gasteiz
—— (2004) Methodological Notes on the Interaction between Researcher and Informants in the Anthropology of Food. In Macbeth, H. and MacClancy, J. (eds) *Researching Food Habits. Methods and Problems*, Berghahn Books, Oxford
—— (2005) *Food Culture in Spain*, Greenwood Press, Hartford, Connecticut
Millán, A. (1998) Acerca del Status Animal. In Ávila, R., Fournier, D. and Ruiz, M. T., (eds) *Estudios del Hombre 7: Ensayos Sobre Alimentación y Culinaria*, Guadalajara
Riera, I. (1996) Las muchas memorias del hambre. In Medina, F.X. (ed.) *La Alimentación Mediterránea. Historia, Cultura, Nutrición*, Icaria, Barcelona
Simoons, F.J. (1994) *Eat Not This flesh. Food Avoidances from Prehistory to the Present*, The University of Wisconsin Press, Madison (2nd Edition, Revised and Enlarged)

14. INSECTS: FORGOTTEN AND REDISCOVERED AS FOOD

ENTOMOPHAGY AMONG THE EIPO, HIGHLANDS OF WEST NEW GUINEA, AND IN OTHER TRADITIONAL SOCIETIES

Wulf Schiefenhövel and *Paul Blum*

Introduction

For the wider Western public, insects have become a nutritional topic only in recent years. Today fashionable restaurants in urban centres, usually of the developed world, present arthropod dishes and shops sell insects not for one's aquarium but for one's frying pan and books are written on insect and other traditional foodstuffs (e.g. May 1984). Thanks to these changes, people have become aware that insects can indeed be food, albeit usually evoking disgust reactions, which, in an interesting biocultural twist, serve as a tickling motivation to overcome (culture-specific, yet biologically grounded) aversion and rejection. Around the same time, the public has seen in TV documentaries of wildlife, etc. the interesting termite-fishing techniques employed by chimpanzees in Gombe (Goodall 1986) and other habitats. Viewers rather suddenly understood that: (a) insects are food, much sought after by our phylogenetic cousins; and (b) chimps use tools to get food otherwise difficult to come by.

William McGrew has highlighted these aspects of chimpanzee material culture (1992) and summarised (2001) primate insectivory and its significance for understanding early human diet. He gives a number of tables illustrating well the various modes and nutritional consequences of this trait so common in primates. Marcel Hladik (2002: 430) talks, again from primatological-anthropological perspectives, about 'la nécessité et du plaisir de manger des

Figure 14.1   woman selling insects

insectes' a food source which can be gathered from, as he coins it, a 'magasin
à grande surface'.

In this contribution, we will briefly explore perspectives of human
entomophagy, review its occurrence and importance for the culture of the Eipo
and their neighbours in the highlands of West New Guinea and discuss some
of the possible roles of insects as a food source in the future.

Insects as Food around the Globe

Possibly the earliest European publication on entomophagy is that of Holt
(1885) which has the suggestive title 'Why Not Eat Insects?' Netolitzky (1919)
wrote on insects as a source for food and medicine and Bodenheimer (1951)
has written a monograph on *Insects as Human Food* which is considered a
classic in this field. The topic of entomophagy became more widely known
through the activities of Gene R. De Foliart of the Department of Entomology,
University of Wisconsin-Madison who (1989, 1992), among others, published
a work-in-progress bibliography, *The Human Use of Insects as a Food Resource*
(Food-Insects Newsletter, www.food-insects.com), an exhaustive and
ambitious documentation of this subject, listing taxonomical and other details
of recent entomophagy in a large number of human societies.

In a similar vein, Hinz (2001, based on Ramos-Elorduy 1997) published the
two tables presented here as tables 14.1 and 14.2.

Table 14.1 Number of insect species eaten by humans in different continents (after Hinz 2001)

Continent	Species
Africa	524
America	507
Asia	247
Australia	86
Europe	27

Table 14.2 Number of insect species (listed by order) eaten by humans worldwide (after Hinz 2001)

Coleoptera (beetles)	336
Hymenoptera (sawflies, wasps)	307
Orthoptera (no corresponding term found)	235
Lepidoptera (butterflies and moths)	228
Homoptera (clear winged bugs)	73
Isoptera (termites)	39
Diptera (flies)	33
Odonata (dragonflies and damselflies)	20
Ephemeroptera (mayflies)	17
Trichoptera (caddice flies)	5
Neuroptera (alder flies)	4
Anoplura (sucking lice)	3
	Total 1,391

Source: Hinz 2001; corresponding English terms were taken from Grzimek 1969.

This distribution reflects the actual number of species contained in the orders (e.g. 350,000 in the *Coleoptera*, 7,000 in the *Trichoptera* and 5,500 in the *Neuroptera*) rather than nutritional preferences for certain species. A few examples may highlight the nutritional and economic importance that insects can have in certain parts of the world.

Mopane 'Worms' in Southern Africa

In southern Africa, on the shores of the Zambezi River, in southern Angola, the Kalahari and as far north as southern Malawi, the blue-green caterpillars of *Gonimbrasia belina* (*mopane* moth, *mopane* emperor moth, *phrane* in Botswana; order: *Lepidoptera*) feed on the leaves of *Colophospermum mopane*

(*mopane* tree, African ironwood, formerly called *Bauhinia mopane*) and grow to a size of 8 to 10 cm. They are harvested, usually roasted (sometimes boiled) and then dried, in which condition they can be kept for several months. Headings and Rahnema (2002) analysed dried *mopane* caterpillars and found that they contain 60.70 per cent crude protein, 16.70 per cent crude fat, and 10.72 per cent minerals. The authors conclude that these 'grubs' are a highly nutritious supplement to the diet of people indigenous to these regions. According to Hinz (2001) up to 18 kg (!) can be collected in one hour; the South African Bureau of Standards gives the figure of 1.6 million kg of dried *mopane* 'worms' being marketed by cooperatives alone; the actual figure will thus be considerably higher. In Northern Transvaal a factory cans this food exclusively. During the caterpillar season, some people rent out their *mopane* trees to collectors and get good cash returns. In recent years though, less caterpillars have been available as food because the *mopane* trees are cut down to produce charcoal (Hinz 2001). Lately, as insect food has become trendy in urban centres around the globe, *mopane* 'worms' are now also served to a well-to-do clientele in South African restaurants (Hampton www.travel.za.net).

The Giant Water Bug in Thailand

In Thailand, especially in the northeast of the country, more than eighty insect species are consumed (Hinz 2001), among them is *Lethocerus indicus* (Giant Water Bug, 6 to 8 cm long; order: *Heteroptera*). Large amounts of these bugs are ingeniously caught by using fluorescent light which attracts the bugs, so that they can be collected in small nets (Yhoung-Aree *et al.* 1997). They are sold alive in local markets but also exported, e.g. to the US and to Germany. The Thai government tries to promote *Lethocerus* and other traditional (and cheap) foods that are becoming less valued in their countries of origin, one outcome of the process of acculturation to Western standards.

Insects as Medicine

It is noteworthy that many insects are consumed for medicinal purposes. One of the better known examples is *Lytta vesicatoria* (blister beetle, Spanish fly; order: *Coleoptera*), which excretes a necrotising secretion, containing *cantharidin*, when in danger. This substance is extremely toxic for humans, but surprisingly not for many of the frogs and other predators that feed on this insect and have, apparently, developed a chemical counter-protection. Cantharidin has been used for a long time by European men (e.g. Henry IV of Germany used it as a drug, effectively producing penile erection with sometimes pathological and painful priapism). It thereby represents one of the very few aphrodisiacs with a verifiable pharmacological principle. The effect is due to a strong irritation of the urethra. It is, more recently, used as a substance (erroneously) thought to increase libido in men and women.

Netolitzky (1913, 1919a, 1919b), Arndt (1923) and Hinman (1933) drew attention to insects and other arthropods as therapeutic agents that still are, as it becomes obvious in the ethnographic literature (Meyer-Rochow 1973), well represented in many ethnic groups. They are, one could argue, perhaps the second most numerous therapeutic elements after medicinal plants.

Hinz (2001) lists various insects which were and are used in different parts of the world, e.g. in Egypt, Greece, the Roman Empire, India, Arabian countries, by Aztecs and particularly in traditional Chinese (Ding *et al.* 1997) and Japanese medicine. A large amount of insect species was orally taken or sometimes used externally as aphrodisiacs but also against a whole range of complaints and diseases, such as pain, rheumatism, circulatory problems, jaundice, measles and as a tranquiliser, tonic, corroborant and the like. Hinz (2001) points out that medically and nutritionally motivated eating of raw insects can sometimes lead to infection from various diseases, as insects can be carriers of parasites harmful for humans.

Insects as Food for the Eipo, Highland Papuans in West New Guinea

Members of an interdisciplinary project of the German Research Foundation (DFG) started fieldwork among the Eipo in the highlands of Indonesian West New Guinea (then called Irian Jaya, now Propinsi Papua) in June 1974. The Eipo are typical mountain Papuans of very short stature (male average body length less than 150 cm), but very muscularly built and having great stamina. Their language belongs to the Mek group of languages and cultures (Schiefenhövel 1976) that straddle the central cordillera and almost reach its northern and southern foothills.

During the first period of fieldwork the Eipo lived with a stone-based tool kit and had had only very limited contact with the outside world. (For English descriptions of their lives see Schiefenhövel 1991; for some aspects of their nutritional traditions see Schiefenhövel 1996; and for their language and mental concepts see Heeschen and Schiefenhövel 1983.)

The Eipo were horticulturists who grew, in swidden gardens with approximately fifteen year periods of fallow, the following crops:

- sweet potato: *Ipomoea batatas* (*kwaning*), their staple food; taro: mainly *Colocasia esculenta* (*am*), important for rituals, the classic New Guinean highland food domesticated about 9,000 years ago (Swadling 1981); a small quantity of wild yam: *Dioscorea sp.* (*ib wanye*); leafy greens: *Abelmoschus manihot* (*touwa*), *Runggia klossii* (*mula*), which provided by far the majority of protein in the diet; some vegetables of the grass family: *Saccharum edule* (*teyang*), *Setaria plicata*, *Setaria palmifolia* (both

lana); – bananas: *Musa X paradisiaca* (*kwalye*); sugar cane: *Saccharum officinarum* (*kuye*); and some other vegetable species; and
* wild food gathered in the forests and especially important as sources of fat, which was otherwise very rare, being Pandanus nuts (*Pandanus brosimos, P. conoideus*); the latter of which had ritual significance. No sodium chloride source other than that contained in their plant and animal food was available to the Eipo. They consumed, however, in a socially important ritual, specially prepared ashes of certain leaves plus a sauce of spices (*tung*) and thereby received some extra potassium chloride.

Pigs (*basam*) were bred and important for ritual feasts, but their meat did not play an important part in the Eipo diet. We estimate that per person not more than 1 g/day of pork was consumed on average; some clans were barred from eating pork because the pig was their totem animal.

Hunting, sometimes with the domesticated dog (*Canis familiaris Hallstroemi; kam*) and snaring/trapping of small marsupials, the only game in this region of the mountains above 1,600 m elevation, also played a minor role in their nutrition, but was considered central for their lives by the men.

Women and girls, in the typical gathering mode of subsistence, collected an amazing variety of small amounts of animal protein from a large number of insect, reptile and bird species. We concentrate here on arthropods, especially insects. On their way to and from the gardens their keen eyes detected leaves in which eggs of insects were laid and developing into larvae. These and all kinds of other insects and arthropods were very efficiently collected, sometimes applying special techniques. These small amounts (see Table 14.3) were put in a special little string bag (*karakna, minmin dob*) '(the place to) put something quickly', worn like a necklace. One of us (P.B.) has documented and measured the contents of these protein containers on various occasions (Blum 1978, 1979). Table 14.4 shows a list of arthropods (mostly insects) that he identified.

Table 14.3 shows the amount of animal food collected by women and girls on various days. These are *ad hoc*, on the spot samples, but they give an impression of the results of this archaic way of gathering valuable little foodstuffs. The quantities gathered are small, especially when one takes into account that in the case of adult, married women (Kilito, Sekto and Wokwokto in the sample) they were usually shared with infants. We thus estimate that an amount of perhaps 20 g of insect food per day was available for each woman and each weaned infant up to approximately five years. For children above the age of three to four years, who are becoming increasingly independent and spend much time in play groups, insect-intake is occasionally higher because they may gather this kind of food and eat it, uncooked, on the spot when they play with their peers in gardens and patches of secondary vegetation. We did not measure this kind of protein consumption, which is more typical for boys than for girls. The latter start early in their lives to be responsible for other members of their families and will often put collected small foodstuffs in their *karakna* for later consumption during the afternoon dinner in the family house.

Table 14.3 Animal food (in g) collected by Eipo women and girls (samples taken on various dates)

Collector	Age	Larvae of Dragonflies	Crickets	Larvae of beetles	Beetles	Caterpillars	Potamids	Frogs	Lizards	Birds	Rats	Total animal food	Total insect food
Furubner	14	–	–	–	20	–	–	–	–	–	–	20	20
Kilito	25	–	–	–	–	–	–	53	15	–	–	68	–
Kilito	25	–	–	7	3	–	–	–	37	–	–	47	10
Kilito	25	–	5	–	–	–	–	–	46	–	–	51	5
Wowokto	22	8	6	72	3	–	7	–	9	–	–	105	89
Sekto	30	–	–	–	–	66	–	–	–	–	–	66	66
Kwamulto	15	40	–	–	–	–	–	–	–	–	–	40	40
Tokonto	19	–	–	–	–	–	–	–	–	–	140	140	–
Engento	16	–	–	–	–	–	–	48	24	–	–	72	–
Yokner	15	–	13	8	6	–	–	–	–	80	–	107	27
Girl	–	–	–	–	–	–	–	–	20	15	–	35	–
Girl	–	–	8	16	–	–	–	–	8	–	–	32	24

Table 14.4 Insects in Eipo nutrition (after Blum 1979)

Gasteracantha sp.	spider
Tetragnathidae	long-jawed orb-weavers (spiders)
Odonata	various dragonflies + larvae
Oreaeschna sp.	dragonfly larvae
Hemicordulia	dragonfly larvae
Ensifera	bush crickets
Caelifera	short-tentacled grasshoppers
Grylloidae	crickets
Pentatomidae	shield bugs, stink bugs
Cydnidae	bugs
Lamprima adolphinae	stag beetles
Oryctes sp.	rhinoceros beetles
Passalidae	bess beetles
Curculionidae	snout beetles, weevils
Cerambicidae	long-horned wood-boring beetles
Gyrinidae	whirling beetles
Hydrophilidae	water-beetles
Scarabaeidae	cock-chafers
Cetoninae	rose-chafers
	and larvae of various other beetle species
Pentamonidae	pentamids (freshwater crabs)

As will be discussed below, it is not the total amount that counts, but the fact that essential amino acids are taken in this way. As mentioned, some insect food is eaten raw but the rest of the catch carried home in the little string bags is placed in bundles of leaves with other vegetables and then placed on the glowing fire or cooked in other ways (e.g. in bamboo containers). A most interesting aspect of Eipo culture is that it provides a 'protein niche' for the ones who need this precious food most: the women and the children. Most bird species and almost all the gathered small reptiles and insects are taboo for initiated males, i.e. from early boyhood on.

Table 14.5 gives the results of a laboratory analysis which was carried out on some of the samples received from Eipo women and girls, to whom we gave, in turn, peanuts – our usual and very much liked 'pay' – to make up for the lost food. We handed out very little salt (the common mode of reward in those days), as we were concerned about its effects on the almost saltless diet of the Eipo. The contents of lipids, protein, and trace elements are comparable to that mentioned by other authors.

Another noteworthy observation is that we did not see signs of *kwashiorkor* or other forms of malnutrition; one exception, especially among males, was iodine-deficiency goitre, quite common in the mountainous regions of the world, which resulted in sometimes enormous nodular strumae of stage IV.

Table 14.5 Analysis of some animal food collected by Eipo women and girls (Bertling Laboratory, Solingen, Germany)

Examined material	Total lipids %	Protein %	Ash %	NaCl %	Cd ppm	Pb ppm	Ca %	Cu ppm	Fe ppm	Zn ppm
Dragonfly larvae (*Oreaescha* spec.)	6.9	30.2	–	–	–	–	–	–	–	–
Crickets	–	28.5	–	–	0.27	1.8	0.11	20	–	62.8
Frogs (*Xenobatrachus giganteus*)	1.5	14.3	3.0	0.14	0.27	8.1	0.7	3.6	100.2	17.3
Lizards (*Sphenomorphus nigriventris*)	3.4	19.4	6.5	0.09	0.45	8.0	1.9	3.4	133.5	33.3
Snakes (*Styporhynchus mairii*)	2.1	21.3	5.6	traces	0.38	7.2	1.6	1.7	52.0	26.0
Birds (*Melidectes torquatus*)	3.3	21.5	4.5	0.1	0.32	6.0	1.1	3.9	108.9	27.4
Marsupials (*Pseudocheirus mayeri*)	1.7	18.9	3.2	–	0.19	–	–	5.9	88.1	32.1
Rats (*Rattus ruber*)	3.4	20.7	4.5	traces	0.36	15.6	1.2	4.5	89.6	29.6

Insects in the Diet of Cultures Adjacent to the Eipo

For lack of space we will only compare Eipo insect consumption with that in the adjacent neighbouring societies in the highlands of West New Guinea. Jan Godschalk has published a monograph on the inhabitants of the Sela Valley, another Mek group southwest of the Eipo (1993), describing their culture in detail. He writes (31–32): '... mostly women and children "collect" ... small animals, such as lizards, frogs, tadpoles, grasshoppers, beetles, beetle grubs, spiders, dragon flies, mice or rats, which are rarely eaten by males' (probably adult males). This is the same pattern as found among the Eipo.

Klaus-Friedrich Koch (1974: 41) states in his monograph on the Jalé (Jalî, Yali) near Angguruk (the western neighbours of the Mek): 'Women, occasionally in small groups, gather insects and their larvae and catch lizards, mice and frogs.' Similarly, Siegfried Zöllner (1977: 39), in his account on the religion of the same ethnic group, mentions that women collect frogs, lizards, grasshoppers, crickets, mice, ant larvae and some kind of woodworm, all of which were considered typical female food, whereas hunted game was male food.

Sibil Hylkema who has written a substantial monograph (1974) on the Nalum (Ngalum), a Mountain Ok group near Abmisibil Airstrip in West New Guinea, not far from the border with Papua New Guinea, concentrates on socio-religious aspects of this culture and does not mention insect food. Of the people near Ok Sibil Airstrip, to the south of Abmisibil, still in Mountain Ok land, Brongersma and Venema (1962: 23) write: 'The Sibillers walked across the strip in rows, picking the voracious caterpillars off the grass stems and eating them with gusto; clearly they thought them a delicacy.'

Even though some monographs on cultures in the West New Guinean Highlands do not mention insect food or name only a small number of species eaten (e.g. the classic book on the Dani, second neighbours of the Eipo to the west, by Heider, 1970: 57–58, just mentioning 'stinkbugs' in the chapter on 'Incidental Collection of Fauna'), it is most likely that entomophagy plays or at least has played a more or less prominent role in the New Guinea Highland and probably in all Melanesian societies (Meyer-Rochow 1973).

Discussion

Various authors have been puzzled by the low to very low protein intake in New Guinea Highland people and by the marked contrast to their muscular built and remarkable stamina (see Attenborough and Alpers 1992). Also very noteworthy is the small body size of these populations, among which the Eipo range at the lower end – most likely an adaptation to limited food, especially protein supply, and the rather cold climate. At night temperatures can range around 13°C in the villages and sometimes below 0°C in the high mountains, where ice and snow can be encountered when crossing the divide.

Some authors dealing with ecological and medical aspects of nutrition in Melanesian societies (e.g. Garnaut and Manning 1974) do not mention insect food at all. This is interesting as it may reflect an ethnocentric bias on the part of the ethnographers or fieldworkers from other disciplines: it is more difficult to detect things which one is not looking for or is not used to from one's own cultural background. Participant observation will reveal, however, that 'bizarre' foods are indeed collected, sometimes employing very sophisticated techniques, and actually represent a very much liked food.

As Marcel Hladik states (2002), biological mechanisms of taste perception and evaluation are guiding humans just as any other animal to important food sources. It can be assumed that because of these inbuilt preferences found in so many primate species entomophagy '... may have been a key feature of human origins' (McGrew 2001: 174) and would thus have been present in very many if not all traditionally living human populations, provided their environment held insects ready for them.

Surely insects are a very healthy food, at least as long as insecticides are (still) absent. They contain around 10 to 20 per cent fat, 30 to 60 per cent protein and are an important source of iron, copper, zinc, thiamine, riboflavin, niacin and other nutrients. The caloric value of termites and caterpillars can be very high (up to 800 kcal/3200 kJ); 50 per cent of the analysed insect species had a higher caloric value than soya beans, when the comparison was with beef, fish, corn and wheat the figures were 63 per cent, 70 per cent, 87 per cent and 95 per cent, respectively (De Foliart's online bibliography).

The importance of entomophagy may lie, as Attenborough and Alpers (1992) also state, not so much in the quantity of protein they usually supply (even though this can be substantial, see the section on *mopane* 'worms') but in their quality, i.e. as a provider of essential amino acids, especially lysine and threonine which are found in high levels in insects. At the same time, the level of lysine and threonine are low in tubers like *Manihot esculenta* (cassava), which contains, on the other hand, two further essential amino acids, methionine and cysteine (De Foliart's online bibliography). Even though taro and yams, ancient Papuan foodstuffs, were not mentioned in these accounts, this pattern of distribution of some essential amino acids in tubers with supplementary ones in insects could be particularly important in cases where the staple diet consists of tubers, as is typical for Highland New Guinea.

In the light of this, it is no longer surprising to see the Eipo and their neighbours radiate with health and muscular power (they regularly outdid both of us, despite our rather sporty backgrounds) and to understand that this source of essential amino acids was responsible for the lack of obvious malnutrition in juveniles and adults. Children, on the other hand, showed clear signs of stunting after weaning. We consider this, however, in contrast to many authors in the medical disciplines, as a non-pathological adaptation (for a discussion of this issue, see Obrist van Eeuwijk 1992).

Given the wide distribution of entomophagy in the primate species, it is most likely that the last common ancestor and the various representatives of our line of hominids which have branched off since then, have utilised insects as food as a species-typical trait (see McGrew 2001). Many ethnic groups around the world still eat insects; sometimes insects constitute vitally important sources of protein, as we have shown for the Eipo. Still, modern Western humans are, on average, quite shocked that these creatures can (and should perhaps) actually be eaten.

A number of authors (e.g. Mercer 1977; De Foliart's online bibliography; Hinz 2001) suggest that, for subsistence purposes and cash income, insects should be farmed as a veritable, ecologically sound and sustainable alternative to very inefficient meat production as for example in the case of pork and beef. Entomophagy could thus again assume its role as a classic hominid strategy to obtain valuable animal protein and fat. Another issue in this perplexing field of nutritional science is that insects often cause substantial loss of plant life, which, in turn, is important for humans either because they directly get food from this source or because of the wider impact on the ecological environment. The simple idea is these degradations could be contained by eating their agents.

Given the pronounced nutritional value of insect food, especially for women and infants, it is the more puzzling and indeed deplorable that entomophagy is disappearing from the menu of many ethnic groups in the developing world. Insects are progressively perceived as 'low status' and 'non-food' there. People have come to prefer instead canned meat and other industrially produced foods. In an interesting twist, the Western urbanised world is at the same time rediscovering this archaic hominid protein source, insects, as a luxury food.

Figure 14.2 Insects served on a plate in a restaurant

References

Arndt, W. (1923) Bemerkungen über die Rolle der Insekten im Arzneischatz der alten Kulturvölker, *Deutsche Entomologische Zeitschrift*, 1923: 553–570

Attenborough, R.D. and Alpers, M.P. (eds) (1992) *Human Biology in Papua New Guinea: The Small Cosmos*. Clarendon Press, Oxford

Blum, P. (1978) *Forschungsprojekt Zoologie II*. Sonderausstellung Steinzeithuete, 8, Museum für Volkerkunde, Abteilung Südsee, Staatliche Museen Preussicher Kulturbesitz, Berlin

—— (1979) *Untersuchungen zur Tierwelt im Leben der Eipo im zentralen Bergland von Irian Jaya (West-Neuguinea), Indonesien. Sammel-, Fang- und Jagdmethoden*, Reimer, Berlin

Bodenheimer, F.S. (1951) *Insects as Human Food: A Chapter of the Ecology of Man*, W. Junk, The Hague

Brongersma, L.D. and Venema, G.F. (1962) *To the Mountains of the Stars*, Hodder and Stoughton, London

De Foliart, G.R. (1989) The human use of insects as food and animal feed, *Bulletin of the Entomological Society of America* 35: 22–35

—— (1992) A concise summary of the general nutritional value of insects. *Crop Protection* 11: 395–399

—— (over the last three decades) *Food-Insects Newsletter* (*www.food-insects.com*) and Ongoing Research Programme

Ding, Z.M., Zhao, Y.H. and Gao, X.W. (1997) Medicinal insects in China, *Ecology of Food and Nutrition* 36: 209–220

Garnaut, R. and Manning, C.H. (1974) *Irian Jaya: The Transformation of a Melanesian Economy*, Australian National University Press, Canberra

Godschalk, J.A. (1993) *Sela Valley: An Ethnography of a Mek Society in the Eastern Highlands., Irian Jaya, Indonesia*, CIP-Gegevens Koninklijke Bibliothek, Den Haag

Goodall, J. (1986) *The Chimpanzees of Gombe. Patterns of Behavior*, Belknap Press of Harvard University Press, Cambridge, Massachusetts

Grzimek, B. (ed.) (1969) *Grzimeks Tierleben: Zweiter Band, Insekten*, Kindler, Zürich

Headings, M.E. and Rahnema, S. (2002) The nutritional value of mopane worms, Gonimbrasia belina (*Lepidoptera: Saturniidae*) for human consumption, Annual Meeting of the Ecological Society of America, Paper no. 1083

Heeschen, V. and Schiefenhövel, W. (1983) *Wörterbuch der Eipo-Sprache (Eipo Dictionary). Eipo-Deutsch-Englisch*, Reimer, Berlin

Heider, K.G. (1970) *The Dugum Dani: A Papuan Culture in the Highlands of West New Guinea*. Aldine, Chicago

Hinz, E. (2001) Über Entomophagie und ihre Bedeutung für die Humanparasitologie. *Mitteilungen der Österreichischen Gesellschaft für Tropenmedizinische Parasitologie*, 23: 1–14

Hladik, C.M. (2002) Le comportement alimentaire des primates: de la socio-ecologie au régime eclectique des hominidés, *Primatologie* 5, 412–466

Holt, V.M. (1885) *Why Not Eat Insects?* Classey, London

Hylkema, S. (1974) *Mannen In Het Draagnet. Mens- en Wereldbeeld van den Nalum (Sterrengebergte)*. Verhandelingen van het Koninklijk Instituut vor Taal-, Land- en Volkenkunde, vol. 67. Martinius Nijhoff, S'Gravenhage

Koch, K.-F. (1974) *War and Peace in Jalémo. The Management of Conflict in Highland New Guinea*, Harvard University Press, Cambridge, Massachusetts

May, R.J. (1984) *Kaikai Aniani: A Guide to Bush Foods, Markets and Culinary Arts in Papua New Guinea,* R. Brown and Associates, Bathurst

McGrew, W.C. (2001) The other faunivory: primate insectivory and early human diet. In Craig, B.S. and Brunn, H.T. (eds), *Meat-Eating and Human Evolution.* Oxford University Press, Oxford, 160–178

Mercer, C.W.L. (1977) Sustainable production of insects for food and income by New Guinean villagers, *Ecology of Food and Nutrition,* 36 (2–4): 151–157

Meyer-Rochow, V.B. (1973) Edible insects in three different ethnic groups of Papua New Guinea, *American Journal of Clinical Nutrition,* 26: 673–677

—— (1979) The diverse use of insects in traditional societies, *Ethnomedizin* 5: 287–300

Netolitzky, F. (1913) Die Volksheilmittel aus dem Insektenreich, *Pharmakologische Post* 46: 825–827

—— (1919a) Käfer als Nahrungs- und Heilmittel, *Koleopterologische Rundschau* 7: 121–129

—— (1919b) Käfer als Nahrungs- und Heilmittel, *Koleopterologische Rundschau* 8: 21–28, 47–60

Obrist van Eeuwijk, B. (1992) *Small but Strong: Cultural Context of (Mal-) Nutrition among the Northern Kwanga (East Sepik Province, Papua New Guinea).* Wepf and Co., Basle

Schiefenhövel, W. (1976) Die Eipo-Leute des Berglands von Indonesisch-Neuguinea: Kurzer Überblick über den Lebensraum und seine Menschen. Einführung zu den Eipo-Filmen des Humanethologischen Filmarchivs der Max-Planck-Gesellschaft, *Homo* 26, 4: 263–275

—— (1991) Eipo. In Hays, T.E. (ed.) *Encyclopedia of World Cultures, Volume II, Oceania,* G.K.Hall and Co, Boston, 55–59

—— (1996) We could be short of food: food and the preoccupation with food in the Eipo Society, Highlands of West-New Guinea. In González Turmo, I. and de Solis, P.R. (eds), *Antropología de la Alimentacion: Nuevos Ensayos sobre la Dieta Mediterránea,* Pinelo, Sevilla, 265–276

Swadling, P. (1981) *Papua New Guinea's Prehistory: An Introduction,* National Museum and Art Gallery in association with Gordon and Gotch, Port Moresby

Young-Aree, J., Puwastien, P. and Attig, G.A. (1997) Edible insects in Thailand: an unconventional protein source? *Ecology of Food and Nutrition,* 36: 136–149

Zöllner, S. (1977) *Lebensbaum und Schweinekult: Die Religion der Jalî im Bergland von Irian-Jaya (West-Neu-Guinea),* R. Brockhaus, Wuppertal

15. EATING SNOT
SOCIALLY UNACCEPTABLE BUT COMMON: WHY?*

María Jesús Portalatín

Introduction

This chapter is about nose-picking and putting the product into the mouth. As regards the relevance of this to the topic of the book, one should consider to what extent this non-food can be considered 'edible'. It is not socially perceived of as 'food' and it is evident that only a certain small amount is ingested, which hardly affects nutrition. Yet, all its components are digested and assimilated by the body. So, theoretically, if all that can be assimilated can be considered at one level to be 'edible', then perhaps we should include nasal mucus in this category, but it would be unusual to call it 'food'.

The act of eating snot can be studied from the perspectives of various scientific and cultural disciplines. Yet surprisingly none of the disciplines except psychology has paid much attention to this practice, which involves pulling out the secretions adhered to the mucin exuded by the nasal mucosa and introducing these into the digestive system through the mouth, rather than down the retronasal passage to the throat. That is to say, what is inhaled from the air and filtered through the mucosa is turned into something that is extracted, put into the mouth, eaten and assimilated through digestion. Until now, I have encountered little written material regarding snot eaters. Therefore, in order to learn more about this phenomenon, I resorted to questioning people who said they had eaten snot in their childhood. Here I have summarise a few angles from which it might be considered. As regards the relationship, or non-relationship, of this topic with medicine, I have not met anybody who has specifically worked on this subject. Yet I believe it to be relevant. So I can only advance a conjecture and raise questions which can be answered *a posteriori*, hoping that others may find it worth researching further.

First, I should like to explore some of the perspectives related to nasal mucus ingestion through the mouth, and the branches of knowledge which are potentially concerned with this activity.

Cultural and Social Perspectives

The first perspectives from which I shall consider this topic are social and cultural. For example, nasal mucus is socially accepted, whereas its ingestion through the mouth is not. In other words, if eating snot is a practice that exists without being accepted in public, under which category should we place it? Is it an aversion and/or a cultural prohibition?

Are there any cultures that accept nose-picking and (oral) mucus ingestion as a natural and daily practice? As far as the so-called Western or 'first world' societies are concerned, the answer seems to be negative. Eating nasal mucus is a behaviour that is not accepted in public from the moment that a child is recognised as being of responsible age by the social group s/he is integrated into.

In other words, children are allowed to pick their noses and eat the snot until they reach the age when they can understand the rules and prohibitions of their social environment. From that moment onwards, this practice is proscribed until it is removed from public behaviour, pleasurable though it may be. Thus, once a person has reached the age when social rules are understood and accepted (that is, from the moment they have the power of reasoning, which is deemed to occur around the age of seven), the spontaneous and natural action of eating nasal mucus, as related to the exploration of the individual universe and the 'I', turns into transgression, rebelliousness and provocation towards the social environment.

During childhood, in order to find a place within their social group, human beings need in the first place, to gain awareness of themselves. For this reason, it is very common for them to explore their whole anatomy and to try to access what is hidden inside through their orifices. That is, they can recognise their external phenotype, but have no information whatsoever about their internal anatomy. They frequently explore their physical identity through the senses (especially smell, touch and taste). So they habitually eat mucus and scabs; they smell secretions; they suck their own blood, etc. Furthermore, children similarly try to define their immediate environment and they commonly eat earth, detritus and any other things which arouse their curiosity and on which they lack information that might help them define or classify it. All these activities are considered part of normal behaviour, unless they persist past the age of childhood. If these consumptions do persist, they become behavioural abnormalities and turn into 'pica', a subject I return to below.

Rules of behaviour that are not written and are yet generally accepted by Western social groups prohibit this kind of spontaneous conduct, which aims at exploring the environment through taste. Doing the same through smell, however, (smelling things and people) is granted greater permissiveness, though it becomes less tolerable as the individual reaches adulthood. Oddly enough, we establish differences with respect to the status of body exudations and their related prohibitions. For example, during sexual intercourse a couple can exchange saliva and all its components, among which are a great deal of micro-organisms, including the very mucus channelled along the retronasal passage. Such an exchange becomes a sign of love or passion and marks the beginning of sexual relations. In this case, not only is the septic salivary secretion considered favourably by humans, but it is also regarded as an exclusive means of intimate communication. Likewise, in some countries, licking the tears of a beloved person (not necessarily one's sexual partner, but also children and parents) is an act which conveys sympathy and deep affection. It is appreciated by the person who secretes the tears and it produces no aversion whatsoever.

In Spain, the diverse sexual behaviours and languages of humans have recently been demythologised. In fact, in 2005, public television has been broadcasting a programme that deals forthrightly and naturally with various sexual techniques. These include the 'black kiss' (licking and/or introducing one's tongue into the partner's anal sphincter), the 'golden shower' (urinating on the body of one's partner) and, of course, oral sex. This last may also include probing the partner's nasal orifices with one's tongue. All these are considered pleasurable acts that shape a sexual relationship without giving rise to concepts of deviation or perversion.

Again, I wonder why eating one's own nasal mucus should be frowned upon. How is it different from the fluid exchanges that occur during sexual intercourse? Evidently, the dissimilarity lies in the fact that the former practice does not produce an ecstasy comparable to orgasm, although to the performer this action is as pleasurable as caressing one's skin or scalp. In addition, it is an autonomous and independent act that does not involve other people. I here quote a remark that I found on the Internet:

Ever since I have had power of reasoning I have been too weak to resist the hedonistic impulse to pick my nose. Yes! Yes! Pick my nose. Who said that hedonism is just confined to sex, evil drugs and contemplative life? If we accept that hedonism is the pleasure of abandoning oneself to the nature of the flesh, then what is more hedonistic than letting your fingers free to accomplish that sublime symbiotic action, the ecstatic mystic union, we could say, the parable of the very carnal act, caressing the nasal cavities, cleaning the dirtiness, clearing our pores and opening them up again to the ineffable pleasure of smell. Until now I have enjoyed this inclassifiable pleasure in solitude, but I cherish the idea of enticing others into this mucophagic universe of mine. Have you ever experienced the immense pleasure of a female tongue licking your little nasal hairs? Can you tell how delightful it is to find your own residue while your tongue runs along your beloved's palate and gums? In confidence, I can't! (http://usuarios.lycos.es)

The Social Image

Once again I wonder: why is the habitual practice of eating snot frowned upon and rejected by society under the argument that it is a bad and ugly thing to do? In other words, why is this practice culturally condemned?

We can gain an idea of the aversion component of this activity by analysing social communication. The expression *'comerse los mocos'* (literally, to eat one's snot) is frequently associated with enduring an unpleasant situation, restraining one's violence. The idiom *'te comeras los mocos'* (literally, you'll eat your snot), on the contrary, is interpreted as an act of humiliation. These references, which I found on the Internet, curiously originate in Latin American countries. I am not sure if this is because it is more common for these people to communicate in this way, or because Spaniards simply disregard this connotation of the expression. What is certain is that in Spain this action is associated with transgression. As an example, I will quote a childhood song that has always been found unacceptable because it causes aversion[1] (personal communication from Jorge Hernández Esteruelas):

Yo tengo un moco
Lo saco, poco a poco.
Lo redondeo,
Y lo miro con deseo.
Yo me lo como,
Y como me sabe a poco …
Volveremos, volveremos
A empezar[2]

The following is another song that I remember personally. By way of anecdote, I will say that the person who taught it to us children was a teacher, a nun from the Catholic school where I was educated until my teenage years.

Por el río Pisuerga, ¡olé!, pasa un gargajo[3]
Se juntó con un moco, ¡olé! Vaya que majo
Como el moco era verde
Y el gargajo amarillo
Los dos juntos hicieron ¡olé!
Carne membrillo[4, 5]

In this case, the reference to ingesting nasal mucus is double (through retronasal and buccal routes) and it entails the transformation into a food, quince jelly, identified as normal and delicious. Thus, this provocation and transgression provides, besides a description, an image of food preference, since quince is a dessert, which is much appreciated. Another similar reference, which originates from Mexico is:[6]

Mocos, pocos, pero a sus horas.
Mira pa arriba, come saliva
Mira pa abajo, come gargajo.[7]

Psychological and Psychiatric Perspectives

I interviewed Dr Velilla, supervisor of the children's Eating Disorders Unit at the University of Zaragoza, Spain, and he confirmed that he does not consider eating one's nasal mucus to be a manifestation of some kind of eating disorder.

The most similar pathology would be 'pica F98.3[307.52]' as classified by the Diagnostic and Statistical Manual of Mental Disorders (DSM IV 1995). The following criteria must be fulfilled in order to diagnose pica:

A the persistent eating of non-nutritive substances for a period of at least one month;

B the ingestion of substances which vary depending on the subject's age. Little children may eat paint, chalk, rope, hair and fabric. Older children may eat animal excrement, sand, insects, leaves and pebbles. Teenagers and adults may ingest earth or dung. For them, no food aversion is present. The eating of non-nutritive substances is inappropriate according to the developmental level;

C the eating behaviour is not part of a culturally sanctioned practice (DSM IV 1995: 69).

If we follow this classification, doubts arise as to whether 'snot eaters' are to be assigned a pathological category, since this particular kind of ingestion habitually continues for longer than a month, but is spasmodic. It doesn't seem relevant to mental development and attitudes to it seem to be entirely cultural. As Dr Velilla argues, this act should be regarded as a disturbance only if it becomes uncontrollable, and if it becomes associated with other kinds of psychiatric pathologies, like schizophrenia, etc. If a related pathology is not observed and the drive remains, it could be regarded as a tic, but only in the case when it is a compulsive act and permanent nose-picking causes deformation and/or wounds in the nasal cavities. Members of the Psychiatric Unit of the Faculty of Medicine of Zaragoza University, in all their long experience, have never encountered such a case (Velilla, personal communication).

Jefferson and Thompson (1995) also discussed whether nose-picking should be considered a psychiatric disorder or just a habit. From a questionnaire sent to a random sample of adults from Wisconsin in the US, 91 per cent admitted to nose-picking, although only 75 per cent thought that nearly everyone else did it. They collected further data on frequency, perforation of the nasal septum and on other bodily habits, such as fingernail-biting. From what they claimed to be the first population survey of this activity, they concluded that nose-picking was almost universal among adults, but that it should not be considered a pathological condition for most people, unless it was excessive and uncontrolled, and they presented some criteria for considering it a disorder, called 'rhinotillexomania' (Jefferson and Thompson 1995).

So, it can be concluded that eating one's mucus cannot be considered a behavioural pathology. Nevertheless, it does appear in cultural prohibitions, although these are not always clearly defined, and despite the fact that it is also an exudation that we necessarily ingest via the retronasal passage. Yet, when it happens that the ingestion path changes (from nasal into buccal) this practice becomes socially proscribed. Why?

Perspectives Related to Medicine

The upper respiratory system, which is covered by mucosa, is the place where cells secrete mucin, which acts as a first filter connecting the exterior with the interior physiological processes. One of the purposes of mucin is to phagocytise external agents, both chemical and micro-organic, through macrophagic cells. Another important function is thermal regulation, as it works as an agent mediating between external and internal temperatures. A further function is that of absorption, which is typical of mucosa in general and true of those found in the respiratory tract. Lastly, it is worth remembering that mucin plays an important role in cranial sinuses, covering their surface to muffle the sounds that penetrate them, allowing them to work as a resonance box. This volume is not the place to outline all the details of the secreting processes and paths taken by mucus, but this chapter is concerned with the mucus which has reached and dried in the nose and is then extracted with the help of the nose-picker's fingers, to be introduced thereafter into the digestive system through the mouth.

Nasal mucus is usually composed of 95 per cent water, 2 per cent glycoprotein, 1 per cent other proteins, 1 per cent inmunoglobulin, lysozyme, lactoferrin, lipids and 1 per cent inorganic salts (Table 15.1).

The high amount of water is particularly worth noting, since it may explain why in an arid climate mucus tends to dry up, causing greater discomfort in the nasal cavities. This would make it necessary to extract mucus with one's fingers, in order literally to pull it off the nasal mucosa, rather than expelling it through

Table 15.1 The usual composition of nasal mucus

- 95% water
- 2% glycoprotein
- 1% other proteins
- 1%immunoglobulin
- traces of lactoferrin
- traces of lysozyme
- traces of lipids

forced expiration. In arid areas one might therefore expect a greater frequency of manual extractions and oral ingestion of the exudations, but this is yet to be shown, because, as far as I know, no data have been collected on these matters.

A more likely area for medical concern would be the risk of infection through the delicate nasal membranes or even directly into the blood supply to the nose. There are some references to this in the literature about rhinotillexomania, as a psychiatric condition. However, in view of the physiological significance of nasal mucus and the vulnerability of underlying nasal membranes, it is interesting that a brief search in the electronic database, Medline, revealed a negligible number of published articles outside of the journals of psychology or psychiatry. A less specialist search via Google, did reveal an article entitled: 'Top doc backs picking your nose and eating it.'[8] The article continues:

> Picking your nose and eating it is one of the best ways to stay healthy, according to a top Austrian doctor. Innsbruck-based lung specialist Prof. Dr Friedrich Bischinger said people who pick their noses with their fingers were healthy, happier and probably better in tune with their bodies. He says society should adopt a new approach to nose-picking and encourage children to take it up. Dr Bischinger said: 'With the finger you can get to places you just can't reach with a handkerchief, keeping your nose far cleaner. ... and eating the dry remains of what you pull out is a great way of strengthening the body's immune system. Medically it makes great sense and is a perfectly natural thing to do. In terms of the immune system the nose is a filter in which a great deal of bacteria are collected, and when this mixture arrives in the intestines it works just like a medicine. Modern medicine is constantly trying to do the same thing through far more complicated methods, people who pick their nose and eat it get a natural boost to their immune system for free.'

Again using Medline, no medical journal source for this article was found, which may reflect either on its reliability or its acceptability for refereed journals, but in view of the suggestions made in it, it seemed worth obtaining some perspectives from immunology on this subject.

Perspectives from Immunology

An Immunological Act?:[9] Auto-vaccination?

It is my intention to advance the hypothesis that nasal mucus ingestion might boost the immune system of the person who eats it, working as a kind of 'self-vaccination'. In vertebrate animals there are two kinds of protective mechanisms. Firstly, natural and non- specific, including:

- cutaneous/mucal barriers with their secretions;
- molecular elements (CRP, complement, interferon and other cytotoxins);

- cellular elements: phagocytes, denditric cells and natural killer cells (NK), able to capture and process foreign substances so that they may be recognised by the specific immune system.

Secondly, acquired or specific protective mechanism, based on the lymphocytes produced in the bone marrow and thymus gland. During their development they are able to acquire specific receptors for the millions of substances, for example the antigens (Ag) which exist in the environment. As nasal mucus passes into the mouth (digestive path), it travels around the non-encapsulated oropharyngeal immune system, that is, tonsils, nasopharyngeal adenoids and Peyer's patches in the small intestine. The result of mucus ingestion is a prolonged contact through the buccal mucosa, which stimulates B-lymphocytes, mostly providing A-immunoglobulins.

Furthermore, by eating mucus, after repeated contact 'memory cells' are more intensely stimulated and reinforced, which increases their effectiveness in recognising antigens; as a result, the immune response is improved and becomes increasingly faster. As a matter of fact nasal mucus facilitates contact with weakened or dead micro-organisms, increasing their exposure to a greater portion of the mucosae (nasal, oropharyngeal and digestive ones) and, consequently, of the non-specific and specific immune system.

A Small Independent Survey

As I have already observed, I found hardly any articles written about 'snot eaters'. So I resorted to asking children and adults directly about this 'transgressional' behaviour. I questioned ten adults, aged twenty to sixty, five men and five women. When asked, 'Do you pick your nose and eat the snot?' all the adults emphatically answered that they did not, showing aversion at the idea. However, when asked, 'Do you kiss your partner introducing your tongue into his/her mouth?' the answer was absolutely affirmative and it was accompanied by positive remarks. Clearly these responses relate to what are considered to be appropriate answers in relation to socially acceptable norms. Isn't consuming another person's saliva more disgusting than picking one's own nose and eating the snot? I wonder.

When I asked, 'When you were a child, did you pick your nose and eat the snot?' some of them answered that this was so, whereas others again gave a firmly negative answer, despite the fact that the interviewer remembered them doing so in their childhood. Apparently, they preferred to forget about this spontaneous act due to their assumption of social disapproval. Those who had answered affirmatively (mainly those who could not deny the evidence, because of a close bond with the interviewer) were asked, 'Why did you do it?' the replies varied and they are summarised below:

- *Because it was something mine* – a comment which coincides with acquiring knowledge of the 'I', typical of childhood.

- *Because I liked it* – at this point I asked them to be more specific and they said they liked the texture of snot and the way it changed from solid into oily inside the mouth. They also commented on its slightly salty taste, adding that it was similar to that of dry blood scabs.
- Other informants answered that it felt like a relief to leave their nose clean in order to breathe more freely, and since the exudation was solid, they considered it could be eaten.
- Lastly, someone answered that they did not realise they were doing it, thus justifying their 'bad action'.

It is worth observing that the answers given by men were more spontaneous, though not necessarily more sincere. The idea of transgressing social rules was endorsed by remarks like: 'I liked keeping them in a box to observe the various shapes they had.' Likewise, someone observed that they stuck the snot they did not eat on furniture, by way of rebellion against the strict family ban on pulling it out of their nose and eating it.

It is also worth noting that the mucus produced in a highly polluted environment, which contains particles typical of urban contamination, factories, etc., is not to these people's liking. Therefore, a new parameter of chemical purity (though not of micro-organisms) must be added. These snot eaters insist that when they have undergone a respiratory infection and nasal secretions turn more fluid acquiring a greenish-yellowish tone, they are eliminated by sneezing or blowing the nose. This reinforces the idea that they only eat the mucus that naturally dries up in the nose, which is considered, I must emphasise, 'normal', whereas they discard secretions with different characteristics produced by chemical or infectious substances.

As far as the children are concerned, I questioned five boys and five girls aged five to twelve. The younger ones always answered that they picked their nose and ate it because they liked it, without discerning whether the pleasure of ingestion was produced by the taste or by the self-cleaning act. The older children showed a tendency to speak in terms of the past, and if their answer was that eating their snot was a natural act, because it belonged to them, I asked them a further question: 'Faeces and urine are also your own, did you use to eat/drink them, too?' The answer was categorically negative and it was accompanied by gestures of aversion. All of them agreed that they did not like the smell, whereas snot had no scent and it had a pleasant flavour and texture. It should not be forgotten that among human preferences concerning food texture, crunchiness is highly significant, and as regards flavours, salty and sweet tastes are the favourite ones. It so happens that dry nasal exudations possess both characteristics, as well as proteins and traces of lipids.

Another parameter to take into account is the climate affecting the areas where the interviewees live. Zaragoza and its province have a dry climate, with a low environmental humidity rate, which causes the mucosa to dry up. For this reason, mucus, besides being dry, becomes a nuisance in the nasal cavity.

Both groups were also asked whether they became ill and whether this happened often in the period when they used to eat their snot. All answered that they regarded themselves as being healthy. Of course, their answers cannot be considered valid data, but it is an interesting factor to be taken into account. These began to ask if a link had been established between health and snot eating. Some of them even asked: 'It is good to eat snot, then?' By 'good' they clearly meant 'healthy'.

Conclusion

After this exposition, I must ask once more: 'Is eating snot good or bad? Is it socially bad, but good healthwise?' It is interesting that it has received so little attention outside of psychology.

Notes

*   Translated by Monica Stacconi.
1. Oral source: Jorge Hernández Esteruelas.
2. Translator's version:
    > I have some snot
    > I take it out slowly.
    > I round it,
    > I look at it with desire.
    > And I eat it,
    > And since I have not enough ...
    > We'll start, all over
    > All over Again.
3. *Gargajo*, according to the Dictionary of the Spanish Royal Academy, is an indelicate connotation of phlegm or voluminous spit. That is, the mucus coming from the retronasal passage, which after a contraction of the diaphragm is orally expelled.
4. Sweet preparation made by cooking quinces, with a high concentration of sugar.
5. Translator's version:
    > By the River Pisuerga, ole! A gob was passing
    > It joined a snot, ole! How nice
    > As the snot was green
    > And the gob was yellow
    > Together they made, ole!
    > Quince jelly
6. Source: Rodolfo Fernández, Guadalajara (Mexico).
7. Translator's versión:
    > Snot, just a little, and in due time.
    > Look upwards, eat saliva
    > Look downwards, eat gobs.
8. http://www.ananova.com/news/story
9. Taken from notes on the immune system, written by my colleague, Dr Enrique Martínez Pedraja, who works for the Aragonese Health Service.

References

DSM IV (1995) *Manual Diagnóstico y Estadístico de los Trastornos Mentales: Brevaio.* López-Ibor Aliño, J.J. (Director general de la edición española) Masson, Barcelona

Farreras and Rozman (2000) *Medicina Interna,* Ediciones Harcourt, Madrid

Jefferson, J.W. and Thompson, T.D. (1995) Rhinotillexomania: psychiatric disorder or habit?, *Journal of Clinical Psychiatry,* 56(2): 56–59

16. CANNIBALISM
NO MYTH, BUT WHY SO RARE?

Helen Macbeth, *Wulf Schiefenhövel* and *Paul Collinson*

Introduction

Human flesh cannot be considered a material frequently consumed by people today. Autophagia, consumption of components of one's own physiology, such as nasal mucus, (Portalatín, this volume), can be extended to include any consumption of scabs, fingernails, dried skin, blood, etc. Such ingestion, even if hidden from public view, is common and would not be considered cannibalism. The consumption of excreta, usually recorded in terms of psychological abnormality (Cantarero, this volume), would also not be considered cannibalism. This chapter is about cannibalism defined as consumption of the flesh and other tissue of another individual of the same species. Holding an anomalous situation between consumption of excreta and cannibalism is placentophagia; while the cells of the placenta are grown from the foetus, the placenta is expelled by the mother. Ethnographic information exists about various rituals concerning the placenta, but apart from small pieces in some ethnomedicine, there was no trustworthy record of placentophagia, until recently. In association with the natural childbirth movement from the 1960s placentophagia was taken up in some 'Western' societies, especially in California, on the basis that it was 'natural', as 'all' mammalian species eat the placenta. The problem with this is that not all mammals are regularly placentophagous and our closest primate relatives also are not placentophagous (Menges 2007). Even the advantage of placental opioid enhancing factor in placentophagia is only relevant to multiparous births, as it reduces the pain during expulsion of the next offspring born. So, Menges (2007) concludes that modern placentophagia is a fashion based on an inaccurate idea of making the human birthing process more 'natural'.

Rare cases of cannibalism among humans today have drawn considerable attention from the media, and the topic of cannibalism has been a growing focus for discussion in the medical and psychological sciences. The reasons for this increase in interest raise further issues which deserve a place in a volume on consuming the inedible. Four distinct areas of discussion have received recent attention in biological literature: cannibalism as a psychological abnormality, in non-human species, as a trigger for prion diseases and as a survival strategy. As well as these biological perspectives there is a rich social literature. In 'Western' societies cannibalism has long caused fascination and disgust (MacClancy 1992). Are we only intrigued because cannibalism is viewed with repugnance, and if so how universal is such repugnance? By understanding the reasons underpinning that repugnance, we can ask *why* the practice is frequently a source of taboo. The materialist approaches to explaining cannibalism, most fully articulated in the work of Michael Harner (1977) and Marvin Harris (1979), have fallen out of favour in recent years, as ethnographers have sought to emphasise its social significance as a highly ritualised activity in ceremonial, sometimes sacred, contexts, where the consumption of human flesh is not necessarily the primary focus. Social anthropologists in general have tended not to focus on the biological intake but on its context and function in 'society', whereas in our cross-disciplinary approach we cannot ignore the physical aspects of cannibalism.

After reviewing the literature on cannibalism from different sources, referring to human and non-human species, we extend the categorisation by Fernandez-Jalvo *et al.* (1999) to the following classification of perspectives:

1. *Nutritional*
   a. incidental (survival during a catastrophe, abnormal scarcity)
   b. long duration (a persistent part of the diet)
   c. biological effects (whether incidental, long duration or ritual)
2. *Ritual*, (funerary, magic, revenge, etc.)
   a. affectionate (endocannibalism)
   b. aggressive (usually exocannibalism)
3. *Demographic* (population dynamics)
4. *Competitive* (e.g. of pre-existing infants, by usurping males)
5. *Dysfunctional* (e.g. individual psychological abnormality)

Endocannibalism (consuming people from one's own group) should be distinguished from exocannibalism (consuming people from 'other' groups), since the beliefs and reasons given for these types of cannibalism are, as might be expected, quite different. In the case of the former, the ethnographic record suggests that, where it exists, cannibalism serves as a social bonding mechanism between the living and the dead, ensuring continuation. Exocannibalism is also described as a social bonding mechanism, but of group(s) to which the consumed does not belong, ensuring either complete eradication of the victim or incorporation of some power. However, where cannibalism is repugnant, accusations of cannibalism, whether factual or not, are commonly invoked in order to create social boundaries by asserting one group's moral superiority over the 'other'. In the same way, some reports of cannibalism among non-

Western populations documented by early travellers and missionaries have been shown subsequently to be false. Such observations led Arens (1979) to go so far as to refer to cannibalism as a 'myth'. Following the publication of Arens's book, articles by ethnographers and others described what they believed demonstrated well-substantiated cases of cannibalism (e.g. Sahlins 1979, 1983; Strathern 1980; Sanday 1986), thereby casting doubt on Arens's basic thesis. Recorded cases of societies which have practised cannibalism in the past are scattered across the world, but strong evidence recurs in ethnographies of Melanesian peoples. The two ethnographic examples we provide in this chapter are both from that region.

The evidence for cannibalism, whether recorded by the observer or derived from trusted informants or from forensic investigations, point overwhelmingly to its existence. In reviewing this literature, what we have found intriguing is the general lack of discussion about reasons for the avoidance of cannibalism. Why *not* eat people?

Psychological Dysfunction and the Media

The existence of exceptional contemporary cannibalism and our society's fascination with it was clearly shown, among other notable cases, in the media's interest in a German, who had contacted what became his victim of cannibalism via the Internet, and later claimed that the victim was a willing participant. Armin Meiwes, the 'cannibal of Rotenburg', said that, as a juvenile, he had had fantasies about slaughtering his younger brother. Later, other male figures became objects of his desire to kill, disembody and incorporate them into himself. He claimed to have received 430 answers to between 10 and 20 emails in which he searched for young able-bodied men aged between 18 and 25 for disembodiment and consumption. One respondent, after weeks of email correspondence, travelled to Meiwes's house, where Meiwes killed him and in the course of the next few months ate about 20 kilogrammes of his 'meat' and then kept searching for other volunteers via the Internet. A student from Austria warned the police, which led to the discovery of this active cannibal. What is interesting is that the judicial process had to resolve whether Meiwes was primarily driven by the wish to kill (i.e. murder) or whether the whole incidence was a consensual act. In May 2006 Meiwes was convicted of murder and given a life sentence. Thus there are legal as well as psychological debates to pursue in discussions of such cases. The BBC website, for example, notes that cannibalism is not illegal in Britain. Murder, of course is.

Although plentiful in recent psychological literature, we cannot include coverage of the impetus for such psychosexual dysfunction, but it is worth noting that Medina Ortiz *et al.* (2006) stress that cases of psychiatric cannibalism are extremely rare. The question remains why is it rare, why considered abnormal?

Nutritional Cannibalism as a Survival Strategy

The 1972 air crash in the Andes and the subsequent consumption by the survivors of their companions killed in the crash has recently been publicly re-explored in books and a documentary film, again feeding public fascination. In brief, the crash killed the pilot, flight crew and some passengers, and those remaining alive, some injured, had no training in survival in a snow-covered mountain range. They melted snow for drinking, had a little fuel from some wooden crates and minimal food; they sheltered in the wrecked fuselage. When an avalanche filled the cabin with snow, others died. Some survivors, but not all, cut off and ate the flesh of the dead, and these 'cannibals' survived for seventy two days. What is clear is that the survival of those who did consume this valuable source of nutrition depended on their overcoming strong socialisation against eating human flesh, which others could not overcome and died. It is extremely unlikely that this famous case stands alone in the history of human survival, and other cases are recorded, from shipwrecked sailors to notorious sieges, from early accounts to recent history. An eighty-year-old informant was a British teenager in Shanghai in 1941, son of the education officer for the Municipal Council (RLH personal communication). He tells of rumours that unclaimed dead on the streets were collected by butchers. That human meat ended up with other meat in some sausages receives credibility from contemporary municipal legislation forbidding it, and a contemporary biochemical test to identify transgression. Many other cases will always remain untold due to strong feelings against cannibalism.

Nutritional Cannibalism in Human Evolution

The existence of cannibalism in prehistoric human evolution has frequently been postulated, but debated, from fossil assemblages, and consideration given to whether it was nutritional or ritual. At both Moula-Guercy, France (Defleur et al. 1999), and at Gran Dolina, Spain (Fernández-Jalvo et al. 1999), human and animal fossilised bones were randomly mixed, both with similar cut marks and breakage, suggesting that they were equally food-related garbage. Finding no evidence indicating ritual, the researchers at each site concluded that this was nutritional cannibalism. Whereas Defleur et al. (1999) referred to their ignorance of possible resource stress, Fernández-Jalvo et al. (1999) reviewed whether the cannibalism was incidental or of long duration and decided the evidence suggested that it was repeated over decades, possibly longer, which would suggest that humans were regularly part of the diet, but the exact survival circumstances remain unknown.

Ritual Cannibalism: Two Examples from Papua New Guinea

It is time to review credible ethnographic examples of ritual cannibalism.

Exocannibalism among the Eipo

The Eipo are a Papuan speaking group in the highlands of West New Guinea, and Schiefenhövel lived among them for a total of twenty-two months starting in 1974, and returning several times through the 1970s and 1980s. He worked with Heeschen who spent four years in the Mek area. It is important to emphasise that the evidence they gathered generally concurs with that given on cannibalism in several reports on other Melanesian societies.

Although none of Schiefenhövel's research team witnessed the eating of human flesh, the Eipo talked about their own experiences of cannibalism in a matter-of-fact way; it was part of their tradition, like killing enemies or infanticide or witchcraft beliefs. As they were very open about almost all aspects of their lives, it is clear that cannibalism was not just an accusation aimed at enemies, but a reality. For example, some informants spoke with clear relish of their preference for hands and feet, apparently because of the mixture of fat and cartilage in these appendages. The three following informant reports from Heeschen's notes (Heeschen 1990) tell their own stories:

Informant Welimde: (on the killing and eating of an enemy)
Namin was a man from the Fa valley, [where the hereditary enemies of the people of the Eipo valley lived].
He had visited one of the villages in the upper Hei valley, where he had a sexual affair with a woman of the village of Larye. On Namin's return he was caught by warriors of a village in the Eipo valley, who killed him. The warriors laid Namin's corpse on a makeshift stretcher and carried him to their village, where they displayed the victim, and then proceeded to a nearby satellite settlement of that village and danced the dance of triumph. [Schiefenhövel notes that it was traditional to dance when an enemy was killed, and the researchers had witnessed such dances (Figure 16.1).] The Eipo then began to cut Namin's body open in the same way that pigs are disembowelled. There were long cuts from the mouth across the chest, and from the abdomen to the anus. After the rib cage had been broken, the intestinal tract from tongue to colon was removed. The penis was cut off. The legs and arms were separated, and the head cut off. Pieces of the body were then steamed in the earth oven. The skull was destroyed with stone adzes, so that the brain could be taken out and cooked. Namin's meat and organs were then distributed to groups of people from the Eipo valley and from villages in adjacent regions who were allies of the Eipo.

In this way, the cannibalistic feast was part of the general political strategy to involve partners in an alliance of war against the common enemy, those of the Fa valley.

Figure 16.1   An Eipo triumphal dance

Informant Bingde: (on reasons for eating a killed enemy)
[Bingde was a young man at the start of the German fieldwork, but, as a
boy, he had participated in a cannibalistic meal.]
We ate these corpses out of anger, because they are different from us. We
destroyed their bodies with our teeth, and we left nothing of them; we even
cracked and ate their bones. When we sat at the meal, the fat dripping from
our mouths and fingers, we were happy that everyone was participating in
the eating of this enemy. This made us feel that we were a communal group
and, at the same time, it rendered it difficult for the enemy to take revenge
on individual people. A piece of the meat was cut even for me, a child.
However, some people in the village said that this was taboo and we should
not eat the meat. Meanwhile, in the village of the dead warrior, people
were weeping and mourning because he was eaten by us.

Informant Bowungde: (a man unwilling to participate in a cannibalistic meal)
[Bowungde was about twenty five years of age at the beginning of the
German fieldwork among the Eipo.]
When they had killed Nanamde, a man from the Fa valley, I was thinking
whether I should participate, but I got sick from the smell of the burned
meat and the smoke. So, I retreated a bit. Keningde (one of the
protagonists of the cannibalistic ceremony) carried the dead man's head
around and tried to scare people with it. I became quite nauseous and
went to a cliff, where I emptied my body.

From these and similar reports, collected by Schiefenhövel, Heeschen and
others, there emerges a pattern of exocannibalism typical of the Eipo and their
neighbours. It is evident that lone travellers were easy prey for a raiding group

of warriors. According to informants in 1974 what happened to Namin (see report above) happened to Mute, a man from an Eipo village, who was on his way back alone from a visit to the south to collect fruits, not locally available. Mute was an easy victim for Fa warriors since he was alone and there was no danger of immediate revenge from other Eipo. He was killed by arrows. The corpse was carried to a Fa village and publicly displayed there; triumph dances followed and Mute was eaten.

Disembowelling of a body, however, did not take place within the villages, but, according to reports, quite far from the village. It would seem that there was a taboo protecting the sanctity of the village itself. In a society with a cultural tradition of cannibalism this is interesting and may reflect some avoidance of polluting the village itself with the disembowelling. As with Bingde's report (above), the ceremonies surrounding cannibalistic rituals generally included the whole community and their allied neighbours, binding them together. In this way, the ceremonies were embedded in the socio-political strategies to keep alliances, and to acknowledge a common enemy. The Eipo themselves explained this ritual as an act directed at utterly destroying one of the hated enemy. 'When we crush the meat and bones of one of them with our teeth, nothing will be left of this evil being' (Schiefenhövel's field notes). This form of exocannibalism, therefore, is not directed at incorporating any symbolic power of the victim, but is part of the rather pronounced martial traditions typical of the Eipo and other ethnic groups in the New Guinean Highlands, where 25 per cent of the men and also many women died a violent death (Schiefenhövel 1991).

Nevertheless, as with Bowungde's report (above), some individuals of the community were able to withdraw and not take part in the cannibalism. What might be the cause of Bowungde's report of nausea? In our culture this does not surprise us, but is there something common to many humans in this rejection of cannibalism, which perhaps must be overcome with ritual even where cannibalism was part of the social fabric? Another point not to be neglected is that by no means all enemies killed were eaten, and this, too, is interesting. Why not?

Endocannibalism among the Fore

We briefly present ethnographic information on the Fore of the Eastern Highlands of New Guinea (Lindenbaum 1979), because of discussions of kuru and the prion diseases (see below) and because it provides an example of endocannibalism. Upon the death of an individual, the Matrikin dismembered the corpse in a traditional way, and different parts were distributed to different relatives; e.g. the buttocks of men went to their wives, female maternal cousins got the arms and legs, and children under ten ate whatever was given to them. The skull was broken open and brains were eaten by specific female relatives. Bones were broken to extract the marrow, then pulverised, cooked and eaten.

Most males over the age of ten did not eat human meat, unless they were old men, and males never ate the meat of females. From these details of distribution, it is clear that these were funerary rituals involving incorporation of family members and belief in the continuation of some essence of the deceased, rather than basic nutrition.

The details that Gillison (1983) provides about the Gimi, neighbours of the Fore, are very similar, with consumption by women related to the deceased, for reasons intrinsic to their belief system, which she describes in detail. Symbolic endocannibalism in funerary rites is found in several ethnographies worldwide (e.g. Chagnon 1968).

The Prion Diseases

As recently as June 2006 there was an article in *The Lancet* about endocannibalism in Papua New Guinea in the 1950s (Collinge *et al.* 2006). The reason for renewed medical interest was the outbreak of bovine spongiform encephalopathy (BSE) in Britain and elsewhere in Europe, followed by cases of a variant form of Creutzfeldt-Jakob Disease (vCJD). This stimulated money and research into the epidemic human prion diseases, of which kuru, a disease found among the Fore of New Guinea, was a clearly reported example.

Kuru

In the 1950s Vincent Zigas, a district medical officer in the then Australian-administered Trust Territory of Papua New Guinea, had found patients with an unexplained fatal, neurological disease, termed '*kuru*' (meaning trembling, shaking) by the local people. Zigas invited Daniel Carleton Gajdusek, an American neurologist, to assist in studying this puzzling disease (Zigas and Gajdusek 1957). Several pathogenetic hypotheses were formulated, genetic (because it seemed to pass down families) and environmental. Quite early in the consideration of cause, the Fore tradition of endocannibalism was considered. It was noted that especially women and their children and a few elderly males were affected. This ties in with details (above) of the distribution of human meat. One of the diagnostic problems for the researchers was the very long incubation period (up to twenty-three years). Gajdusek had carefully conducted autopsies of kuru victims and, in his laboratory at the National Institute of Health, Maryland, he injected infected brain tissue into chimpanzees. It took fifteen years before the chimpanzees developed the kuru symptoms. Gajdusek described this new disease as transmissible spongiform encephalopathy and believed that a 'slow virus' was causing it. He saw the resemblance to scrapie, to Creutzfeldt-Jakob disease (CJD) and to similar neurodegenerative disorders (Gajdusek 1990). In 1988 Gajdusek received the Nobel Prize for his role in kuru research.

The Fore stopped their endocannibalistic mortuary rites; and eventually no more cases of kuru were reported. Later, it turned out that kuru, like similar diseases (e.g. vCJD) was caused by misfolded prions, not 'slow viruses', and a relevant detail is that the Fore typically cooked brain tissue in bamboo containers at temperatures no higher than 95°C (Lindenbaum 1979), which would not destroy prions.[1]

Prion diseases are not all identical, but form a group of rare neurodegenerative disorders. Until BSE, only two forms in humans were relatively well-known, kuru and CJD. The media frenzy about the so-called 'mad cow disease' with TV pictures of cows staggering, led to some changes in public behaviour. When vCJD was postulated to have resulted from consumption of BSE-infected beef (Will *et al.* 1996), this not only had a further impact on public behaviour, but also stimulated a wave of research into prions and prion diseases. Contemporary medical researchers began to review information on kuru, e.g. Collinge and colleagues (2006) describe that there may have been an incubation period of as long as fifty years for some cases of kuru, which should be considered a warning about the uncertainty of the number of vCJD cases that could still result from the BSE outbreak.

Evidence from Genome Studies

Meanwhile, a new source of biological information may throw light on how common cannibalism and kuru death may have been. Prions are not external pathogenic elements, but proteins produced in our body, coded in a single gene (prion protein gene or PRNP) and thus, part of our own genome. An error in the folding of the protein makes it anomalous and once misfolded, this induces other molecules to become misfolded, initiating a process that may be very long. The initial misfolded protein may be of internal (e.g. a point mutation in the prion protein gene produces CJD) or of external origin (e.g. from eating a misfolded protein). Finally, there are some variants of the PRNP which give individuals carrying them a different susceptibility to developing the disease, if exposed to it. These are especially in the codons 129 and 219 of that gene, which have a very heterogeneous distribution worldwide (Soldevila *et al.* 2003). Codon 129 polymorphism has been shown to be relevant to susceptibility to the prion diseases originating from cows (e.g. vCJD). This is not the place to enter into the precise molecular biology, but homozygosity at codon 129 has been shown in all the cases of vCJD. Mead *et al.* (2003) found an excess of heterozygotes at codon 129 in the currently surviving Fore women of Papua New Guinea of an age that would have been involved in ritualistic cannibalism, but who had not died of kuru. Mead *et al.* (2003) therefore concluded that this excess was due to heterozygote advantage and went on to suggest that a balancing selection existed in the presence of the prion disease, kuru, and endocannibalism. Moreover, they studied several worldwide populations and claimed that the polymorphism at codon 129 was very ancient, arising from a long human history of the resistance it confers to prion disease, based on cannibalism in prehistory. However, Soldevila *et al.* (2006), while not querying Mead *et al.*'s (2003) findings of higher than expected heterozygosity among the Fore, questioned the conclusion of balancing selection and the worldwide distribution. Following mathematical analyses of the worldwide distribution of this codon, from gene resequencing data in many individuals from many populations, Soldevila *et al.* (2006) concluded that there was a mathematical flaw in Mead *et al.*'s (2003) analyses and that 'a general pattern of balancing selection, presumably related to prion diseases and cannibalism can be rejected in human history' (Soldevila *et al.* 2006: 237). While not discarding the existence of cannibalism, they showed that general and persistent cannibalism across time and space in the human past cannot be defended from this contemporary DNA evidence.

While further details on this are beyond the scope of this chapter, the past history of human encounters with prion diseases is relevant. There is some dissimilarity in prion chains between species, probably explaining the relatively infrequent cross-species leap from scrapie in sheep to humans. Soldevila *et al.* (2006: 237) believe that the results from their studies of the distributions of the alleles of codon 129 are 'consistent with a positive selection scenario, but not a simple one'. Their conclusion is that worldwide variability in the patterns of frequency of alleles of that codon was probably caused by 'a complex history of episodic or fluctuating selection' (p. 237). So, one might postulate periods of prion disease epidemics in those episodes. For prion diseases to spread epidemically, it can be assumed that diseased tissue has to be consumed either through conspecific cannibalism or through prion code similarity of the species consumed. So, simply by following the trail of DNA codes, an indication exists that periods of cannibalism at population level may have occurred in human history, but not consistently, or at least the prion infectivity was not consistent. We referred briefly above to prehistoric human cannibalism, where the authors postulate a nutritional explanation; so, we again ask why might cannibalism have only been episodic.

A Social Anthropological Interpretation

It is clear from the ethnographic examples above that cannibalism among both the Eipo and the Fore occurred in highly ritualised contexts, related to their belief systems. Much of the discussion of cannibalism in social anthropological literature has revolved around functionalist interpretations. Thus, cannibalism has been seen as a means of reproduction of lineage, society and population and as a way of constructing and maintaining group cohesion and social boundaries. The consumption of one's enemies is a recurring theme, and the ethnographic record suggests that this is the principal form of exocannibalism. A desire for dominance, perhaps revenge, appears to be significant, and two mutually exclusive outcomes may be postulated – the total extermination of the foe or the incorporation of some power into one's own lineage. Sahlins (1979, 1983) provides one of the most articulate accounts of the origins of cannibalistic practices, with reference to the Aztecs. He emphasises the ritualistic and symbolic functions of cannibalism, viewing the practice as one aspect of a highly complex sociocultural framework through which the Aztecs interpreted their relationship with nature, the divine, one another and members of other societies with whom they came into contact.

The conclusion from social anthropological literature is that cannibalism is a cultural phenomenon, and must be interpreted as such if one is to make sense of the practice. However, in persuading us that it fulfils certain social functions in *some* societies, the literature renders the question posed above yet more problematic: why *not* eat people? Perhaps the most fruitful avenue for pursuing this is to adopt a structuralist perspective; any phenomena which are somehow anomalous or contradictory in relation to major classifications are often 'marked out' by human societies in some way, in order to maintain the coherence and 'purity' of the classifications which humans use to interpret life. This marking might be through rituals, through being labelled as 'sacred' or through taboos; the important point is not how they are marked but the reasons why. In *Purity and Danger*, Mary Douglas (1966) identified that the physiologies and behaviours of those species tabooed in early Jewish society did not correspond with the 'ideal type' of each major category. Edmund Leach (1964) adopted this approach when he suggested that tabooed words in both English and Indonesian derived from those animals which had an anomalous status in terms of the relationship between humanity and nature.

Extending this argument to cannibalism, the reasons why the practice is 'marked out' by every society may become clearer. Humans represent the ultimate anomalous animal. In nutritional terms, humans are an obvious source of food, and yet we think of 'food', even if of animal origin, as belonging quite firmly to 'matter' not 'people', and thus, in social terms, we are classed as 'non-food'. From this perspective, then, to attempt to draw a distinction between those societies where cannibalism takes place (or has taken place in the past) and those where it has not, is to posit a false dichotomy. If we accept that where it occurs cannibalism operates in fulfilment of a particular social function and in a ritualised context – and in no contemporary or historical society can we find evidence of it being a routine means of satisfying nutritional needs – then taboo and ritual are essentially two sides of the same coin. They both serve to 'mark out' the behaviour surrounding the consumption of an anomalous source of nutrition.

In keeping with the overall emphasis of this volume, however, it is clear that social anthropological interpretations are only part of the story to be born in mind with biological perspectives.

Cannibalism in Non-human Species

Among the increased references to cannibalism in biological literature the reasons for cannibalism in non-human species are frequently discussed. Whereas spiders and other non-mammalian species are most common in this recent literature, including reports on laboratory experiments (e.g. Mayntz and Toft 2006), we shall refer only to mammalian species. Research into cannibalism in laboratory mice has a long history, with both female and male cannibalism, usually of infant mice. The explanations for this are various; while overpopulation or litter size is one claim, male/male competition is another. Elwood and Kennedy (1991) demonstrated that male mice had a tendency for cannibalism of unrelated infants, while acting paternally to their own offspring. Yet, Wuensch (1988) revealed that under laboratory conditions female deer mice showed a preference for conspecific flesh over dead mice of another species, an explanation which sounds nutritional. Goodall (1977) described several cases of chimpanzee cannibalism, and in each case the victim was an infant, usually the infant of a 'stranger' female. Ebensperger (1998) reviewed all species where infanticide was recorded, revealing that it was variable whether the victim was eaten.

What appears to be lacking in the literature of ethology, but is surely of equal, or greater, interest is why conspecific cannibalism is generally avoided among mammals. Why are the events of cannibalism, though relatively rare, of sufficient interest to be discussed, but not its avoidance? As conspecific flesh must provide an ideal selection of protein chains for nutrition, its avoidance is interesting. McGrew (personal communication) suggests that, for a start, only carnivores have the anatomical tools to be cannibalistic. Secondly, most mammals, even carnivores, avoid fatal fighting and many avoid carrion. However, as hominids have had butchery tools for around 2.5 million years, and members of the human species do kill each other, the reason for avoidance of cannibalism in the majority of human societies may be social, as suggested above.

Conclusion

Across several disciplines, this chapter has exemplified cases of cannibalism and some of the causes suggested. We raised the questions of why the consumption of human flesh, including placenta, is repugnant in so many cultures, and why its avoidance is rarely discussed. Only in societies where it is repugnant would it be a description of abuse about enemies, and thus a demarcation of social boundaries. This idea had led to the views that accusations of cannibalism were *only* unfounded descriptors of 'other' groups and that descriptions of cannibalism were fantasies of early travellers or gullible researchers. Why was there such a problem in believing (as Arens 1979) that actual cases occurred and were sometimes parts of cultural systems?

Above, we presented a hypothesis from within social anthropology about why humans are viewed as 'non-food'. However, when other mammalian species are considered, as above, are there other hypotheses to examine? The consumption of meat is an efficient form of nutrition, providing proteins and minerals required by the body, and these are most similar in conspecific flesh. Examples of survival depended on it. On the other hand, several pathogens can most easily be passed on within the same, or closely related, species. Are the sociobiological options, then, the benefits of ideal protein concordance for survival versus the costs of conspecific diseases? Meanwhile, biomathematicians (e.g. Getto *et al.* 2005) have produced analyses of the advantages or disadvantages of conspecific cannibalism at non-human species population level. However, not everyone is comfortable with the leap from such zoological, mathematical, cost/benefit analyses to cultural belief patterns in humans. So, while one could build up the above evolutionary scenario for avoidance, based on health risks, its transmission to taboos and repugnance in cultures necessitates a theoretical explanation based on the co-evolution of genes and cultures, or on a biologically selective evolutionary process for cultures. A simpler point, perhaps, is that social species cannot cooperate efficiently if individuals regularly view each other as possible meals. A suggestion which draws the biological and the social together, for human and non-human social species, would be the beneficial biological evolution of 'empathy' as an emotion aiding cooperation in social species. In summary, while cannibalism does occur under some circumstances and in some cultures, it is generally avoided by humans and other mammals. We have asked why, and suggested some perspectives, but this question could become as thorny as discussing the universality of incest rules.

Finally, where the bread and wine of Christian symbolism fits into this, we leave for the theologians to explain.

Note

1. (en.wikipedia.org/wiki/Bovine_spongiform_encephalopathy).

References

Arens, W. (1979) *The Man-Eating Myth: Anthropology and Anthropophagy*, Oxford University Press, Oxford

Chagnon, N.A. (1968) *Yanomamö. The Fierce People.* Holt, Rinehart and Winston, New York

Defleur, A., White, T., Valensi, P., Slimak, L. and Crégut-Bonnoure, E. (1999) Neanderthal Cannibalism at Moula-Guercy, Ardèche, France, *Science*, 286, 128–131

Douglas, M. (1966) *Purity and Danger*. Routledge and Kegan Paul. London

Elwood, R.W. and Kennedy, H.F. (1991) Selectivity in paternal and infanticidal responses by male mice: effects of relatedness, location and previous sexual partners, *Behavioral and Neural Biology*, 56(2): 129–147

Fernández-Jalvo, Y., Carlos Diez, J., Caceres, I. and Rosell, J. Human cannibalism in the early Pleistocene of Europe (Gran Dolina, Sierra de Atapuerca, Burgos, Spain) *Journal of Human Evolution*, 37(3–4): 59–622

Gajdusek, D.C. (1990) Subacute spongiform encephalopathies: transmissible cerebral amyloidoses caused by unconventional viruses. In Fields, B.N., Knipe, D.M., Chanock, R.M., Hirsch, M.S., Melnick, J.L., Monath, T.P. and Roizman, B. (eds) *Virology* (2nd edition) Raven Press, New York, 2289–2324

Gillison, G. (1983) Cannibalism among women in the eastern highlands of Papua New Guinea. In Brown, P. and Tuzin, D. (eds) *The Ethnography of Cannibalism*, Society for Psychological Anthropology, 33–50

Goodall, J. (1977) Infant killing and cannibalism in free-living chimpanzees, *Folia Primatologica (Basel)* 28(4): 259–289

Harner, M. (1977) The ecological basis of Aztec sacrifice, *American Ethnologist* 4: 117–35.

Harris, M. (1979) *Cultural Materialism: The Struggle for a Science of Culture*. Random House, New York.

Heeschen, V. (1990) *Ninye Bun. Mythen, Erzählungen, Lieder und Märchen der Eipo im Zentralen Bergland von Irian Jaya (West-Neuguinea), Indonesien.* Reimer, Berlin
—— and Schiefenhövel, W. (1983) *Wörterbuch der Eipo-Sprache. Eipo-Deutsch-Englisch.* Reimer, Berlin

Leach, E. (1964) Anthropological aspects of language. Animal categories and verbal abuse. In Lenneberg, E.H. (ed.) *New Directions in the Study of Language*, MIT Press, Cambridge, Mass, 23–63

Lindenbaum, S. (1979) *Kuru Sorcery. Disease and Danger in the New Guinea Highlands*, Mayfield, Palo Alto

Mayntz, D. and Toft, S. (2006) Nutritional value of cannibalism and the role of starvation and nutrient imbalance for cannibalistic tendencies in a generalist predator, *Journal of Animal Ecology*, 75(1): 288–297

Medina Ortiz, O., Contreras Galvis, D., Sánchez-Mora, N. and Arango López, C. (2006) Cannibalism in paranoid schizophrenia: a case report, *Actas Españolas de Psiquiatría*, 34(2): 136–139

Menges, M. (2007) Evolutionbiologische Aspekte der Plazentophagie (Evolutional and biological aspects of placentophagia). *Anthropologischer Anzeiger* 65(1): 97–108

Sahlins, M. (1979) Cannibalism: an exchange, *New York Review of Books*. 26(4): 45–47.
—— (1983) Raw women, cooked men and other 'great things' of the Fijian Islands. In Brown, P. and Tuzin, D. (eds), *The Ethnography of Cannibalism*, Society for Psychological Anthropology, Washington, 72–83

Sanday, P.R. (1986) *Divine Hunger. Cannibalism as a Cultural System*, Cambridge University Press, Cambridge.

Soldevila, M., Andrés A.M., Ramírez-Soriano A, Marqués-Bonet, T., Calafell F, Navarro, A. and Bertranpetit J. (2006). The prion protein gene in humans revisited: lessons from a worldwide resequencing study. *Genome Research* 16(2): 231–239

Soldevila, M., Calafell, F., Andrés, A.M., Yagüe, J., Helgason, A., Stefánson, K. and Bertranpetit, J. (2003). Prion susceptibility and protective alleles exhibit marked geographic differences. *Human Mutation* 22(1): 104–105

Schiefenhövel, W. (1991) Eipo. In Hays, T.E. (ed.) *Encyclopedia of World Cultures*, *Volume II, Oceania.* G.K.Hall, Boston, 55–59

Strathern, A. (1982) Witchcraft, greed, cannibalism and death. In Bloch, M. and Parry, J. (eds) *Death and the Regeneration of Life*. Cambridge University Press, Cambridge. 111–133

Will, R.G., Ironside, J.W., Zeidler, M., Cousens, S.N., Estibeiro, K., Alperovitch, A., Poser, S., Pocchiari, M., Hofman, A. and Smith, P.G. (1996) *The Lancet*, 347(9006): 921–925

Wuensch, K.L. (1988) Female prairie deer mice prefer conspecific flesh over contraspecific flesh, *Journal of General Biology*, 115(3): 277–283

Zigas, V. and Gajdusek, D.C. (1957) Kuru: clinical study of a new syndrome resembling paralysis agitans in natives of the Eastern Highlands of Australian New Guinea. *Medical Journal of Australia* 2: 745–754

17. FROM EDIBLE TO INEDIBLE
SOCIAL CONSTRUCTION, FAMILY SOCIALISATION AND UPBRINGING*

Luis Cantarero

The Social Construction of What is Edible

Human beings are omnivorous. Among the great variety of organic products available they have always discarded certain foods and chosen others, which have become accepted foods with nutritional functions and allowed the species to survive. However, food is more to humans than a biological fact.

As Berger and Luckman (1966) put it, society directly intervenes in the functioning of the organism, above all in sexual and nutritional matters. Although sexuality and nutrition are biological impulses they are extremely pliable in animals and human beings. Due to their biological constitution human beings feel the urge to seek sexual relief and food; yet, this constitution does not indicate where sexual satisfaction is to be sought, nor what is to be eaten. As these authors go on to explain, sexuality and food are channelled along specific directions, in a social rather than biological way; this channelling not only sets limits to these activities, but also directly affects the functioning of the organism. Thus, the individual who is successfully socialised is unable to interact sexually with an 'improper' sexual object and likewise he/she is likely to vomit when given an 'unsuitable' foodstuff. In other words, certain intrinsic biological functions like orgasm and digestion become socially structured (see Berger and Luckman 1966).

What Berger and Luckman contended in the 1960s[1] without being specialists in human food, had already been highlighted three decades earlier by anthropologists like the Briton, Audrey Richards, (1932) and the North American, Margaret Mead, (see Guthe and Mead 1943, 1945), who carried out the first cultural studies on this subject matter.

Both the former and the latter agree that a social approach is needed in order to achieve a deeper knowledge of the subject we are considering. More specifically, there are two of these authors' ideas which I would like to emphasize: firstly, that food is socially defined (what must be eaten) and secondly, that the organism physiologically responds according to such social definition (the foodstuff which is considered 'unsuitable' is vomited).

The first assumption is backed by sufficient ethnographic data and both biologists and nutritionists agree that the limits of what can be eaten are fixed by the community and the process by which the concepts of food and non-food are created is one which can be analysed. What is edible is the outcome of culture and more specifically of social interaction, whereby we learn and whereby social definitions are changed or perpetuated. From birth, the Other (that which is not 'I') teaches us 'proper' food habits in accordance with criteria that are established by the relational context. In adult life our tastes, preferences and practices are anchored to this early experience and are further configured by social contact.

In what way is that which is considered edible incorporated into subjectivity? The answer is to be found in social constructionism (Gergen 1996), the consequence of post-modern thought. Thirty years after Berger and Luckman had analysed the social construction of reality, Gergen laid the foundations of constructionism, basically suggesting that human knowledge and actions are the result of community relationships.

The antecedents of this postulation can be found in the symbolic interactionism developed by philosopher and psychologist, G.H. Mead, in his posthumous work published in the 1930s (Mead 1934). Dealing with the internalisation of social reality, this author focuses his attention on primary socialisation and the linguistic and communicative aspects of social interaction, maintaining that the 'I' is shaped through this interaction. There is no 'I', nor significant action which is independent from the 'Other'. In the decade of the seventies, other authors, like Vygotsky (1978), believed that daily life cannot be understood without interacting with other subjects, sharing with them an intersubjective world. Thanks to relationships, the child internalises language, developing higher mental functions. Likewise, sharing socially produced signs transforms human speech, mentality and actions.

If this argument is applied to the topic of food, it can be said that edible/inedible is linguistically defined within social relationships. The definition is liable to cultural modifications, although certain discourses may become hegemonic.

It can thus be considered that what is regarded as 'natural', 'normal', 'obvious' ... 'food', is a relational agreement that may not be permanent and may undergo mutations. Derrida (1968) made an important contribution in this respect, when he used the method of deconstruction towards the late 1960s, to show that all postulations concerning the 'truth' are under suspicion. In order for transformations to take place, new perspectives and different terminologies are needed from those which created the dominant *status quo*. That is to say, if it is discursive practices that generate the conception of the world and initiate and maintain the process whereby opinions and actions are created, then it is through discourse as well, that changes are performed.

Today, the creation of discourses which associate symbols and values with foods is in the hands of a number of organisations that compete in the development and dissemination of such associations. The analysis of these discourses may uncover the underlying ideology, which serves economic, political and religious interests. Those who create reality by producing 'sermons', present themselves as neutral, but are in fact 'employees' to an ideology, understood as the fulfilment of specific interests.

In the field of food there are several examples which prove that moral, political and economic organisations define what is good according to their particular concerns. In the sphere of ethics, Fischler (1996) gives a good example concerning the Mediterranean diet. In the political sphere, it can be observed in the way that the mass media deal with food crises, while as regards industry, this process is exemplified by daily advertising. By associating values with products, producers seek to increase their sales. According to the principle of incorporation (Rozin and Nemeroff 1989; Fischler 1992) subjects acquire the symbolic qualities of ingested food. Thus, ingestion goes beyond the satisfaction of hunger, deep into the sphere of mentalities and internalises an ideological language which is 'artificially' built.

To sum up, reality is constructed within society, that is, human beings create meanings. This linguistic definition is spread through interaction and it becomes part of the collective social representations, of intersubjectivity. As already mentioned, an association is the result of discourses; thus, others can arise which may bring about transformations in the conception of food. Millán (1998) cogently develops this idea. With reference to meat, he explains how the status of animals is altered according to the sociocultural context. In this author's opinion, today we are witnessing a process of upward socio-animal mobility (humanisation) which materialises in the defence of animal rights and hampers the death of beings which are becoming increasingly like us. This process implies various issues (Millán 1998), but the relevant one to us is that the animal has turned from a food object into an animal subject and the modification of this mental image (the outcome of a particular historical process) makes ingestion difficult.

Once the social definition of food has been created, the human biological organism responds accordingly, structuring not only its practices but its own physiological functions as well. In other words, the pleasurable or disturbing feeling experienced by the body in relation with consumption is caused by this social definition. The repulsion felt towards products considered 'disgusting' triggers physical sensations of malaise like vomit. Some people even spit or spew in order to do away with the nasty sensation. Both are psychosomatic reactions, that is, bodily responses that arise due to psychological discomfort; in our case this happens when foods that are regarded as socioculturally inappropriate are eaten (Schiefenhövel 1997). Human beings may eat them without experiencing such reactions provided they cannot categorise such foods according to their mental schemes (Western people, for example, may enjoy dog meat if they do not know what it is, otherwise they would soon start gagging).

In other words, absorption is explained in terms of what is 'good to think'. French sociologist Fischler (1992) believes there is a cognitive operation which verifies whether the potential foodstuff suits cultural categories and particular culinary rules. If this is not so, a violent affective state arises, associated with manifestations like sickness and vomit. The philosopher Korsmeyer (2002) gives a compelling description of this phenomenon when she says that the discovery of having ingested something repellent or forbidden makes our whole body shake in horror.

Consequently, the disgust resulting from the ingestion of foods that are not defined as such is an emotion produced by ideas, perceptions and cognitions shaped in social and cultural contexts within which it has a meaning (Miller 1998). It is a response to the disorder of a socially constructed order.

Consuming the Inedible: Family Socialisation and Upbringing

As seen in the previous section, there are organic products which are constructed as food as a consequence of social interaction. Once the categorisation has been made, they acquire biological functions (as well as social functions, of course). In this section I consider non-organic products that also become food, if we regard them from a psychological, rather than nutritious, perspective. It is worthwhile remembering here Garine's notion of cultural arbitrary (1979). As he argues, food selection is not always rational from an ecological and nutritional point of view. Human beings are able to consume, consciously, foods that they know to have a negative or neutral effect on their organism. By consuming them, they do not seek a nutritional benefit nor an adaptation to the environment, but the satisfaction of cultural and psychological needs.

Thus, when a non-organic product is consumed, in the West we usually talk of food transgressions. Generally these are ingesta which, as explained already, have no nutritional functions. For this reason, all these foods are considered inedible or non-food, despite the fact that they are ingested under particular circumstances: earth (geophagia), paint, glue (usually sniffed), soap, nails (onychophagia), glass, matches, hair (trichophagia), chalk, faeces (coprophagy), etc.

These kinds of consumption, due to their characteristics, are regarded as psychopathological by Western society and culture, and the people who perform them are considered 'neurotics'. However, I believe they have an important psychological purpose: they are the expression of an indisposition and eliminate certain anxieties which have been acquired at an early age. In this sense, we can assert that they have a worthy function: they 'feed the psyche' and, thus, they can be considered food, psychologically speaking.

The *Diagnostic and Statistical Manual of Mental Disorders* (DSM IV) published by the American Psychiatric Association (1994) classifies a nosological unit called Ingestion Disorders and Food Behaviour in Childhood and Infancy. Basically, this unit comprehends two kinds of behaviour: Pica – ingestion of non-nutritious substances like the ones described above – and ruminations – regurgitation and repeated chewing of food. All these 'unhealthy' practices according to the DSM have a function within their culture of reference. Ethnographic data show, for example, that ruminations, which are considered unhealthy in the West, are common and understandable in other cultures. Eibl-Eibesfeldt (1993) explains, for instance, that infants are fed pre-chewed food mouth-to-mouth in several cultures and sometimes they also receive water in this manner. Among the Bushmen and the Yanomami, food and water are also transferred with saliva. Mothers are the ones mainly responsible for this transference, although it is also performed by children.[2]

The behaviours included in the Pica category are, likewise, cultural. For instance, Miller (1998) reports that the Zunis perform rituals which include eating human and dog excrement. Korsmeyer (2002) explains that when the anthropologist Jack Goody conducted fieldwork in Western Africa, he was told to put some of the village earth into his mouth should he feel threatened by the people around him. In this way he would be protected by the natives.

These consumptions are not deemed proper eating from a biological standpoint: they are symbolic acts with psychological functions in the West (sickness), and social functions within other cultures (for example, an expression of trust and dependence).

In other words, pica includes what in the West is defined as 'anomalous' behaviours, cultural disorders resulting from family socialisation and education. Unfortunately, the psycho-sociocultural study of such behavioural patterns has so far been insufficient. Within the field of psychology, only psychoanalysis has paid attention to the link between the mother's first influences and the psychosexual development of the child; yet, the role played by such early influence on food practices has been only marginally uncovered. Sociologists and anthropologists have shown even less interest in the origin of 'psychopathological eating'. Due to this lack of investigation we can only formulate a few hypotheses in relation to the link between socialising and upbringing practices and the development of what is regarded as pica; it is to be hoped that new light will be thrown on this matter by future research.

On principle, I believe that eating non-organic products is the symptom of an anxiety disorder generated at a very early age and which the subject has not been able to overcome. As a matter of fact, it is during growth when the individual, thanks to social interaction, becomes the subject of the wish (in Lacanian terms) within a specific sociocultural context. The Other is essential in the construction of the child's subjectivity and, of course, in the shaping of his/her representations and food practices (including those which are deemed pathological).

According to Freud (1997), for example, the first stage of psychosexual development is the oral one. Oral gratification is the earliest drive and the origin of food transgressions, since it is during this stage that the potentially most disturbing fantasies of the psyche are produced (Korsmeyer 2002).

During the first years of our life, sexuality and nourishment are closely related. The pleasure generated by satisfying hunger is a 'sexual' pleasure. By sucking our mother's breasts we eliminate the physiological need for nutrients experiencing pleasurable emotions. For this reason during this stage the mouth is at the service of two pleasures: the erotic and nourishing ones. Little by little, sexual satisfaction must be separated from food. When this does not occur food disorders arise. Paraphrasing Freud (1997) it could be said that if the functional duality of the labial area causes sexual satisfaction to appear along with food-related activities, the same factor may enable us to comprehend why nutrition disorders should appear if the erotogenic functions of the mouth are disturbed.

One of the manifestations of infantile sexuality is thumb sucking, an activity which produces pleasure: it helps to get to sleep, for example. The child finds satisfaction in its own body (it is auto-erotic) and the purpose is not the absorption of food, but the search for a peaceful state, already experienced during the suckling period. As Freud argues, this may be how the importance of the labial area as a source of satisfaction is reinforced. In adult age this reinforcement might give rise to excessive alcohol consumption. On the other hand, if some kind of repression took place during childhood, an adult might possibly suffer from food repulsion and hysterical vomiting and, due to the duplicity of the mouth function, even from sexual problems.

In the case of children, repression of eating habits provokes frustration and induces thumb sucking. Mothers try by all means to eliminate this practice considered 'abnormal', either through punishment or reward. Neill (1960) recorded a few examples in this respect.[3] Among others, he cited one case in which frustration undergone at the moment of eating induced a child to suck his thumb. The general practitioner said that the child should not be allowed to acquire bad habits and instructed the mother to tie his arms or rub the tip of his fingers with some badly tasting substance (Neill 1960).

In another instance, a mother promised her son that if he stopped sucking his thumb she would give him a radio. Indeed, a hard conflict for a child! Thumb sucking is an unconscious act that lies beyond the check of one's will. The child may make a brave, conscious effort to eliminate the habit: yet she/he will relapse time and again and, as a consequence, she/he will be acquiring an increasing burden of guilt and pain.

I agree with Neill that thumb sucking is also the commonest consequence of feeding schedules. The tyranny exerted by parents, who follow the practitioner's advice to the letter, interferes with the children's nature and forces them to eat, not when they are hungry, but when the Other tells them to do so. Already from birth, in many Western hospitals until recently, infants were taken to the mother in order to be fed according to clinical timetables, and were fully introduced into the organisational industrial system. Immediately after delivery, the child's discipline was prioritised over pleasure.

According to Freud (1997), other kinds of repression are connected to excrement. Parents know that children aged one or two do not feel repugnance towards faeces, but curiosity. To a certain extent, culture and education determine the moment when disgust arises (Miller 1998). An inadequate repression of the child's interest may become dangerous, turning coprophagy into a sexual perversion. In human beings excretory and sexual organs are contiguous and as can be easily deduced, both are related and may be confused. Given such circumstances the consumption of faeces is motivated by the repression of infantile sexuality.

Coprophilia (and its eating derivative coprophagy) may also be related with a need for love and the teaching of personal cleanliness. Neill (1960) narrates that a small child was sent to his school because he kept dirtying his trousers. For this reason, his mother had hit him and eventually, driven by desperation had obliged him to eat his own faeces. It turned out that this child had a younger brother and that difficulties had appeared along with the latter's birth. According to the child's logic, he had been deprived of his mum's love. If he had done what his younger brother did, dirtying his trousers just as the baby dirtied his nappies, then he would have recovered his mother's love.

As Neill argues, a complex arises in a child according to the way he/she has been instructed. When the mother says 'Don't be disobedient' or 'Dirty', or even 'Stop it', the element of good and evil appears and the question is turned into a moral issue, while it should be only a physical matter. For this reason, telling a coprophiliac child that he/she is dirty is the wrong way of dealing with him/her. The most appropriate attitude is allowing him/her to lose interest in excrement providing him/her with clay or mud. In this way the child will sublimate this interest without repression.

Interpersonal relationships as a cause for the refusal of food:[4] the unwillingness to eat, or rather, eating nothing, may become a challenge for demanding parents who feed the child when he/she does not wish to be fed. In this case, when parents replace the demanded love with food, the child refuses it. Following Lacan (1996) we could assume that this kind of refusal is more typical of upper-class than lower- and middle-class children, since, as this author argues, love is giving what one does not have. It may be inferred that the difficulty rich people find in loving lies in that they possess too many objects.

As a matter of fact, having everything may be as negative as pretending to have everything. In the world of appearances craving for distinction implies elaborate food training practices such as table manners, which are maybe too hastily imposed on children. The consequences are soon apparent. In Neill's opinion, the sad truth is that the children with the worst table manners are those who show the best social conduct. This author makes a distinction, which I share, between manners – taking into account others, having group conscience – and etiquette – the outward appearance of good manners – and concludes that the latter are feigning, performance, appearance, search for approval and, all in all, the result of the servility required by the Other.

All such repressive food training practices, which are regarded as 'natural' in our context, have become widespread. By this, I do not mean that children must not be encultured, but a balance must be sought between an adequate socialisation which facilitates collective life and an excessively disciplined socialisation which causes discomfort.

Behaviour must not be the outcome of one's automatic response to authority, but the result of naturalness and even more of analysis, reflection and criticism. Compliance with some of one's parents' requirements, like, for example, eating a bit of everything, eating fruit and vegetables, finishing all the food on a plate, not putting into one's mouth more than can be chewed, washing one's hands before meals, etc., is aimed at avoiding punishment and making a good impression. These behaviours are usually thoughtless, mechanical and repetitive, the outcome of associative learning. When the stimulus that causes them (the authoritarian Other) disappears, they often cease to occur. Children who want to provoke adults, or rather, wish to show that what is ordered has nothing to do with their own desire, may use behaviours which are opposite to the 'adequate' ones.

To sum up, by correcting children constantly we make them feel inferior, offending their dignity. Forcing a child to eat Swiss chard if he/she hates it, for example, is absurd and cruel. This is not to be understood literally, though, but in a wider metaphoric sense. At present children are obliged to consume foods which are considered appropriate by adults, i.e. those foods which it is thought protect their offspring from those diseases which are at present frequently discussed. Nowadays it is becoming increasingly common to hear the mass media in Spain speak of an increase in childhood obesity due to a decline in the 'Mediterranean Diet' and a lack of physical activity. Parents end up interiorising this danger and requiring children to eat healthy foods, as well as motivating them to do exercise. When this demand becomes stifling, symptoms become manifest in their children. Symptoms also arise from the repression of 'unhealthy' practices. In any case, adults should put the child's happiness before their hyperprotective diet. All the fruit and vegetables in the world will not cure psychic disorders if these are due to repression.

Conclusion

I do not believe that a specific training practice can be associated with the development of a particular kind of 'abnormal' food consumption like the ones included in the category of pica. I think, however, that a disciplined, cruel and absurd upbringing style results in submissive children who are repressed, devoid of freedom and become the object of their parents' narcissism.

Unfortunately, our contemporary Western context facilitates the appearance of various kinds of symptomatologies. This is a context which advocates a style of upbringing based on the 'must be', which stifles the ability to experience joy and is grounded in the importance bestowed on the world of appearances. Within this environment anxiety symptoms arise and manifest themselves through the consumption of non-organic substances. These kinds of consumption are the metaphorical expression of anxieties originating in early interaction and are an alert signal addressed to the oppressive Other. Therefore, such eating practices have a psychological function which is easily understandable from this perspective, and they must be considered food. If such practices are to be avoided, socialisation and food training processes must be taken into account, since there lies the origin of these behaviours. When the symptom appears it might be consequential not to deal with it, due to the function it performs. If it must be tackled, treatment must not centre on it, but on its significance. It is to be expected that thanks to therapy the 'patient' will understand the meaning of the symptom and will be able to turn it into words, and express it only through language.

Notes

* Translated by Monica Stacconi.
1. The first edition of the cited work, in its original version, dates to 1966.
2. Personal communication by Elena Espeitx.
3. A.S. Neill created a school around what was considered a radical point of view. Summerhill was founded in 1921, at about 160 km from London. Its philosophy of education focused on the child's good will, on working with joy and pursuing happiness, on developing the intellect as well as the feelings and abandoning excessive discipline while favouring freedom, etc. Neill's accomplishment can be appreciated in his own works (2001, first edition in English: 1960).
4. On the refusal of food ingestion see Cantarero 2000 and 2001–2002.

References

Berger, P.L. and Luckman, T.H. (1966) *The Social Construction of Reality,* Allen Lane, London
Cantarero, L. (2000) Resistencias alimentarias en un centro de protección de menores, *Trabajo Social y Salud,* 36: 179–193
—— (2001–2002) Memoria y preferencias alimentarias humanas, *Studium,* 8–9: 215–226
Derrida, J. (1968) La Différance, *Bulletin de la Societé française de Philosophie* (juillet–septembre)
Eibl-Eibesfeldt, I. (1993) *Biología del Comportamiento Humano,* Alianza, Madrid
Fischler, C. (1992) *L'Omnivoro. Il Piacere di Mangiare Nella Storia e Nella Scienza,* Mondadori, Milano
—— (1996) El modelo alimentario Mediterráneo: Mito y/o Realidad. In Medina, F.X. (ed.) *La Alimentación Mediterránea: Historia, Cultura, Nutrición,* Icaria, Barcelona: 361–383
Freud, S. (1997) *Tres Ensayos para una Teoría Sexual,* Biblioteca Nueva, Madrid
Garine, I. de. (1979) Culture et nutrition, *Communications,* 31: 70–92
Gergen, K.J. (1996) *Realidades y Relaciones: Aproximaciones a la Construcción Social,* Paidós, Barcelona
Guthe, C.E. and Mead, M. (1943) *The Problem of Changing Food Habits,* Bulletin of the National Research Council, n° 108, National Academy of Sciences, Washington, D.C.

—— and —— (1945) *Manual for the Study of Food Habits,* Bulletin of the National Research Council, n° 111. National Academy of Sciences, Washington, D.C.

Korsmeyer, C. (2002) *El Sentido del Gusto: Comida, Estética y Filosofía*, Paidós, Barcelona

Lacan, J. (1996) *El Seminario 4. La Relación de Objeto*, Paidós, Barcelona

Mead, G.H. (1934) *Mind, Self and Society*, University of California Press, California

Millán, A. (1998) 'Acerca del status animal', En *Ensayos sobre Alimentación y Culinaria*, Estudios del Hombre, n° 7, Universidad de Guadalajara (México), 133–149

Miller, W.I. (1998) *Anatomía del Asco*, Taurus, Madrid

Neill, A.S. (1960) *Summerhill, a Radical Aproach to Child Rearing*, Hart Publishing, New York

Richards, A. (1932) *Hunger and Work in a Savage Tribe: A Functional Study of Nutrition Among the Southern Bantu.* Routledge, London

Rozin, P. and Nemeroff, C. J. (1989) The laws of sympathetic magic: a psychological analysis of similarity and contagion. In Stigler, J., Herdt, G., and Schweder, R.A. (eds) *Cultural Psychology: Essays on Comparative Human Development*, Cambridge University Press, Cambridge, 205–232

Schiefenhövel, W. (1997) Good taste and bad taste: preferences and aversions as biological principles. In Macbeth, H. (ed.), *Food Preferences and Taste: Continuity and Change*, Berghahn Books, Oxford

Vygotsky, L. (1978) *Mind in Society: The Development of Higher Psychological Processes*, Harvard University Press, Cambridge

18. THE USE OF WASTE PRODUCTS IN THE FERMENTATION OF ALCOHOLIC BEVERAGES

Rodolfo Fernández and *Daria Deraga*

Introduction

This chapter discusses the subject of waste products used in the fermentation process of alcoholic beverages in Mexico. Emphasis is placed on human excrement as a fermentation accelerator in the production of *pulque*, a traditional drink of the highlands of Meso-America since before Hispanic times. Supposedly these waste products were in the past also used in the making of *tequila* and *mezcal*, two very popular distilled alcoholic beverages of Mexico.

Due to the fact that there exist both a general taboo and an aversion about the use of human excrement in the elaboration of food and drink, the research carried out for this chapter has had its difficulties, but at the same time has produced information on local myths, and lay theories on the subject. Many producers of these drinks tend to deny the use of any non-consumable material in the fermentation process; some even state that this idea has been created as a negative publicity tactic by the beer manufacturers. These conflicting stories will be discussed.

International Perspectives

One of the first steps of this investigation was to find out if this practice was linked to some European tradition introduced into Mexico by the Spaniards during colonial times. A main source of our information on this was Maria de Jesús Portalatín, who comes from a wine-producing family in Aragon, Spain. She asked her father-in-law about the use of scatological material in the process of making wine. His answer was that this did not happen, but he did

Figure 18.1 Three Mexican men drinking outside a *pulqueria*, c. 1910. Reproduced with the permission of Fototeca del Instituto Nacional de Antropología e Historia, México

emphasise that animal blood was used to filter wines, as were egg whites. She also mentioned that through the old custom of treading the grapes with bare feet during the pressing phase of wine production, tough calloused skin was almost certainly introduced. One can also imagine other organic material that was probably introduced by the bare human feet, which had walked around the vineyards: for example, horse and cow dung.

Use of Faecal Material in Mexico

As far as we have been able to determine, this custom of deliberately using faecal material for furthering or accelerating fermentation seems to be localised to Mexico, and we decided to investigate this with informants in rural parts of Mexico.

As regards mezcal, a typical alcoholic beverage distilled from the agave plant, when visiting a traditional and extremely rudimentary distillery in Mexico's south-eastern state, Oaxaca, we asked about the use of human intestinal waste products in fermentation, and got negative responses to our questions. One very incensed man stated: 'Such filthy things! Of course not!' Our literature-searching about the production of this drink also provided no evidence of the practice.

Our investigation of this in the production of the well-known alcoholic beverage, tequila, produced in Mexico's western state of Jalisco, also proved negative, although some did say that it was possible but hard to prove. The big distilleries deny any such possibility, even that it may have existed in the past. They defend their hygiene and a highly controlled level of quality in their production.

As our research continued, we decided to focus on pulque, a very popular alcoholic beverage in the central highlands of Mexico, dating back to pre-hispanic times. Pulque is a fermented, not distilled, drink made from the juice extracted from the agave plant, also known as *maguey*. Our main interest was the use of the *muñeca* (meaning literally in Spanish a 'doll'), which in this case refers to a piece of cloth wrapped around human excrement and used in the fermentation process of pulque.

Pulque

First, we would like to include a description by Vargas *et al.* (1998: 187–188) on the production of pulque, which can be translated as:

> The raw material of this drink is the maguey juice ... The juice is collected daily, morning and afternoon, in a special gourd. In the summer, collection is done at midday as well in order to prevent dilution due to rainwater. Then it is transferred to the fermentation vats made of rawhide. The fundamental element for the fermentation is the starter, a mixture held

secretly by pulque producers which can be prepared in different ways using varied substances. Once the fermentation has been established, part is passed on to the other vats. When the official taster decides it is time, the process is suspended, and the fermented juice is emptied into barrels for consumer consumption.

When we continued our research into the use of the *muñeca*, among other waste products, we came across totally opposing views, both in the literature and from the personal communications of informants. Some sources claim that the use of the *muñeca* is just a myth, and that no such custom exists or existed. Others state clearly, that, yes, it was used as an accelerator in the fermentation process. Still others say with conviction that this product was used in the *pulquerias* (special places were people go to drink pulque), in order to accelerate fermentation or to enhance the flavour.

During the latter half of the nineteenth century, beer was introduced into Mexico, and in order to convince future consumers of the benefits of drinking beer, and to discourage them from purchasing pulque, the use of the *muñeca* was publicised as a very unhealthy custom. In contrast, beer was described as beneficial and healthy. Many now claim that it was the beer industry which invented a myth about the use of the *muñeca*, and that this custom never really existed. They blame this 'myth' for being the main reason that the consumption of pulque has gone through a definite decline, especially since the 1920s in central Mexico, where pulque had been a very popular drink. German Diego, a newspaper reporter, wrote:

A myth about pulque is that when the beer companies were established in the country, a campaign was started to discredit and defame pulque. Of course bribes were paid to the sanitary authorities to close down the pulquerias, places where pulque was consumed throughout the Mexican Republic. This was done on the pretext that they infringed on all sorts of laws, from sanitary to public order. Of course these accusations passed from calamities into myths, without recognition that the beer companies profited from spreading the idea that pulque was fermented by using animal or human excrement. NOT TRUE! It was the slimy secretion from the nopal that was used for fermentation (http://germandiego.s5.com/pulque/ acapulquito.htm 05/05/05: author's translation).

Juan López Cervantes (2005) describes traditions and customs in his neighbourhood in a very colloquial manner, including the so-called myth of the *muñeca*.

To accelerate the fermentation process, nopal extract, the core of the nopal or the plant itself was used to ferment the pulque. From this came the myth that a sock with excrement in, the *muñeca*, was put in; no, no. What happened was this; they accelerated the fermentation of pulque because by not being fermented, it was not digested well. It was like drinking the fresh juice extracted from the maguey plant. This, a knowledgeable drinker would right away call 'watered down' or 'baptised', things like this. But it was not because the *muñeca* was involved. Of course they were not very clean apparently, because they handled it with dirty hands; they were not clean, never clean. Why should we even mention cleanliness? Let's talk honestly. However, everyone drank it this way; of course once in a while, overindulging would cause problems. Supposedly there were cases where medical doctors prescribed pulque to women during pregnancy and lactation as a food supplement for the child. This could also be a myth (www.acd.com.mx/obras p lectura/consejo/EL PULQUE/pulque.htm 05/05/05).

One other source of information comes from Canadian tequila expert Ian Chadwick who states: 'Pulque makers sometimes use various fruits to accelerate fermentation. In traditional pulque, a *muñeca* (doll) was used – a rag or sock filled with human faeces and dipped to start the fermentation process' (Chadwick 2005).

Continuing with our references, Rubén Hernández, writer for the newspaper *Reforma* of Mexico City, published the following:

The campaign to discredit pulque that started in the 1920s, according to Ramírez Rancaño, brought on the slow decline of the pulque industry, which hit bottom during the 1970s.

Antonio Rivas, pulque producer in the Apan, Hidalgo zone, underlines that for years myths have only brought the depression of the industry on even more, and have fomented the image of unhealthiness which surrounds the drink. One of these is known as the famous *muñeca*; faecal material used with the purpose of enhancing fermentation. The fact that people believe this story is precisely due to the lack of knowledge of its preparation. (Ruben Hernández, 'Que siga la tradición pulquera') *Reforma*, Mexico, 18th September 2003. http://mx.geocities.com/master_chobojo/ nuestro_México/tradicion-pulquera.htm: author's translation

A French magazine published the following: '*Certains vous diront que la fermentation est aidée par l'emploi d'une muñeca. Le bon pulque n'en a pas besoin, normalement. Je vous laisse chercher par vous-même la signification exacte de ce terme.*' (www.mexeko.net/population.htm 05/05/05).

The negative publicity created against pulque was at its peak during the 1920s and again between 1934 and 1940, according to Ruben Hernández, as cited above. He credits this to the President of Mexico during those years, Lazaro Cardenas, who instigated a campaign of anti-alcoholism with emphasis on the dreadful properties of pulque. Meanwhile, the beer companies took advantage of this, and according to Hernández, began covering the cost of the snacks or *botanas* that were served while consuming beer in certain bars and cantinas. Hernández states that pulque was said to be the cause among drinkers of degeneration and stupidity, and was considered unhygienic. Beer was being publicised as a family drink, very hygienic and modern. He continues by commenting that beer was advertised as nutritious and therapeutically beneficial as a diuretic, and a blood circulation stimulant, also good for raising low blood pressure and cleansing the kidneys, plus ideal for mothers when breastfeeding babies (Hernández, 2003).

Hernández showed how pulque diminished in its consumption among the people of the central highlands due to the negative propaganda concerning the use of the *muñeca* in the fermentation process. He also commented on how the beer companies prospered, taking advantage of the situation, but he did not elaborate on how beer companies overpowered and basically pushed aside pulque, thus dominating the market.

Nowadays it is difficult to reintroduce or introduce pulque among people who were not raised in the area of the Mexican highlands, where the agave plant exists and pulque is made. It takes time to get used to the drink, due to the fact that it is rather slimy, and has a potent flavour and odour. It was never a drink that was widely spread over the whole country. The agave does not grow well in the lowlands, but thrives in a dry high altitude environment, thus the *maguey* plant and its product, pulque, have been limited to the highlands.

As far as the *muñeca* goes, we believe that it was used in the past, but whether a myth or not, we do not believe that its use was really the cause of the decline in the consumption of pulque.

Extent and Territory of the Use of the *Muñeca*

What we do not know is the extent and territory of this practice. According to an informant in the mountains area of West Mexico, Jesús Torres, there was a *pulqueria*, where the proprietor, a woman, put human faeces, the *muñeca*, into the pulque she served to clients who were disagreeable or behaved badly in her establishment. Others say that it was not uncommon that the *muñeca* was inserted for further fermentation or for enhancing the flavour, in the local pulque drinking places. A pulque producer, Juan Ledezma Esparrza, from the town of Yahualica, located in the highlands of the state of Jalisco, stated that he knew of the use of the *muñeca*. He claimed that a person who cleaned out some containers, *tinacales*, where pulque had been fermented in a *pulqueria* in the nearby town of Tepatitlan, had found a *muñeca*. This point was further supported by two chemists, experts in tequila production in Jalisco, Arcelia Rabago and Leopoldo Solis. They stated that the use of the *muñeca* was not done in the original production facilities, but rather in the *pulquerias*. They also added that the name '*perro con clavo*' (dog with a nail) was used to refer to this practice. They mentioned that one of the reasons the *muñeca* was used was that it produced phosphates which in turn accelerated the fermentation.

These chemists cited one other example for non-eatable products used in the production of spirits from the agave plant, which was the use of human urine in its maceration process. It is also worth mentioning as an inedible product, the use of containers made of cowhide for gathering the *maguey* juice, called *aguamiel*, as part of the process of producing pulque.

Conclusion

As a finishing note, we would like to comment that knowledge of this custom, the use of the *muñeca*, considered a myth by some and a fact by others, is slowly disappearing from Mexican culture. The general taboo about human intestinal waste material as a fermentation accelerator, considered by most as a disgusting idea, has been the main factor in a lack of information on the subject, and, in consequence, the fact that knowledge has not been and will not be passed to future generations. Documentation here of this facet of pulque production is valuable as a way of helping to preserve a part of a tradition which may soon be lost, as new generations will have no memory of its existence.

References

Chadwick, I (2005) www.ianchadwick.com/tequila/pulque.html 5th May 2005
Diego, G., (2005) http://germandiego.s5.com/pulque/acapulquito.htm 5th May 2005
Guerrero, R. (1985) *El Pulque* (2ª. Edición Reformada), Editorial Joaquín Mortiz-INAH, Col. Contrapuntos, Mexico
Hernández, R. (2003) Que Siga la Tradición Pulquera, *Reforma*, México, 18th September 2003
Jiménez, A. (1972) *Nueva Picardía Mexicana* (4ª. Ed), México, Editores Mexicanos Unidos, Mexico
López, Cervantes, J. (2005) http://www.acd.com.mx/obras%20p%20lectura/consejo/EL%20pulque/pulque.htm
Vargas, L., Aguilar, P., Esquivel, G., Gispert, M., Gómez, A., Rodríguez, H., Suárez, C, and Wacher, C. (1998) Bebidas de Tradición. In *Beber de tierra generosa. Historia de la bebidas alcohólicas en México*. Fundación de Investigaciones Sociales A.C, México, 171–202
www.acd.com.mx/obras p lectura/consejo/EL PULQUE/pulque.htm 5th May 2005
www.mexeko.net/population.htm 5th May 2005

AFTERWORD

EARTHY REALISM: GEOPHAGIA IN LITERATURE AND ART

Jeremy MacClancy

Anthropology, by definition, has no geographical limits. We research ourselves and others anywhere on the globe. Moreover, as an almost boundless discipline, anthropology has remarkably few intellectual limits. So long as the topic of study is social, in one dimension or another, its investigation can usually fit within the remit of our remarkably broad discipline.

Geophagia is no exception. We investigate its incidence, nature and contexts wherever it occurs (see, e.g., the relevant chapters in this volume). And just because eating earth is not a common-day or customary practice in the modern West does not mean there is not a topic here for us to study. In fact, the very opposite: for in order to gain a more rounded idea of Western conceptions and approaches to geophagia, we need to look at popular modes of representing the practice to Western audiences. That is the aim of this contribution. I start with its occurrence in novels, then move on to illustrations.

Literary Representations

The first point has to be that there are so few references to geophagia in literature. I have, over the past two years, repeatedly badgered friends, colleagues and associates in neighbouring disciplines for examples, only to trawl a meagre shoal.[1] It is possible that there are a host of references in the indigenous literatures of the areas where it is most practised (Africa, Asia, the American South), but I have yet to learn of them.

The earliest reference I found is from John Steinbeck's great novel of the labour-migrant Okies, *The Grapes of Wrath* (Steinbeck 1939). Impoverished, under-nourished, these poor whites trek to California only to find that a sustained, gross exploitation is their most likely lot. One evening, the matriarch of the novel's main family notices her malnourished, pregnant daughter eating something:

'What you nibblin' on?'
'Jus' a piece a slack lime. Foun' a big hunk.'
'Why, tha's jus' like eatin' dirt.'
'I kinda feel like I wan' it.'

The matriarch controls her physical reaction, then confesses that she had done similar things herself when pregnant: eaten 'a big piece a coal' and been admonished by her mother. The daughter makes her predicament plain: 'Got no husban'! Got no milk!'. Her mother replies that it is only her daughter's state which stops her from hitting her (1939: 309).

Perhaps the most striking point here is that Steinbeck clearly does not wish to sensationalise the activity. On the contrary, he appears to present it as just another behaviour of the group he is describing: the dust-bowl migrants of the 1930s. In this sense, it is but a further item in their sorry list of activities. Steinbeck seems to be acknowledging the liminal status of this sort of consumption: it is both recognised and devalued; accepted and discouraged. Whether it is to be taken as distinctive of the poor is left unclear. If it is meant to be understood in that vein, then Steinbeck appears to have included it as a way to inform middle-class readers of what the rural impoverished get up to. Further, it may have even been a way for this campaigning novelist to remind his leisured readers that geophagia was emphatically not a past custom, but a living one in the United States of their time, and thus an added reason for condemning the contemporary social injustices suffered in the land.

Next comes Lionel Shriver's *The Female of the Species* (Shriver 1988), a tale of a female anthropologist who lives among an isolated African people denigrated by their neighbours. To the Masaai, these isolates are worthy only of derision:

(The) Il-Ororen of the Puddle had grown superstitious and easily awed ... They had eaten clay for too long and their smiths made dull arrows, their women made pots with holes; their minds would hold no more cleverness than their pots would hold water. They had forgotten how to raid and be warriors. (Shriver 1988: 21–22)

Shriver uses geophagia as cross-tribal put-down. It is made an ethnic slur by a Masaai pastoralist who prided himself a warrior and drinker of livestock-blood. Fighters are not made of clay. Earth they leave for unconstrained agriculturalists with no self-respect. Once again, there is no sensationalism here; geophagia is accepted as a local custom; it is just not one for males who wish to be men.

Barbara Kingsolver's *The Poisonwood Bible*, published the next year, is an epic novel about an evangelical missionary's tribulations in post-independence

Congo, narrated by his wife and daughters. In the Congo, one of the girls observes the desperate reactions of mothers who lose their children in an epidemic:

> Inside a grove of trees the mothers threw themselves on mounds of dirt that covered their children. Crawled on their hands and knees, tried to eat the dirt from the graves. Other women had to pull them away. (Kingsolver 1989: 336)

Years later, another daughter, now a student in the USA, finds this scene returns in her dreams. Here it serves as a potent reminder of how local children died and, by corollary, how her baby sister perished in the village. Why did she die, and not another sister? The survivor can think of no answer (p. 468). Thirty pages later, she takes her half-Congolese niece to an Atlanta supermarket. The child scans the shelves, then asks her

> 'But, Aunt Adah, how can there be so many *kinds* of things a person doesn't need?'
> I can think of no honourable answer. Why must some of us deliberate between brands of toothpaste, while others deliberate between damp dirt and bone dust to quiet the fire of an empty stomach lining? (p. 498).

Kingsolver uses dirt-eating here as a contrast between the States and the Congo, between an overstocked affluence and a need-driven desperation. For her, it is an index of the radical differences between the two areas. To this extent, her literary deployment of geophagia could be seen as a mild sensationalism, an extra-lively means of underscoring the gap between the wasteful riches of the West and the grubbing of Africans in the soil beneath their feet, in order to survive. The morality of the contrast is heightened by Kingsolver's use of 'dirt' rather than earth, and then reinforced by reference to 'bone dust', almost animal-like in the images it calls up.

And yet, this transatlantic, transeconomic, cross-cultural contrast is undercut by the mother's reference, earlier in the novel, to doing the same herself, years before. She remembers she was brought up poor, in Mississippi, and innocent of the world beyond. Married at seventeen to a Free Will Baptist and soon pregnant, she finds her new condition troubling: 'When I was carrying the twins I had such desperate cravings I sometimes went out at night on my hands and knees and secretly ate dirt from the garden' (Kingsolver 1989: 226). Thus Kingsolver uses geophagia to both divide and unite: to underline the material difference between a wealthy West and an impoverished Africa, and at the same time, to bring together women, whether grieving Congolese mothers or a pregnant Southerner, in their common, female despair. In this sense geophagia can play an edgy, double role, which Kingsolver uses to powerful, pedagogic effect.

The most famous literary use of geophagia, however, is not by a US writer, but by a Latin American one, Gabriel García Márquez, in his celebrated *One*

Hundred Years of Solitude. Rebeca, a distant relative of obscure origin, who appears not to speak Castilian but an Indian tongue, is adopted by the novel's central family. All she eats are 'the damp earth of the courtyard and the cake of whitewash that she picked off the walls … Whoever had raised her had scolded her for that habit because she did it secretively and with a feeling of guilt' (García Márquez 1970: 43). The family manage to cure Rebeca of 'her pernicious vice' and she appears to settle down and grow up as a normal girl. When an adolescent, she falls in love. But her lover's letters stop arriving.

> Mad with desperation … she ate handfuls of earth in the garden with a suicidal drive, weeping with pain and fury, chewing tender earthworms and chipping her teeth on snail shells. She fell into a state of feverish prostration, lost consciousness, and her heart went into a shameless delirium. (p. 68)

She regains her health as soon as her stepmother agrees to the engagement (p. 71). But frightened by her stepsister's declaration she would stop at nothing to prevent the marriage, Rebeca spends 'whole hours sucking her finger in the bathroom, holding herself back with an iron will so as not to eat earth' (p. 77). A death in the family forces the engagement into 'an eternal relationship', with the consequence that 'Having lost her bearings, completely demoralized, Rebeca began eating earth again' (p. 91). The prolonged mourning over, a huge 'protomale' arrives, her stepbrother. When he looks her over lasciviously, without shame, she loses

> control of herself. She went back to eating earth and the whitewash on the walls with the avidity of previous days, and she sucked her finger with so much anxiety that she developed a callus on her thumb. She vomited up a green liquid with dead leeches in it. She spent nights awake, shaking with fever. (p. 95)

All of which promptly stops with their copulating and, a few days after, their marriage. When he later dies, in an apparent suicide, she dons her weeds and shuts herself away, forever. García Márquez summarises that she had first tried to find peace 'in the taste of earth', then 'in the tempestuous bed of her husband', only to find it at last in the house where she confined herself 'where memories materialized through the strength of implacable evocation and walked like human beings through the cloistered rooms' (p. 161).

García Márquez's approach to geophagia is predominantly psychologistic rather than cultural. He presents earth-eating as solely the chosen therapy of a very particular woman to assuage her distress, primarily at the frustration of her loves. Rebeca's pronounced individuality has several sources: for such a geographically confined novel, where the populace come from a specific place in rural Colombia, it is telling that its only practitioner of wall-licking is one whose precise origin is unknown, and whose kinship is unclear. Furthermore, in a novel replete with extraordinary individuals, Rebeca's character is peculiarly salient; even in Macondo, her emotional extremes are exceptional, whether presocial, frustrated in love, in love, or in mourning. On top of that, all other participants in the novel, and some of them have very marked personalities or unusual powers, regard her dietary disposition in strongly negative terms, as a vice, and a pernicious one at that. Indeed, in old age, when the details of the personality have been forgotten or never learnt by most, this reclusive widow is mainly known in the town, in stereotypical terms: as the woman who once ate earth. Nibbling on soil and casting a greedy eye at whitewash marks her out, even in a site as strange as Macondo.

Looking at the novel as a whole, García Márquez exploits the phenomenon of geophagia as a means to emphasise the singularity of rural Colombia. It is a way to feed his much-vaunted, much-criticised style of 'magical realism'. In a mythical land, supposedly grounded on local lore and folk memory, the mundane is interlaced with the magical, and the fantastic is presented as everyday. Geophagia could slip easily into a Latin American novel which focuses on the rural past, as a customary, albeit occasional, but still relatively unremarkable cultural practice. Instead, García Márquez chooses to exploit its oddness to Western audiences to thicken the description of his pop-ethnographic novel. On this reading, geophagia is a perfect device for his ends: it is both real in the world today and deeply strange to all those unaware of its worldwide incidence. This is a frank sensationalism for the sake of selling books. And, judging by its sales, his strategy worked.

The Cuban writer Reinaldo Arenas reacted strongly to García Márquez's characterisation of the practice. Though in his autobiography he too revels in excess – in his case in depth of emotion or sexual indulgence – Arenas takes pains to stress that his juvenile geophagia, when growing up poor in the mountainous interior of Cuba, was more quotidian than anything else:

> Nevertheless, my first sexual relations with another person were not with one of those lads, but with Dulce Ofelia, my cousin, who ate earth just like me. I ought to go ahead and clarify that all this business of eating earth was nothing literary or sensational: in the countryside, all the kids did it; it did not belong to the category of magic realism, or anything of that style; one had to eat and as what there was was earth, perhaps for that reason it was eaten. (Arenas 1992: 28–29)

Visual Representations

Here also my trawl yielded little. It seems explorers and travellers either were ignorant of earth-eating or chose to ignore it. To my knowledge, there are no drawings or engravings of geophagics engaging in the act. Instead, there are only representations of Whites' attempts to halt the practice. All these illustrations come from contemporary accounts, whether apologist or critical of slavery.

The earliest of which I am aware is the drawing by Jacques Arago (1790–1885) of a slave sketched during his two-month visit to Brazil in 1817–18, as the official draughtsman on a French scientific expedition (Figure 1). Dismayed by what he saw of the slave trade in Rio de Janeiro, he learnt that the mouth-mask was imposed to prevent earth-eating, which, slaveholders claimed, was practised by suicidal slaves sunk in misery and wishing to escape punishment by whipping. His illustrated multi-volume account of the voyage was a great success in France, and the lithograph of the masked slave reproduced many times (Handler and Steiner 2006).

Next comes Jean-Baptiste Debret (1768–1848), a French artist favoured by the Imperial Court in Rio, whose drawings and paintings of indigenous Brazilians and local slaves are among the most important visual documents about life in Brazil in the first half of the nineteenth century. Plate 10 of the second tome of his multi-volume *Voyage Pittoresque et Historique au Brésil* (Debret 1836; Figure 2) depicts neighbours paying a visit to the homestead of a long-established Portuguese settler family. Debret explains,

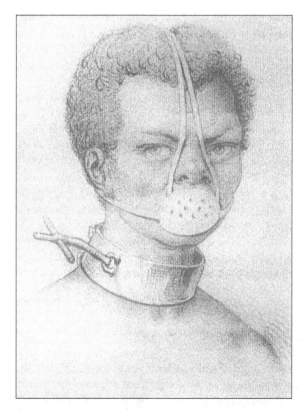

Figure 19.1 Brazilian slave, from Arago, *Souvenirs d'un Avegule*, 1839 (Handler and Steiner 2006: 56)

Figure 19.2 'A countryside visit', after Debret, *Voyage Pittoresque et Historique au Brésil*, 1836

Figure 19.3 Brazilian slave, with tin-mask, from Ewbank, *Life in Brasil*, 1856, p. 437

Figure 19.4 Tin-mask used on slaves, from Ewbank, *Life in Brasil*, 1856, p. 437

Figure 19.5 Brazilian slave with face mask, *Le Magasin Pittoresque*, 1846 (Handler and Steiner 2006: 61)

Behind the mistress of the house, one of her young slaves, fulfilling the boring job of whisking away flies and their cousins, by shaking two tree-branches which she holds in her hands, provides a European with the example of how one can make her captivity worse, by the distressing spectacle of a tin mask which covers the victim's face; a baleful index of the resolution she had shown to kill herself, by eating earth (Debret 1831: 47).

In a footnote he observes that this geophagic 'force of character' is called a vice by slave owners, and that practitioners of it could be identified by a yellowy whiteness of their inner eyelids (ibid.)

In the mid-nineteenth century a British-born American writer, Thomas Ewbank, visited Brazil for six months, and ten years later produced his much-acclaimed memoir of the trip, *Life in Brazil* (Ewbank 1856). A convinced abolitionist, he depicted slaves in iron masks (Figures 3 and 4), 'the reputed ordinary punishment and preventative of drunkenness' (ibid. 437), which he viewed as also a means to render them faceless and devoid of human characteristics. A similar mask is depicted in the illustration by 'M. Bellel' for a short article on Brazilian slavery in *Le Magasin Pittoresque* (1846, vol. 14: 229; Figure 5). The anonymous author of the article states that slaves who had tried to escape, only to be recaptured, were condemned to the hardest labours

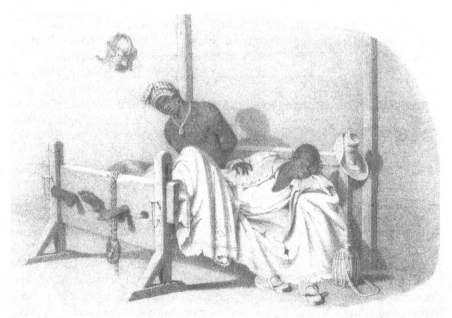

Figure 19.6 'Bed-stocks for intoxication' (note the face mask hanging on the wall), Bridgens, *West India Scenery*, 1856, Plate 32

Figure 19.7 'Negro Head', Bridgens, *West India Scenery*, 1856, (Detail of Plate 34)

and usually enchained. Some, despairing that they could not flee anew, might then be masked, to prevent them from committing suicide by either drinking themselves to death or eating earth.

Use of these masks was not exclusive to Brazil. In 1836 Richard Bridgens, an English engraver and apologist of slavery, who had visited Trinidad, included depictions of these confining instruments in the illustrations to his *West India Scenery* (Bridgens 1836; Figures 6 and 7). An unflinching supporter of racist ideas, he said these tin masks were tied to those 'addicted to the unaccountable propensity of dirt-eating' (ibid: page accompanying Plate 34).

Commentary

What has our meagre trawl shown us? Several things – above all that a practice as widespread and as various as geophagia can be used by writers for a diversity of ends: to highlight social inequities in the wealthiest nation on earth; as an inter-ethnic slur; to simultaneously heighten the contrast between Africa and America, and to deny it, by pointing out its common occurrence among both Whites and Blacks; to add a dash of sensationalist colour to an already well-stocked novel of the quotidian fantastic; to simply record its occurrence and so rebut sensationalist claims for the practice in his home region. Our clutch of artists have used it for a much narrower range of interests: to throw into relief an extreme of slavery, whether for critical or apologetic reasons. In contrast to the twentieth-century novelists whose work I have mentioned, these nineteenth-century painters viewed geophagia as inexplicable and/or an index of desperation. In not one case do these artists attempt to fathom the wider cultural dimensions of the practice. They view earth-eating solely through the prism of slavery.[2]

I close with two queries. To what end will future writers and artists put geophagia? Above all, and most interestingly, how will indigenous authors and painters represent earth-eating – if they choose to bother?

Notes

1. I thank Sera Young for directing me to some literary uses of geophagia, and Jerome Handler for permission to reproduce Figures 1 and 5.
2. This pathologising approach to geophagia was general among Europeans in the Caribbean at that time (Handler 2006). On the continuing stigmatisation of the practice in the USA, see the suggestive article by Henry and Matthews Kwong (2003).

References

Arago, J.E.V. (1839) *Souvenirs d'un Avegule; Voyage Autour du Monde, Enrichi de 60 Dessins et des Notes Scientifiques*, Hortet et Ozanne, Paris

Arenas, R. (1992) *Antes que anocheza. fore Night Falls*, Tusquets, Barcelona

Bridgens, R. (1856) *West India Scenery*, London

Debret, J.-B. (1836) *Voyage Pittoresque et Historique au Brésil, ou Séjour d'un Artiste Française au Brésil. Tome II*, Paris

Ewbank, T. (1856) *Life in Brasil, or, A Journal of a Visit to the Land of the Cocoa and the Palm*, Harper and Brothers, New York

García Márquez, G. (1970) *One Hundred Years of Solitude*, Jonathan Cape, London (orig. pub. 1967, Sudamericana, Buenos Aires)

Handler, J. (2006) Diseases and medical disabilities of enslaved Barbadians, from the seventeenth century to around 1838 (Part II). *Journal of Caribbean History* 40(1): 177–214

—— and Steiner, A. (2006) Identifying pictorial images of Atlantic slavery: three case studies. *Slavery and Abolition* 27(1): 51–71

Henry, J. and Matthews Kwong, A. (2003) Why is geophagia treated like dirt? *Deviant Behaviour* 24(3): 353–71

Kingsolver, B. (1989) *The Poisonwood Bible*, Faber and Faber, London

Shriver, L. (1988) *The Female of the Species*, Viking, London

Steinbeck, J. (1939) *The Grapes of Wrath*, Heinemann, London

INDEX